RESPECTABLY QUEER

RESPECTABLY QUEER

Diversity Culture in LGBT Activist Organizations

Jane Ward

Vanderbilt University Press

NASHVILLE

© 2008 by Vanderbilt University Press
Nashville, Tennessee 37235

12 11 10 09 08   1 2 3 4 5

This book is printed on acid-free paper
made from 30% post-consumer recycled content.
Manufactured in the United States of America

Library of Congress Cataloging-in-Publication Data

Ward, Jane.
Respectably queer : diversity culture in LGBT activist
organizations / Jane Ward.
p. cm.
Includes bibliographical references and index.
ISBN 978-0-8265-1606-0 (cloth : alk. paper)
ISBN 978-0-8265-1607-7 (pbk. : alk. paper)
1. Gay liberation movement—United States.
2. Sexual minorities—United States—Political activity.
I. Title.
HQ76.8.U5W37 2008
306.76′6080973—DC22
2008017951

For Melissa,

the most defiant queer I know

Contents

Acknowledgments

One year ago, I finished writing an earlier version of this book and started looking for a press with whom to publish it. One editor told me, "OK, you have two minutes to explain what's new and different about your book. Go!" Another editor offered her guidance: "You need to pay more attention to the issue of marketability. How many people will buy a book about gay organizations?" While these responses were discouraging at first, I also appreciated the irony of being asked to develop a "sexier" marketing plan for a book in which I was critiquing market-based approaches to queer difference. It was a welcome firsthand reminder of the tension between sales and substance, business and politics. It helped keep the stakes of the book in view.

It is in light of these experiences that I am especially grateful for the colleagues and friends who supported this project long before I knew how to describe it in a two-minute pitch. Faculty and graduate students from the University of California, Santa Barbara, patiently helped me conceptualize the project in its early stages, including William Bielby, Karl Bryant, Dana Collins, Reginald Daniel, Richard Flacks, Glyn Hughes, Matt Mutchler, Susana Peña, Tony Samara, Eve Shapiro, Richard Sullivan, Judith Taylor, and France Winddance Twine. Amory Starr modeled for me what it means to weave critical theory into daily life, and Rachel Luft provided the enduring friendship, bountiful salads, and incisive feedback that made it possible for me to think, write, and be myself. Verta Taylor was, and still is, an invaluable mentor and role model whose energy and dedication to her students know no ends. She has, quite literally, helped me solve a hundred logistical and intellectual problems. My deep thanks and admiration go to Beth Schneider, who is in many ways responsible, whether she likes it or not, for igniting both my feminism and my queerness. Beth saw this project through from beginning to end, and somehow always knew how to strike the perfect balance between stern adviser and loving guide.

Donald Barrett, Rachel Einwohner, James Holstein, Ken Plummer, Jo Reger, and Christine Williams were among the editors and reviewers who provided insightful comments on earlier versions of some chapters. Thanks also to Jodi O'Brien, Nicole Raeburn, Ellen Reese, and Salvador Vidal-Ortiz, each of whom supported this project by reading drafts or attending talks and asking difficult questions. Max Madrigal, Ken Dase, Joey Moore, and all of the members of the Disposable Boy Toys provided comfort and a sympathetic ear during difficult stages of the research process. More recently, my friends Margaux Cowden and Lieba Faier pushed the project, and my thinking in general, in new interdisciplinary directions. I am also grateful to Michael Ames at Vanderbilt University Press for his belief in the project and his patience with my many questions.

Morris Kight and dozens of other LGBT activists in Los Angeles made this project possible through their longstanding commitment to progressive queer politics in L.A. I have great respect for their efforts, and I could not have written this book were it not for all of the dedicated employees and volunteers at the L.A. Gay & Lesbian Center, Christopher Street West, and Bienestar who shared their insights with me. My mother Shirley Ward and brother Alex Ward inspire me to speak up, break rules, and embrace critique wholeheartedly, lessons I will always carry with me. I would especially like to thank Kat Ross, my partner in all things, for her unwavering love and her interest in every single one of my thoughts. She's my wife, husband, colleague, and feminist comrade. Finally, I'd like to thank my friend and anchor Melissa Dase, who has pored over every word of this book more than twice, read through it early in the morning and in the middle of the night, and believed in the project when I was too tired to do so. Queer theories may come and go, but Melissa will always be my queer home. This book is dedicated to her.

Sections from three chapters of *Respectably Queer* were published previously and are reprinted here with the permission of the publishers. Parts of Chapter 3 appeared in "Producing Pride in West Hollywood: A Queer Cultural Capital for Queers with Cultural Capital," in *Sexualities* 6, no. 1 (2003): 65–94. Parts of Chapter 5 appeared in "Not All Differences Are Created Equal: Multiple Jeopardy in a Gendered Organization," in *Gender & Society* 18, no. 1 (2004): 82–102. Parts of Chapter 4 appeared in "White Normativity: The Cultural Dimensions of Whiteness in an LGBT Organization," in *Sociological Perspectives* 51, no. 3 (2008).

Respectably Queer

CHAPTER I

Introduction:
The Co-optation of Diversity

Everybody wants diversity. Progressive activists know that diversity is the lifeblood of struggles for democracy and justice, and that making room for difference is the foundation of social change. Business leaders know that embracing race and gender diversity "makes sense"—it's good for a corporation's public image, it helps to expand consumer markets, and it ushers in a broader range of business practices that give companies a competitive edge. Politicians, media representatives, universities, and various state institutions know the value of diversity too; they know that respect for diversity has become a centerpiece of American culture and citizenship, and that those who do not respect diversity are the new villains in the morality tale of equality and difference in the United States. As Walter Benn Michaels explains it in his polemical book *The Trouble with Diversity: How We Learned to Love Identity and Ignore Inequality*, "If there's one thing Americans can agree on, it's the value of diversity."[1]

Many writers have revealed the ways that mainstream approaches to diversity make strides toward racial and gender inclusion while doing little to challenge global capitalism or correct for longstanding socioeconomic inequalities. They have traced the rise of probusiness liberalism, or neoliberalism, in the 1990s, including the formation of media, corporate, and state interests in identity and diversity.[2] These studies have shown that neoliberalism is characterized not only by the expansion of corporate control into all realms of economic, political, and social life, but also by the co-optation of social justice concepts—such as freedom, equality, and diversity—which are now invoked by corporate elites in an effort to protect their own financial interests.[3] This book builds upon these crucial efforts to understand the evolving relationship between diversity, social justice, and political economic processes. Yet its focus is on the more micro side of neoliberal identity politics: how the meaning of diversity is constructed and contested in daily interaction, and put to both personal and institutional use. To undertake this project, I turn to a perhaps unlikely site: the struggle over the meaning and ownership of diversity among queer activists in Los Angeles. I take queer politics as my point of departure not only to show how neoliberal, or market-driven, ideas about difference are becoming embedded in the daily life of a progressive movement that has long been concerned with diversity, but also to illustrate what happens when mainstream and "respectable" diversity politics come into conflict with a movement rooted in efforts to *defy* respectability. How do queer proponents of diversity respond when diversity is anything but unusual, defiant, or "queer"?

Although celebrating diversity and making demands for racial, gender, and socioeconomic equality are now commonplace within lesbian and gay organizing, some queer activists are growing aware that these changes have done little to transform either the LGBT movement's white and middle-class culture or its more general investments in normalcy and assimilation. To understand these developments requires not only consideration of whether LGBT projects are diverse or oriented towards multi-issue politics, but also attention to the complex relationship between diversity practices and *normativity*, or "conventional forms of association, belonging, and identification."[4] To make my case, I will show how lesbian and gay activists embrace racial, gender, socioeconomic, and sexual differences when they see them as predictable, profitable, rational, or respectable, and yet suppress these *very same* differences when they are unpredictable, unprofessional, messy, or defiant. Even progressive activists are compelled to revert to instrumental conceptualizations of difference, privileging those forms of difference that have the most currency in a neoliberal world and stifling differences that can't be easily represented, professionalized, or commodified.

Though the misuses of diversity are outlined here in detail, an equally important goal of this book is to illustrate some of the hopeful and unexpected effects of mainstream diversity politics. LGBT projects have witnessed a new wave of challenges to the co-optation of diversity, including the emergence of promising efforts to remake diversity into a more substantive form of resistance and to disavow the concept's mainstream roots. This study offers a window into how activists are interrogating the normative logics that have become embedded in the concept of diversity and its deployment as an institutional device. In each of the three organizations examined here, some activists dare to challenge the ways that their differences are being put to institutional use—challenges that I will argue are rooted in *queer* modes of critique. Their strategies reinforce the crucial importance of multi-issue activism; however, they also form a defiant and queer response to respectable diversity politics. They offer a new direction for thinking about, and moving beyond, the limitations of mainstream diversity politics. In sum, they offer a new way of imagining diversity itself.

At a fundamental level, the arguments presented in this book hinge on the meaning of *queerness*. By most accounts, efforts to reclaim the term "queer"—and its longstanding association with gender and sexual abnormality —gained momentum in the 1980s among activists who embraced gender fluidity and aligned themselves with a broad array of sexual transgressions (e.g., nonmonogamy, kink, BDSM, role-play, etc.).[5] The terms "lesbian" and "gay," in contrast, were (and still are) fast becoming associated with assimilation and normalcy, or efforts to convince the mainstream public that lesbians and gay men are "just like everyone else." Today, queer identification is commonplace on college campuses and in progressive activist environments, even as significant numbers of lesbians, gay men, and heterosexual allies remain offended by the use of the term. Some are offended if queer is used at all, given its enduring stigma; others are critical if it's used "incorrectly" to refer to historical figures or less-than-radical people or political projects. In other words, the meaning of queerness is hardly a resolved matter.

It seems most accurate to say that queer has *multiple* meanings and political and cultural modes of operation. Within queer studies, and from my own standpoint, queer is most usefully understood as "a political metaphor without a fixed referent"—a metaphor that describes various modes of challenge to the institutional and state forces that normalize and commodify differences.[6] This is the definition of queerness I will return to throughout this book. From this perspective, queer is abnormal, defiant, and generally unmarketable to straight consumers, and these characteristics are precisely the reason that queerness remains invaluable as a mode of resistance. Yet many people view queer in precisely the opposite terms. From the vantage point of television networks, queer is the winning ingredient of successful television shows such as *Queer Eye for the Straight Guy*, which makes same-sex sexuality familiar, palatable, and interesting to straight audiences. On *Queer Eye*, queer refers to a glossy and marketable form of connoisseurship, one in which homosexuality is linked to other "excesses," such as the consumption of high fashion and gourmet foods. Fine tastes are, it seems, also queer.

In this book, I often use the terms "queer" and "LGBT" interchangeably as I describe nonprofit lesbian and gay organizations in Los Angeles that some would insist are too mainstream for queerness. Yet as I will show, these organizations are sites of glossy and marketable queerness, as well as the defiant and unmarketable variety. As such, they exemplify precisely the tensions embedded in queer politics itself. That said, ultimately I *do* wish to preserve the distinctiveness of "queer" as a mode of intersectional critique, and I offer a precise definition of queer intersectional critique in the final chapter of the book.

Celebrate Diversity!

In 1995, longtime lesbian activist Urvashi Vaid published the controversial book *Virtual Equality: The Mainstreaming of the Gay and Lesbian Liberation Movement*. The book posed what some would argue is a still relevant question: How is it that antigay violence, blatant homophobia, and living in the closet remain commonplace after more than fifty years of lesbian and gay activism? Drawing on her experiences as past director of the National Gay and Lesbian Task Force, Vaid pointed to the political compromises made by lesbian and gay elites in order to achieve "virtual" equality while the majority of lesbians and gay men continued to suffer homophobic discrimination. The problem, she argued, was one of political strategy: "We consciously chose legal reform, political access, visibility, and legitimation over the long-term goals of cultural acceptance, social transformation, understanding, and liberation."[7] These tactical choices were not the choices of *all* queer activists, Vaid explained. Instead, they reflected the movement's largely top-down approach, or the failure of wealthy white gay men and lesbians in national organizations to mobilize a diverse, multi-issue grassroots movement. Perhaps had the movement's leadership been more diverse and inclusive, we would have chosen different strategies altogether—strategies that would have brought us closer to liberation.

Vaid has not been the only critic of the single-issue, or gay-only, approach of the lesbian and gay movement, nor the only one to draw attention to the identity-related tactics of the movement's predominantly white, upper-class leadership. In fact, in light of well-documented race, class, and gender inequities in lesbian and gay politics, the movement's strategic focus on "diversity" has been the subject of recent debate. Many LGBT movement symbols—rainbow flags, "Celebrate Diversity!" T-shirts, "We Are Family" bumper stickers—symbolize queer pride for people "in the know," but they also invoke the value of difference and inclusion more broadly. By some accounts, it has been this pervasive focus on diversity that represents the hypocrisy of lesbian and gay politics, given the sharp contrast between queer diversity rhetoric and the predominantly white and middle-class leadership of the movement.[8]

Yet other accounts emphasize that the lesbian and gay movement has fared better than other identity movements with regard to diversity and inclusion. A study by sociologist Elizabeth Armstrong indicates that early gay liberation efforts were particularly successful at building a gay movement that could balance unity and diversity without paralysis. According to Armstrong, "Other movements understood politics as endorsing the creation of communities of similarity. In contrast, the gay movement focused on freedom of individual expression, making it hypocritical to exclude any form of gay political expression. . . . 'Difference' was defined, paradoxically, as a point of similarity."[9]

Whether a movement characterized by single-issue politics and top-down decision making, or a model of unity built upon diversity, what these analyses have in common is their focus on the tactical choices of queer activists and the particular character of lesbian and gay movement strategies. They consider how queer activists have built, or failed to build, a multicultural and multi-issue movement. They ask important questions about the unique evolution of queer politics and whether the queer movement has lived up to its revolutionary potential: What kinds of queer projects have succeeded at organizing across difference? Where have queer projects failed to be inclusive and why? How might the queer movement serve as a model for other movements?

This book engages some of these same questions, but takes a different approach by focusing on the larger cultural context in which queer politics—indeed, all identity politics—are now practiced. To this end, my analysis is aimed at the complex relationship between queer politics and what I call "diversity culture," or the broader culture's growing interest in intersecting forms of difference. Considerable attention has been given to what is distinctive about the queer movement's engagement with diversity. In contrast, I show that in the context of diversity culture, queer diversity strategies look remarkably nondistinctive, subject to the inevitable strengths and weaknesses of mainstream multi-identity projects, and, dare I say, *unqueer*. I suggest that the question to be asked is not *whether* queer activists are engaged in multi-issue politics, but why and how multi-issue politics have become so commonplace in lesbian and gay organizing, and with what effects.

To be very clear, my intention is not to diminish the crucial importance of multi-issue approaches to social justice. Instead, my goal is to sharpen our tools for evaluating when and how multi-issue justice has been achieved, and to do this by showing that even multi-identity projects can be used to preserve the culture and interests of dominant groups. To make my argument, I tell the story of three multicultural queer organizations in Los Angeles, each of which has been transformed by the diversity-awareness and multi-issue agendas of its members. These activists *do* call attention to race, class, and gender diversity to promote inclusion and power-sharing among their ranks, as well as to address the intersections of homophobia, racism, poverty, and sexism in their programmatic work. Yet across racial, gender, and socioeconomic lines, they are also learning from the corporate model to "leverage" their diversity to gain a competitive advantage, or to receive personal and institutional rewards for being publicly vocal and articulate about racial, economic, and gender differences and inequalities. Queer activists use diversity rhetoric to compete with nonprofit groups to garner corporate funding and mainstream legitimacy, enhance their public reputation or moral standing, establish their diversity-related competence or expertise, and accrue "liberal capital." I argue that this instrumentalization of diversity has increased the demand for utilitarian and easily measurable forms of difference—creating the most room for those who embody predictable and fundable kinds of diversity, adversity, or transgression.

The good news is that these instrumental approaches to diversity have led to the proliferation of important queer multi-issue projects (e.g., homeless shelters for queer youth of color, child care at queer pride events, employment services for transgendered people, etc.). Yet, in striking contrast, they have also helped to reinforce the continued centrality of normative, upper-middle-class values, logics, and culture in the queer movement. This process is exemplified by the rise of a new breed of liberal elites: people with professional diversity skills, multicultural connections, a mastery of diversity-speak, and their "finger on the pulse" of diverse communities. Throughout my discussion, I have tried to keep all of these outcomes in focus, so as to reveal the complexity of evaluating what constitutes "successful" multi-identity politics.

Broadly speaking, I add here to a growing critique of neoliberal diversity politics, and I situate this critique in the context of a movement known precisely for its emphasis on difference and nonnormativity. While a detailed discussion of neoliberal economic policy is beyond the scope of this study, I view neoliberalism as the backdrop upon which movement goals (such as equality and diversity) are placed in seemingly harmonious relation to market goals (such as increasing competition and skill). Anthropologist David

Harvey defines neoliberalism as a political economic theory "that proposes that human well-being can best be advanced by liberating individual entrepreneurial freedoms and skills within an institutional framework characterized by strong private property rights, free markets, and free trade."[10] As a theory about human well-being and liberation, neoliberalism refers not only to economic policies and institutions that have expanded elite financial interests within the last thirty years, but also to the political and moral principles that have helped to justify these transformations. These principles include equality, democracy, and inclusion, which are reframed as the very corporate ethics that enable Americans to leverage human differences (including race, gender, culture, sexuality, etc.) in the service of capital.[11]

Commitment to diversity is now at the heart of what historian Lisa Duggan has called "neoliberal 'equality' politics," or the rise of a New Left focused on cultural expression, identity-based rights, and mainstream inclusion, yet simultaneously supportive of global capitalism and its aspirations.[12] Duggan uses national LGBT projects, such as the professionally produced and corporate sponsored March on Washington, as an example to illustrate the easy relationship between corporate diversity culture and identity politics. In both realms (the corporate and the queer), the glossy presentation of diversity is often a matter of good public relations or a tool leveraged by the powerful to accomplish various ideological and institutional goals.

Critics of the mainstreaming of queer politics have exposed the significant influence of corporate identity practices on queer projects. But how do these business-world identity practices root themselves in nonprofit, activist realms? How do they take root within activists themselves? What conflicts and gaps emerge when "celebrating diversity" doesn't come "naturally," when it stifles rather than welcomes, and when its normative underpinnings begin to be exposed and questioned? What happens when vulgarity, public sexuality, and various forms of queer raunchiness collide with the respectable world of diversity awareness? What unsettling gaps emerge when diversity trainings don't make sense to "diverse" people, or when they become the most tedious and dreaded days of the year? What happens when prevailing diversity discourses—the ones that diverse people are compelled to use to describe themselves and others—simply don't fit? In a world in which diversity offers people and institutions a competitive edge, what happens when some people win the competition and others lose? These are the questions addressed in this book.

The Co-optation of "Diversity"

To answer these questions first requires understanding the broader context in which diversity politics take shape. The notion that difference is, or should be, the foundation of unity and collective identity is hardly unique to LGBT politics. Instead, the "unity through difference and equality" frame has become a ubiquitous component of corporate diversity management, as well as a central theme in popular culture. Today, this diversity frame typically goes further than asking Americans to celebrate differences; it also teaches us that disapproving of the most blatant forms of racism, sexism, homophobia, and classism have become a routine part of the way that "good" Americans think, work, and produce culture.[13] Some examples are offered here by way of introduction, and Chapter 2 takes up this issue in greater detail.

The story of "diversity" really begins with the story of "multiculturalism"—a principle and set of practices that deflect attention away from the most persistent and structural forms of racism and toward the celebration of cross-cultural racial/ethnic differences. While multiculturalism emerged in the 1970s to address racial disparities in U.S. public education, by the 1990s it had spread to almost all other institutional realms, including business, government, arts institutions, the military, and local and national political organizations.[14] As Avery Gordon and Christopher Newfield have argued, multiculturalism challenged the notion of an American monoculture, but also replaced this notion with itself, or with presumably shared values of equality and difference that were to be the new foundation of national unity.

Despite downplaying racism and ignoring white privilege, sociological research indicates that multiculturalism did have a politicizing effect on whites. In dramatic contrast with the pre–civil rights era, the majority of white Americans now view racism as a serious social problem and, by implication, a violation of social norms.[15] These attitudes are bolstered by the remarkable increase in the representation of racially subordinate groups on television and the role played by Black culture, in particular, in reshaping visual and musical culture in the United States.[16] The importance of racial inclusion and diversity is also powerfully, and perhaps primarily, affirmed by corporate discourses that have transformed social justice concepts (inclusion, equality, diversity) into practical business standards. According to the corporate diversity model, celebrating cultural differences is not simply about being fair, it's about being profitable.[17] Corporations that understand cultural differences and market their products and services to racial/ethnic groups not often targeted by advertisers can expand their consumer base and develop the loyalty of these emerging markets.

However, studies of these developments also illustrate their unsettling contradictions, or the ways that multiculturalism has enabled new and more subtle forms of racism to emerge. Reflecting what Eduardo Bonilla-Silva has termed "racism without racists," most whites view racism as a current and serious problem, but are quick to locate the problem elsewhere by insisting that they, personally, are not racist.[18] Similarly, while years of activism have led to increased representation of people of color on television, conservatives have also used this development to encourage complacency and suggest that racism is largely a problem of the past.[19] And, though the notion that diversity is integral to business success bodes well for ongoing efforts to achieve workplace equality, the instrumental focus on profits also leaves many questions unanswered about whether, and for whom, profits are a sustainable foundation for social justice. What happens if, or when, diversity stops being profitable?

These developments, and their contradictions, do not only apply to race, but to multiple forms of inequality and difference that are now of interest to marketers and the corporate media. During the early 1990s, at the same time as the multiculturalism boom, industry and media outlets announced the arrival of "postfeminism"—a new era in which gender inequality had become passé, and therefore virtually nonexistent. At the heart of postfeminist discourse was the claim that, after two decades of equal opportunity initiatives and legal reforms designed to eliminate sex discrimination, women of the 1990s had achieved both parity in the workplace and sexual liberation in their personal lives (or, as women's magazines were inclined to state, women had "made it" in "both the boardroom *and* the bedroom!").[20] Advertisers jumped on the postfeminist bandwagon and learned to co-opt "pop feminist" language and concepts in their efforts to reach the female market (e.g., appeals to "sisterhood," playful critiques of men and masculinity, negative images of the sexism women experience at the hands of competitor companies).[21]

Yet the very same corporations have expressed little concern for the growing number of women and children living in poverty or the sweatshop conditions suffered by their own women workers. Corporate feminism, exemplified by Martha Stewart's do-it-yourself synthesis of business savvy and domestic individualism, offers women consumers personal and local empowerment gained through the global exploitation, inhuman treatment, and low pay of women workers. While the arrival of postfeminism was, and still is, being celebrated and "confirmed" by media images of women who appear to have it all, the actual advancement of most women has been limited, in part due to a growing international backlash against feminism.[22] Other feminist writers point out that even among economically and socially advantaged women, visibility and institutional power continues to be offered only to those who are willing to foreground their sexuality.[23]

Similarly, acceptance of blatant forms of homophobia also declined in the 1990s and were replaced with compassion and tolerance exemplified by the running gay joke on the hit television show *Seinfeld*: " 'So and so' is gay, *not that there's anything wrong with that*!" During the late 1990s, friendships between heterosexual women and gay men became a particularly popular subject in film and television, providing straight audiences with the opportunity to disavow the homophobic attitudes of some characters and identify with the accepting attitudes of others.[24] While public opinion polls indicate that Americans remain divided on the morality and legality of homosexuality, positive media images of gays and lesbians have risen dramatically in last fifteen years, along with a rise in corporate domestic partnership benefits and advertising campaigns targeting queer consumers.[25] However, as within profeminist advertising, ad campaigns designed to reach lesbians and gay men have co-opted the language and symbols of queer pride (rainbow flags, coming out discourse, references to queer icons and inside humor), yet have simultaneously reduced queer people to quintessential consumers and "private individuals with 'tastes.' "[26]

In sum, the co-optation of multiple social justice discourses and the rejection of various identity-based inequalities has become a centerpiece of corporate and popular culture. Encapsulating all of these trends is the idea and practice of "diversity"—or the celebration of multiple differences within political, cultural, and institutional realms. Implied in the logic of diversity is that practical and fair-minded people are interested in multiple human complexities, understand that people should not be reduced to any single component of their identity, and recognize that cross-cultural understanding is not only fair, but also practical and profitable. In some cases, diversity refers not simply to a list of identities and cultural differences, but also to their *intersections*. This is particularly true of reality television, in which "reality" is heightened by the embodiment of more than one form of difference in a single "character."[27]

As I will show, the mainstreaming of intersectionality has far-reaching influence, including into queer projects that receive broad public support for moving beyond single-issue politics and engaging in the politics of diversity. Grassroots queer organizations, once among the forerunners of identity politics, can now draw on ready-made multi-identity frameworks available in broader political and institutional realms, or they may find that they are compelled to do so in order to be legible to funders and the general public. Contrary to the notion that multi-identity discourses always signify a more progressive political analysis than their single-identity counterparts, multi-identity frameworks can also be used to strengthen claims to legitimacy, normalcy, and professionalism. In fact, as I discuss in my analysis of the case studies, downplaying the differences posed by queer sexuality, and emphasizing other forms of difference or inequality that are less threatening in one's local context, is now a common strategy used by queer leaders to garner legitimacy and respect for their cause. If placing rhetorical emphasis on multiple (and watered down) forms of difference is smart, respectable, and American, then talking about diversity kills two birds with one stone—simultaneously addressing progressive demands for multi-issue justice while also strategically building alliances with corporations, the state, and a sexphobic general public. Yet I will argue that it's impossible to do both at once, as these projects ultimately undo one another. Hence, another important thread in my analysis is the exploration of this slippage between diversity and multi-issue politics—a slippage that begs for reexamination of what counts as intersectional resistance.

Selling Gay Identity

In order to understand how mainstream diversity concepts have taken root in queer projects, we must start by looking at the relationship between private business and the LGBT movement. Other writers have argued that the gay and lesbian movement—and gay identity itself—has always been strongly tied to market forces. For instance, historian John D'Emilio has shown how industrial capitalism's break from the nuclear family as the unit of production enabled the emergence of public sexual culture, including city streets, bars, and cafes where people with shared sexual interests could meet and congregate.[28] It was in small businesses that the "gay community" first took form.

Yet it's not simply that industry created the conditions in which gay *community* became possible; marketers to gay men and lesbians have also played their part in producing, or reproducing, gay *identity* itself. As Alexandra Chasin argues in *Selling Out: The Gay and Lesbian Movement Goes to Market*, advertising to lesbians and gay men exploded in the 1990s and solidified the notion that lifestyle choices and consumption were at the heart of the lesbian and gay experience and were the "route to political enfranchisement as well as social acceptance."[29] Eager to be recognized as full participants in U.S. political and consumer cultures, lesbians and gay men have responded to marketers' construction of the gay consumer with open arms and wallets. Indeed, as I know all too well from my own troubled relationship to shopping, it is difficult to resist the allure of being an important and seemingly powerful consumer who can buy her way to respect and dignity, or who can buy just the right balance of normalcy and individual expression. This allure extends powerfully to oppressed groups, including people of color, women, and queers. In fact, being normal is fundamental to being a gay consumer; it means being "just like other Americans" who desire freedom, choice, prosperity, and full access to the financial rewards of American citizenship. However, as Chasin points out, this construction is ultimately damaging to the LGBT movement. It not only lends support to the misconception that all lesbians and gay men are white, middle class, and invested in being normal, but it also drains queer politics of its most countercultural and critical impulses.

The ideological centerpiece of lesbian and gay niche marketing is the argument that targeting gay consumers is about "business, not politics"—it simply makes good financial sense to court the business of professional and affluent gay consumers. Corporations are not the only entities to espouse this logic. The gay press, leaders of national lesbian and gay organizations, and many rank-and-file activists have welcomed the marriage between money and the movement. They've spent thousands of hours building alliances with corporate sponsors and encouraging their constituencies to assert their buying power by supporting "gay friendly" (or simply "gay tolerant") businesses and boycotting those with antigay policies. In contrast with the "business, not politics" argument, such strategies reveal the inseparability of business and identity politics in the current era. As communications theorist Katherine Sender points out, it's not simply that marketers are *misrepresenting* the real or authentic queer politics—instead, they are helping to imagine and create what it now means to be queer.[30]

All of these trends are part of what historian Lisa Duggan has called the "new homonormativity," or the promotion of a lesbian and gay politics organized around the pursuit of rights traditionally granted to white, middle-class heterosexuals, such as privacy, domesticity, and consumption. Building on Michael Warner's term "heteronormativity," which refers to all of the ways that heterosexuality is taken for granted in both cultural and institutional life, Duggan draws our attention to what is now taken for granted about gay identity and culture—namely, that what lesbians and gay men want most is access to a mainstream, safe, and respectable existence filled with high fashion, stylish home decor, and the possibility of parenthood. This pervasive and often inaccurate message about what "we" want is communicated to lesbians and gay men not only through marketing and popular media, but also internally, by LGBT movement leaders and the gay press. According to Duggan, homonormativity has redefined the very terms of LGBT politics, such that *equality* now means "narrow, formal access to a few conservatizing institutions."[31]

Chasin, Sender, and Duggan offer vital and hard-hitting criticisms of the way that capital is shaping national lesbian and gay politics, but what does this trend mean for local queer organizations and the activists within them? What do homonormative politics look like at the local level? Chasin briefly illustrates that many queer organizations have become economically dependent upon corporate funders who offer financial sponsorship in exchange for access to loyal consumers. Many corporations now gain access to the gay dollar through relationships with queer organizations that can help them brand their product as *the* official cell phone, sports car, credit card, beer, and so on, for the queer "community." Queer organizations can offer corporations name and logo visibility at LGBT pride parades, film festivals, fundraising dinners, and other high-profile events, and are eager to accept grants and sponsorships from corporations in exchange for access to queer consumers.

But this trend toward *economic* dependency is not the only way that LGBT organizations are reliant upon corporations. In this book I argue that queer projects have also become *culturally* and *ideologically* dependent upon corporations. In addition to accepting corporate grants and sponsorships (which are arguably needed), queer activists also turn to the business model for ideas about how to manage and represent their own internal race, gender, and socioeconomic differences; how to handle conflict and inequality; and how to transcend gay-only politics and achieve diversity. Corporate marketing techniques and diversity practices not only inform how LGBT activists sell *gay* identity to funders and the public, they also influence how LGBT activists represent a much broader range of identities and social justice issues—to the public, to each other, and to themselves. While critical research on the gay market tells us much about the reframing of gay identity, here I consider a different question: How have corporate-originated ideas about *race, gender, and socioeconomic class* been imported into the LGBT movement?

As illustrated in the following chapters, diversity is now the primary mode of political engagement with difference in the United States, and queer organizations, like almost all organizations, are fast at work on diversity-related projects. As I will show, the influx of profit-based ideas and practices into queer organizations has resulted in the availability of a model for how to approach diversity from an instrumentalist perspective, one that prioritizes organizational effectiveness and the mastery of respected diversity techniques over queer subculture and its unique forms of challenge to systems of dominance. I illustrate that corporate diversity considerations can be easily translated for use in the movement realm by teaching activists to prioritize questions such as the following: Do our advertising materials convey multiple forms of diversity? Have we tapped all possible funding sources interested in diversity? How does our diversity measure up to that of other queer organizations? How will diversity increase our overall effectiveness? And so on. While such questions may be important, they are also the questions that have reduced queer diversity to its instrumental function, or to a matter of public image, a marketable skill, and a new realm of liberal competition.

While private business provides the model for leveraging diversity to meet institutional and financial goals, this instrumental approach extends into public realms as well. As I explore in Chapter 5, many queer organizations are economically dependent upon public foundations and government entities that, like corporate donors, help to set movement priorities by determining which identities and political issues are most deserving of financial support. This dynamic is one outcome of what critical race scholar Dylan Rodriguez refers to as the "non-profit industrial complex," through which state, corporate, and philanthropic organizations partner with one another to ensure elite control over progressive social movements.[32] In this system, distributors of large grants, such as foundations, not only determine which political struggles survive, grow, or receive public attention, but they also encourage competition, managerialism, and careerism among activists.[33] In competing for grants, activists are encouraged to package themselves as "culturally competent" professionals (i.e., in touch with the diversity of their surrounding communities, but also institutionally savvy) and to package their cause as more urgent than those of their competitors. Rather than building a broad-based and collaborative social justice movement, the nonprofit industrial complex is characterized by bureaucracy, resource scarcity, and competition.

Within queer politics, the competition for limited nonprofit resources has been exemplified by the tension between HIV/AIDS projects and other non-HIV related gay liberation projects. As many writers have argued, lesbian and gay identity politics were overshadowed by the AIDS epidemic in the 1980s and 1990s,[34] a dynamic that made lesbians—an ostensibly "low-risk" population—less compelling in the eyes of philanthropists interested in "the spectacle of AIDS."[35] Securing public funding for queer programs became contingent upon demonstrating "high risk," or a life-or-death health threat comparable to AIDS and legible to philanthropists. This risk-based economy links diversity and social justice with a relatively narrow set of health issues, issues that describe the needs of some groups (such as queer men of color) but elide the needs of others (such as queer women of color). Just as conceptualizations of difference emerging from within corporations are often simplistic and static, philanthropy's interest in "target" or "at-risk" identity groups is often based on narrow ideas about which populations are fundable and in need, and which are not. As I will show, this dynamic represents another form of diversity instrumentalism, in which activists embody, or fail to embody, a marketable or fundable social problem. In sum, the corporate diversity model need not be imposed directly by corporate actors in order for bodies, communities, and inequalities to be assigned an economic, or otherwise instrumental, value.

The Instrumental Uses of Diversity

A few years ago, a white feminist student of mine applied for a job managing the LGBT resource center at my university. She accurately anticipated that she should be prepared to answer interview questions about how she would bring in more students of color to the resource center and address the multiple and intersecting forms of inequality facing LGBT students on campus. These sorts of multi-identity questions are now commonly asked of people interviewing for jobs in community-based organizations. In my student's case, the questions simultaneously communicated a history of racial discrimination on campus—for instance, few people of color had been involved with the LGBT center—as well as a shared understanding that eliminating racism was a queer and collective concern. After being offered the job, the student shared with me her belief that being prepared to speak about multiple issues was central to her success in the interview. She knew that she needed to be articulate about racism to get the job managing the LGBT resource center. But how does this kind of multi-identity discourse matter and what does it mean? Two years later, the LGBT center's white reputation on campus had not changed, and it continued to be run primarily by progressive white lesbians and gay men who were committed to, and articulate about, race and gender diversity. The present generation of queer activists is regularly held accountable to multi-identity politics and the varied needs and interests of the diverse lesbian and gay communities they serve. However, as in my student's case, being armed with an intersectional analysis and engaging in multi-issue politics accomplishes more than taking a step toward social justice. Multi-identity discourses also have instrumental and institutional functions, such as getting the job, the grant, the skills, or the connections.

My analysis focuses on three primary instrumental functions of diversity programs and rhetoric in queer organizations: public image management, establishing diversity expertise and professional diversity standards within the field of queer organizing, and marketing diverse queer people and projects to funders interested in specific identity groups. Each of these approaches to diversity moves toward race, class, and gender inclusion and equality, yet each simultaneously prioritizes organizational financial interests and the professional interests of queer movement leaders over the political, social, and economic interests of the queer grassroots. As in many workplaces, diversity skills are a new form of cultural capital for leaders and staff in queer organizations, signifying both professional skills and political alignment with the diversity focus of the LGBT movement. But who is benefiting the most from this form of capital, and how is it being put to use?

DiversityInc, an online corporate diversity magazine, publishes an annual and much-anticipated ranking of the "Top 50 Companies for Diversity." Dozens of similar corporate diversity rankings and reports are produced by various special-interest groups each year.[36] As these rankings illustrate, diversity is often treated like a competitive sport, in which corporations vie for consumer loyalty and target markets. Ironically, the winners in the diversity game are wealthy multinational corporations, not individuals or groups positioned at the intersection of multiple forms of injustice, or the people we might crassly term "the most diverse." Following the corporate model, many queer organizations have bought into the idea that multi-identity rhetoric and programs will give them the competitive edge needed to win grants and promote growth. Similarly, the diversity projects undertaken by queer organizations are often rooted in the logic that reliable knowledge about diversity comes from the top down, or from "professionals" who have been trained to manage, represent, and celebrate multiple forms of identity-based difference.

Yet who gets edged out as diversity is ushered in? Ironically, the case studies reveal that working-class queers and queer people of color are often marginalized as organizational channels for managing and celebrating diversity are created and new forms of diversity knowledge and skill are concretized. Working-class queers are perceived as underskilled when it comes to diversity, while queers of color are offered access to leadership as long as they can adapt to white-normative ways of engaging with diversity and queer politics. Just as the professionalization of diversity has kept white and middle-class interests intact in the broader political-economic environment, so too does diversity culture threaten to undermine the potential of grassroots organizations to envision and work toward sustainable structural change.

Defiant Diversities Strike Back

If diversity politics are failing, then what constitutes success? In each of the queer projects analyzed here, the emphasis on diversity has promoted growth and legitimacy and has resonated for many queer activists invested in the prosperity and improved public image of queer people. Across the boundaries of race, gender, and class, some queer activists are deeply invested in their normalcy, their essential selfhood (their gayness, or Latinoness, or femininity, or transgenderism, etc), their "at-risk" identities, and their membership in a nostalgic and naturalized LGBT "community." Others, however, have been on the losing end of queer normalcy, fundability, and identity consolidation. They've tried and failed to do diversity the professional way. They've been burned out by countless diversification projects (trainings, meetings, retreats, etc.) that misrecognize, diminish, or attempt to compute their differences. They've struggled to find a place within economies of risk and need, and found that doing so requires countless indignities and bizarre identitarian spin. These "strugglers" are most often historically oppressed groups—working class queers, queer people of color, and dykes of color in particular. Yet in the context of the queer movement's rising incentives to address racism, sexism, and poverty, it is not enough to say that queer politics has failed to recognize the intersectional formation of oppression. Instead, it's more accurate to say that many queer projects have taken up intersectionality in the most conventional of ways, inviting the most presentable, predictable, and legibly urgent issues to the fore. For instance, as I discuss in Chapter 3, the right to child care at queer pride festivals is a feminist issue, a race and class issue, and a queer issue. But so too is the right to public sexuality and an environment free of the glorification of innocence, reproduction, and nuclear family formations. When these rights come into conflict, a respectable diversity politics chooses children and innocence; queer diversity politics chooses public sex.

Fortunately, the mainstreaming of diversity has produced internal challenges from activists uninterested in rhetorical, professional, and respectable approaches to difference. At the empirical level, this study shows how activists draw upon three primary modes of resistance—antiprofessionalism, antidiscursivity, and anticommodification—to rebel against "diversity as usual." At the theoretical level, I will argue that in an era in which normativity and mainstreaming function as the primary means of disabling identity movements, "queer"—as a political metaphor for defiance against the institutional and state forces that normalize and commodify difference—offers a necessary contribution to all struggles for intersectional social justice.

To flesh out the stakes of this argument, I draw on three bodies of scholarship. First, feminist intersectional theory has become the dominant framework used by scholars and activists to understand the relationship between multiple inequalities. Its primary assertion is that inequalities are interlocking and multiplicative—one form generally reinforces others and affects how they will be experienced. Rooted in an analysis of sexism in the civil rights movement and racism in the feminist movement, intersectional theory developed largely in response to the limitations of single-identity politics.[37] Feminists of color, in particular, have demonstrated that single-identity movements exclude constituents and fail to see the complex mechanisms behind the very injustice they intend to address. In this vein, I look to a growing body of intersectional research on social movements. These studies have begun to ground intersectional theory by examining how activists address dominant institutions, the public, and community members from a multi-issue perspective.

Critical race theory also heavily informs my analysis, providing a crucial foundation for sorting through the complexities and contradictions of diversity. Critical race theorists have exposed the damaging structural effects of seemingly progressive developments in race relations, including increased media representation of people of color, school and workplace multiculturalism campaigns, and the development of new antiracist norms. While these changes have resulted in greater levels of visibility and inclusion for many people of color, such gains are often made without posing challenges to the power and privileges of white elites. This study expands upon these critiques of race-based multiculturalism by examining the additional complexity of popular diversity discourses that attempt to describe and celebrate multiple axes of difference.

Last, I turn to queer theory to drive home the limitations of current approaches to identity politics and to shed light on the relationship between diversity and normativity. Queer theorists emphasize that while constructing provisional collective identities has proven to be a necessary tactical move for marginalized groups, group identities are also vulnerable to countless forms of regulation and co-optation made possible by the shared belief that identities are (a) real, fixed, coherent, and knowable, and (b) unified by a common struggle for normalcy, safety, prosperity, reproduction, and the like. Such considerations are rarely taken into account in research on social movements, and I draw on queer theory to illustrate the ways in which even multi-identity politics are vulnerable to the undermining effects of co-optation and commodification.

I conclude by offering a "queer intersectional" framework as a new means of evaluating what constitutes intersectional resistance, one that draws important distinctions between instrumental diversity strategies oriented toward short-term institutional legitimacy, on the one hand, and hybrid multi-identity practices rooted in deeper and more sustainable forms of resistance and critique, on the other. "Queer intersectionality" is an approach that strives for racial, gender, socioeconomic, and sexual diversity, but also resists the institutional forces that seek to contain and normalize differences, or reduce them to their use value.

Into the Field: Studying Queer Los Angeles

This project did not begin as a study of queer organizations. Instead, in January 2000, I moved to Los Angeles with the intention of interviewing gay men employed in the beauty and entertainment industries. At the time, I hoped to investigate gay men's role in the construction of female beauty, and this interest had developed from my surprise and disappointment when gay male friends and fellow activists repeatedly expressed sexist judgments about women, their bodies, and their failed consumer choices ("How *could* she wear that!"). Yet during my initial interviews, I began to feel that the project was simply too narrow. In Los Angeles, the rhetoric about money, beauty, equality, and diversity—in sum, the quest for fabulousness—extended far beyond gay men's beliefs about women. As I moved through lesbian and gay activist and professional circles in Los Angeles, I encountered a sea of liberal humanists who were interested in talking about much more than gender and sexual politics. Even white gay male television writers (who happened to be the first group I interviewed) sidestepped my apparently passé questions about sexism and redirected the discussion to "diversity issues" more generally, especially racial diversity. During these interviews, I began to wonder how this broad diversity agenda had penetrated the ranks of chic gay male

Hollywood. In some ways, it was a welcome surprise, though I was cautious. "Diversity" was what was on people's minds, and thus the project evolved.

These initial interviews kept drawing my attention to the relationship between LGBT politics and popular ideas about the benefits of diversity. Given this development, I decided to shift my focus to the current state of LGBT identity politics and to locate the study in local queer organizations in Los Angeles—sites where queer activists were engaged in daily work of negotiating and representing queer differences. While I had not originally selected Los Angeles as the site for a study of LGBT organizations, it proved to be an ideal city in which to examine emergent tensions within queer identity politics. In her book *Mapping Gay L.A.*, Moira Kenney notes that both popular and academic accounts of the lesbian and gay movement have overlooked Los Angeles, in part because the decentralization of queer communities in Los Angeles makes them less visible and more difficult to characterize than those of New York and San Francisco. Yet Kenney adds that the enigmatic character of queer life and politics in Los Angeles, and specifically the lack of a single gay enclave, is what makes it a particularly important site for the examination of how diverse people and communities lay claim to place—including bars, neighborhoods, streets, and local organizations.

I chose the three organizations that are the subjects of this book because each is marked, both spatially and culturally, by its own distinct relationship to difference and inequality in Los Angeles. I was introduced to Christopher Street West (CSW), the organization that produces Los Angeles' LGBT pride festival and parade, when friends told me that the organization was reportedly run by white gay men and had long been known for the exclusion of women and people of color. CSW is located in the predominantly white, gay male, and upper-middle-class city of West Hollywood, also known as "Boys Town." The second organization, the L.A. Gay & Lesbian Center (the Center), claims to be the oldest and largest lesbian and gay social service organization in the world. The Center is located in the heart of Hollywood, the area of Los Angeles famous for the glamour of the entertainment industry, but also home to the highest concentration of homeless youth, many of whom are queer. It is difficult to live in L.A. and not hear about the Center simply by word of mouth, as it is well-known for the countless services it provides (mostly for poor and working-class queers) as well as for its lavish fundraisers and celebrity supporters. Bienestar, the subject of the third case study, is an HIV-focused health organization that is run primarily by and for gay and lesbian Latinos. Latinos are the largest ethnic group in Los Angeles County and Bienestar is arguably the county's most visible organization for queer people of color.

Each of the organizations is engaged in a different kind of queer project from the others, but each is also representative of similar organizations in other large cities. Christopher Street West is one of twenty-five pride festival organizations in California alone and part of a rapidly growing network of state, national, and international pride associations that exchange information about how to produce such events. Lesbian and gay community resource centers, like the L.A. Center, are the most common type of LGBT organizations in the nation. There are approximately 120 such centers in the United States, ranging from small offices that offer basic counseling and referrals to multisite complexes offering services as broad as housing for homeless youth, art galleries, coffee houses, and theater arts facilities. While both CSW and the Center are nearly forty years old, Bienestar is part of a slightly newer organizational field that formed in the early 1990s. AIDS service organizations (ASOs) targeting specific racial/ethnic communities are now a common feature of most large cities in the United States, due largely to the rise in HIV infections among gay men of color in the 1990s.

Getting In and Getting Close: Reflections on Queer Fieldwork

I began research for this project in January 2000 and ended almost three years later in September 2002, by which time I had conducted thirty-one open-ended, tape-recorded, and transcribed interviews (one to two hours in length) and had put in, quite literally, thousands of hours of participant observation in the three organizations. My goal was to become as involved in the inner workings of the three organizations as possible, but within professional and personal ethical limits. At CSW, I joined the organization's board of directors as the chair of the Volunteer Relations Committee and took field notes as I helped produce the 2000 pride event over the course of eight months (from March through October 2000). Inspired by other feminist workplace ethnographies,[38] I gained access to the L.A. Gay & Lesbian Center by taking a job in the development department as the director of corporate and foundation fundraising. I had already begun interviewing Center employees in February 2000; however, I was able to deepen the study of the Center during my eighteen months of employment there (from April 2001 to September 2002) and was also able to take notes at staff meetings and other Center events. I was least closely involved as a participant at Bienestar, though I received significant access to the organization through my then-partner, who was employed as the coordinator of Bienestar's queer women's program. My partner's sponsorship not only increased my access to Bienestar, but also facilitated the development of my friendships with women in the organization.[39] For nine months, from June 2000 to February 2001, I attended dozens of meetings, events, and social gatherings at Bienestar. In each of the case studies, I used a grounded theory approach to analyze my fieldnotes, allowing my hypotheses to surface and transform throughout the research process.[40] I also employed what sociologist Mitchell Duneier has called "diagnostic" ethnography; I repeatedly checked my observations against both participants' accounts and the theoretical frameworks with which I was engaged.[41]

In addition to participant observation, I conducted a few formal interviews with leaders, staff, volunteers, and other stakeholders in each of the organizations: five interviews at CSW; twenty interviews at the Center; and eight at Bienestar.[42] The number of interviews generally reflected the size of each organization. All participants in this study were assigned pseudonyms and assured that their identities would remain confidential. This form of confidentiality, and use of human subjects in this research, was approved by the University of California's Internal Review Board.[43] I also received formal permission to study CSW and the Center from the organizations' board members and executive managers, respectively. Given tensions between women employees and male directors at Bienestar (described in Chapter 5), I did not formally request approval from Bienestar's board to study the organization; however, leaders in the organization, including one board member and the executive director, consented to an interview "for my dissertation about gender relations at Bienestar."

Receiving these kinds of permissions does not resolve many of the interpersonal and political tensions that arise when conducting fieldwork, particularly when one is committed to feminist, queer, and critical race approaches. Studying Bienestar, for instance, was complicated by my discomfort with being a queer white woman inside a distinctly and exclusively Latino organization—an organization that was founded, in part, in response to the racism of white gay men and lesbians. In addition to wanting to be unobtrusive, I was ambivalent about relying upon my partner, a Latina, to provide me with access to participants and vouch for my trustworthiness. Well aware of the history of white scholars' misrepresentations of people of color, I had several long discussions with my partner about whether I should be "airing the dirty laundry" of a community not my own. During these conversations, we decided together how to define the boundaries of my participant observation and determine when the presence of a white researcher would not be threatening or disrespectful at Bienestar's meetings and other events. Though my account of Bienestar has undoubtedly been shaped by my racial privilege and outsiderness, ultimately I decided that including Bienestar, a vitally important queer organization in Los Angeles, resulted in the better outcome.

In weighing these considerations, I was also guided by recent theorizing about cross-race research, a literature that ultimately brought me back to questions of intersectionality. As sociologist France Winddance Twine points out, neither race nor gender, class, or sexuality is the only relevant signifier of power and difference between researchers and participants, and therefore most researchers are neither completely inside nor outside the social world they are studying.[44] In fact, as my analytic focus and research questions evolved, so did my perception of myself as an insider or outsider, or as someone with more or less social power than the people I was studying. As I explain in Chapter 3, my study of CSW involved being the only woman on an all-male board of directors. This situation, combined with my initial interest in rumors about lesbian exclusion at CSW's pride festival, suggested that I was studying people with more power than myself, or "studying up." Yet later, as my interest shifted to conflicts over cultural capital at CSW, my status as a middle-class doctoral student volunteering alongside working-class gay men came into focus. At CSW, I was both insider and outsider, and studying both "up" and "down."

Striking the right balance between intimacy and professional distance was also a challenge that emerged repeatedly throughout my research. For example, some would argue that involving an intimate partner in one's research choices—such as I did in my study of Bienestar—is a violation of the principles of objectivity and nonintervention. Traditionally, ethnographers have been encouraged to strive for scientific objectivity or to avoid the ways that becoming invested in a particular research outcome or being "too close" to research participants might bias the research process.[45] Yet feminist, queer, and critical race scholars have challenged this perspective by demonstrating that the research process is often infused with intimacy, sexuality, power disparities, dangerous possibilities, and various political and personal tensions that underlie relationships between researchers and participants.[46] In contrast with the objective science model, queer, feminist, and critical race scholars are often motivated to understand (through research) our own experiences and surroundings, including the cultures, communities, workplaces, and political movements to which we belong.

Queer scholarship, in particular, is often made possible by the use of unconventional research methods, or what could arguably be called "queer methods." Queer researchers have studied their own experiences inside gay bars,[47] in cybersex exchanges,[48] and in public bathrooms (sites where gender and sexuality are highly regulated);[49] some have also described the presence of love and desire between themselves and their informants.[50] This kind of queer research produces firsthand knowledge about gendered and sexual practices, subcultural formations, and the maintenance of sex and gender taboos, and it could not be accomplished without fully entering queer worlds. It could be argued, then, that queer methodology, which reflects queer subculture generally, is oriented toward intimate connections with participants, access gained through subcultural belonging, and greater comfort with the presence of sexuality in the presumably asexual realm of research. Indeed, my own queer identification was often the glue that bonded me to participants in this study, many of whom became my friends and political allies as we marched together, argued with each other, exchanged gay sex jokes, and planned the revolution.

The Chapters to Follow

In the remainder of this book, I argue that queer critique makes a necessary contribution to all forms of multi-issue, or intersectional, activism. This argument unfolds through the book's six chapters. The first half of Chapter 2 reviews the activist and theoretical roots of intersectionality, as well as sociological arguments about the conditions that enable successful multi-identity politics. In the second half of the chapter, I contrast these sociological approaches with queer theory's take on identity politics, and I analyze the rise of diversity culture as a powerful example of the contradictions embedded in multi-identity organizing. Overall, Chapter 2 sets the stage for the case studies by arguing for the need to critically reexamine what constitutes "successful" intersectional politics.

Chapters 3 through 5 tell the stories of the three queer organizations, with emphases on both the processes of mainstreaming and efforts to resist these processes. Chapter 3 considers the emergence of diversity-related knowledge and skills as a new form of cultural capital among queer activists. Here I examine conflicts between the "vulgar" and antiprofessional working-class organizers of the Christopher Street West L.A. pride event and lesbian and gay professionals, the gay press, and local gay politicians in Los Angeles. The chapter documents a series of press exposés and political interventions that drew attention to the "incompetence" and poor social skills of the event organizers, criticisms that also pointed to a need for a "more professional" team of organizers who could speak articulately about race and gender diversity and ensure the visual representation of diversity in the pride parade. My analysis is focused on the convergence of political values that lend support to multiple issues and differences, and upper-middle-class values that emphasize the importance of professionalism, visual aesthetics, and diversity "skills." Often lost in this process, I will argue, is the voice and representation of working-class activists and alternative conceptualizations of diversity that foreground subculture, spontaneity, and what Leila Rupp and Verta Taylor have called "the politics of vulgarity."[51]

Chapter 4 emphasizes the growing influence of mainstream diversity concepts on the queer movement, with particular focus on the influx of corporate diversity management practices into large community-based queer organizations. Here I focus on the contested racial identity and culture of the L.A. Gay & Lesbian Center, an organization with a national reputation for multiculturalism, a growing presence of people of color in leadership, and more than 50 percent people of color on staff. However, despite the organization's discursive and programmatic emphasis on racial diversity, the Center maintained a local reputation among many queer people of color as the white LGBT organization in Los Angeles. I illustrate that the white culture of the organization was marked not only by the whiteness of many members, but also by the excessive and instrumental focus on documenting and celebrating its own diversity to funders and other organizations—a strategy brought to the organization by leaders who drew on their previous corporate sector experience with diversity management and community relations. Internal critics of the organization resisted the Center's incitement to discourse about diversity, calling instead for a "just do it" approach rooted in ethics and actions.

Chapter 5 shifts the analytic lens from professional diversity discourses emerging from within white corporate culture to some surprisingly similar discourses of risk and need that have been heavily informed by grassroots HIV activism within communities of color. Bienestar, the subject of Chapter 5, began as a lesbian and gay Latino organization but expanded its mission to include HIV, health, and multiple forms of risk facing gay and lesbian Latinos in Los Angeles. Yet the story of Bienestar's transformation highlights the often flawed and dangerous logic of at-risk identities, and specifically the way that being able to demonstrate one kind of risk and fundability—risk easily comparable to that posed by HIV—has become a necessary task for lesbians wishing to lay claim to programs and resources within queer organizations. Chapter 5 shows that this economy of risk represents yet another form of diversity instrumentalism, in which full access and participation rests upon the ability of identity groups to embody a fundable social problem and articulate their belonging using prevailing—and often ill-fitting—discourses of risk and need. Defying this economy, lesbians at Bienestar organized for their place in the organization based upon reciprocity and accountability, rather than fundability.

In Chapter 6, I build on the activist strategies presented in the case studies in order to argue for a disavowal of the mainstream roots of diversity. While some view the broad circulation of diversity concepts as a measure of movement-level success and a reflection of progress in the larger culture, I conclude the book with the argument that the queer movement should be held to more rigorous standards regarding the practice of "queer intersectional resistance." Chapter 6 points the way toward such a model by offering a synthesis of queer and intersectional theory, and suggesting a new method for evaluating what constitutes "successful" multi-identity politics.

Chapter 2

The Mainstreaming of Intersectionality: Doing Identity Politics in a Diversity Culture

A song by Le Tigre, a popular feminist techno-punk band based in New York, is titled, "They Want Us to Make a Symphony out of the Sound of Women Swallowing Their Tongues." It begins with a gentle male voice asking a young woman what possible obstacles women still face after so many gains have been made by the feminist movement. For the entire remainder of the song, different young women swallow their tongues in attempt to answer, their voices stop and start, they stutter and fail to articulate any complete words until the song screeches to an end. It is a difficult question to answer, in part because there are, of course, so many answers. The song comments on the current state of the feminist movement, particularly as it exists in relation to a dominant culture that resists gender equality primarily by insisting that it has already been achieved. This dynamic, not unique to feminism, is an obstacle also faced by the racial justice movement and, to a lesser extent, the queer movement. Identity movements in the United States, and activists within them, evaluate their successes and failures under the conditions of what I call "diversity culture," in which multiple inequalities violate social norms and are therefore imagined to be uncommon or steadily vanishing. Many scholars have critically examined the shape and function of diversity and multiculturalism projects in the broader sociopolitical environment; however, it is also important to understand the effects of diversity culture on grassroots movements themselves and on the very projects from which we expect our newest and most cutting-edge identity discourses and practices to emerge.

Virulent opposition and countermovement organizing often stimulates or strengthens social protest by providing activists with a visible threat against which to mobilize.[1] Conversely, it is difficult to sustain a social movement when a large segment of the public believes it is no longer needed, and it is especially difficult when the lines between activists, the general public, and the enemy are unclear. These lines are blurred when activist discourses about equality and diversity begin to influence mainstream culture, which is arguably a sign indicating that the goals of the movement are being met. However, they are also blurred when the reverse happens, or when mainstream diversity discourses become integrated into the frameworks and strategies of grassroots movements themselves. The latter process is the focus of this chapter.

I use the term "diversity culture" to refer to the ways in which celebrating identity-based diversity and equality have become a part of daily life.[2] Of course, at one level, the infusion of social justice discourse into everyday life is what cultural activism (consciousness raising, political performance art, community and cultural centers, etc.) is all about.[3] However, in diversity culture, being critical of inequality also serves economic and ideological interests unrelated to social change, or to dismantling the systems that reproduce race, gender, and socioeconomic hierarchies. Major corporations launch advertising campaigns that depict social problems and invoke social change as a means of selling their products, even when their own business practices are the driving force behind the inequities being invoked.[4] As I write, a current example is national banking giant Washington Mutual's 2006 print and television campaign advertising free checking accounts. The campaign is organized around disparaging images of white male banking elites at competitor banks that, presumably unlike Washington Mutual, enable the "rich to keep getting richer." One print ad depicts a balding white male banking executive stating, "Free checking for life? Over my butler's dead body!" Not long ago, the marketing strategies of financial institutions relied upon the imagery of the business-savvy white male banker to whom customers could entrust their finances. Today, even banks—the very symbols of global capitalism—recognize that they might better reach consumers through a self-parodic and critical commentary on wealth, whiteness, and/or masculinity.

Similarly, at the political level, conservative politicians such as President George Bush expand anti-immigrant and anti–affirmative action legislation while also actively recruiting people of color and white women into government office and working with diversity consultants to develop strategies for appealing to these constituencies ("Viva George Bush!"). Such developments exemplify the recent neoliberal merging of diversity and equality rhetoric with the goals of free-market capitalism and conservative political agendas.[5] While this movement toward diversity is often superficial and tokenistic, more substantive forms of power and inclusion are becoming increasingly available to minority groups (white women, people of color, and queers) willing to assimilate into the cultural and political mainstream. As historian Lisa Duggan has argued, people of color willing to advocate for color-blind racial politics or lesbians and gay men committed to being "normal" are "currently a relatively small, emergent minority—but [they are] a highly visible new formation within neoliberal politics."[6]

At the individual level, diversity culture has also expanded the range of people who feel a sense of ownership over social justice discourses, including members of dominant groups (like myself) who may speak authoritatively (like I do) about forms of oppression they have not experienced. Ten years ago, men in my women's studies courses sat in the back row of the classroom registering expressions of guilt and anger on their faces. Now they are commonly the most vocal students in my courses, speaking up eagerly and often to share stories about their girlfriends' and mothers' experiences of sexism and to denounce the sexist attitudes of their fathers and male friends. While in many ways this is a promising development, I have also watched it produce a greater silence among women students who report in course evaluations that they find it difficult to get a word in edgewise.

Contrary to the view that more representation and visibility will generally benefit oppressed groups, it is also important to consider that when stigmatized identities become the subject of popular discourse and representation, they also become increasingly subject to certain forms of social control. For instance, increased representation of African Americans, particularly on network television, has both advanced *and* in some ways undermined the struggle for racial equality by enabling white conservatives to point to "evidence" that racism is a problem of the past.[7] Whites have also consumed and appropriated Black popular culture to such an extent—giving each other "daps," wearing hip-hop clothing, and affectionately referring to one another using the term "nigga"—that many scholars and activists have questioned the political value of visibility itself.[8]

In diversity culture, multiple identities (and the histories and struggles they invoke) are talked about, represented, and celebrated, but they are also managed, commodified, and reduced to easy-to-understand stereotypes. Diversity culture reflects a new era in which social justice concepts are widely available and in which talking about identity-based oppression has become a television cliché. Token representatives of oppressed groups are now a staple of reality television shows, such as MTV's *The Real World* (e.g., the flamboyant white gay man, the angry Black man, the oversexed Latina, etc.). It is not simply diversity that producers of reality programs are after, but the interaction and conflict that occurs *between* these groups, particularly with respect to their different experiences of oppression. The embodiment of multiple identities in one "character" represents another form of reality television's engagement with multiple identities. Intersectionality, as embodied by people who are, for example, both Latino and queer, functions to heighten the realness, and yet also the freakiness, of the show.[9]

In this sense, diversity culture also refers to the mainstreaming of intersectionality. A concept first theorized by feminist scholars and activists of color, intersectionality is "a non-additive conception of identities that sees systems of domination as interdefining one another."[10] Clearly, mainstream versions of diversity—almost always additive in their approach—are a far cry from intersectional analyses. Yet in many ways, the broad circulation of diversity concepts makes intersectionality appear to be no longer news, even in mainstream culture. In both corporate and popular culture in the United States, the word "diversity" is intended to evoke shared beliefs about the current state of American identity politics—that we live with a shameful history of race and gender discrimination; that we no longer consider these inequities to be justifiable; that we recognize people to be complex, different, and irreducible to any one aspect of their multi-layered identities; that we appreciate and celebrate our differences because they are key to our individual and collective knowledge, skills, and effectiveness (in business, knowledge production, culture-making, etc.). For example, the Verizon Corporation, voted #1 in the 2006 *DiversityInc* "Top 50 Companies for Diversity" list, explains the goal of its diversity strategy as follows:

> to have an aligned and integrated workplace where diversity is
> transparent, and where Verizon is an inclusive organization that
> leverages the diversity of employees, customers, and suppliers for
> increased productivity, profitability and an enhanced reputation. Our
> definition of diversity includes the whole range of human differences,
> including age, ethnicity, education, sexual orientation, work style, race,
> gender, and more. Over time, we have made diversity an integral part
> of our business.[11]

According to Verizon, diversity is about more than representation (such as showing diverse faces in marketing materials); it is about being an "inclusive organization." Diversity is not just another word for harmonious cross-racial understanding; it's about "the whole range of human differences." And, inclusion and multiple differences are not simply worth mentioning to be fair; they are an *integral* part of business success.

In the early 1980s, arguments about the multiplicity of identities and inequalities—or the triad of "race/class/gender"—represented the cutting edge of feminist theory. Today, multiplicity is an emergent theme in film and television, a central component of corporate marketing and diversity rhetoric, and a centerpiece of liberal identity politics. In the workplace, the ability to understand and utilize multiple forms of difference simultaneously is not only a marketable skill, but a signifier of good judgment and professionalism. Correspondingly, in the realm of nonprofit organizing, multi-identity political discourses sometimes garner more, not less, institutional legitimacy. As I will show in the chapters to follow, queer projects transcend gay politics not only to be fair and inclusive, but also to enhance their reputation and gain legitimacy in the eyes of other nonprofit organizations, funders, state agencies, and the press.

There is little doubt that the neoliberal merging of business values with equal rights discourses has profoundly affected the strategies of contemporary social movements. Yet sociological research on diversity in social movements has given very limited attention to this trend. A growing body of sociological research has, however, focused on the need for new conceptual frameworks and organizing models that account for the intersection of multiple differences, identifications, and inequalities that structure social life. Recent studies of social movements, in particular, have begun to engage theories of intersectionality in order to understand how activists develop political awareness of multiple injustices. Here I build upon and depart from these approaches by emphasizing the broader context in which political organizing occurs. I show that given the complexities and contradictions of neoliberalism, we remain without a clear sociological understanding of what intersectional resistance looks like in an increasingly diversity-obsessed world. Hence, in part 1 of this chapter, I trace the development of intersectional theory as a response to exclusion in identity movements and I describe the solutions to achieving diverse, multi-identity movements that have been offered by sociologists studying intersectionality. In part 2, I build on queer and critical race frameworks to offer a deeper critique of diversity culture and to analyze the ways in which even intersectional and multi-identity approaches are vulnerable to co-optation.

Part 1. Diversity vs. Intersectionality: The Meaning of Multi-Issue Justice

At the same time that social movements work to eliminate one form of injustice, they are often the site of other forms. This has been the seemingly unavoidable underside of most identity-based social movements, which have focused on singular conceptualizations of injustice in order to make their demands more accessible to constituents, the media, and dominant institutions. In her book *Workplace Justice: Organizing Multi-Identity Movements*, Sharon Kurtz refers to this tendency as the "single-identity problem," a problem that has been a long-standing barrier to the mobilization and effectiveness of large and highly visible social movements, such as labor, feminist, and nationalist movements.

The focus on simplistic and singular constructions of identity reflects the ways in which inequalities—racism, poverty, sexism, heterosexism—are ranked by movement leaders who have the public authority and institutional power to define the priorities of the movement.[12] One of the most noted examples is the exclusion experienced by Black women in both racial justice and feminist movements in the United States. Male leaders in the civil rights and Black nationalist movements of the 1950s through the 1970s denied women access to the most visible and powerful positions in the movement, reinforcing the link between Blackness, race politics, and masculinity in public discourse.[13] Similarly, in the first wave of the U.S. women's movement, Black women were not only excluded from white women's suffrage organizations, but many white suffragists made their case for voting rights by asserting that white women's votes would help to strengthen white supremacy.[14] In the 1970s, second-wave white feminists continued to make use of racial arguments to mobilize a largely white feminist movement, but this time by comparing gender inequality to racism. This racism/sexism analogy had long been used by white women to gain support for women's causes by arguing that gender oppression was equally unjust as racial oppression (a claim made by white suffragists), or by positioning race-based movements as models for women's movements, a particularly popular tactic among white feminists during and after the civil rights movement of the 1950s.[15]

While the racism/sexism analogy was an effective tool for mobilizing the white feminist movement, it also denied the historical and institutional differences between structural racism and patriarchy, and incorrectly assumed the experiences of Black women "to be synonymous with that of either Black males or white females."[16] As legal scholar Kimberlé Crenshaw has argued, the institutional effect of the racism/sexism analogy has been to treat people of color and women as mutually exclusive groups, thereby conceptualizing racism as discrimination against men of color and sexism as discrimination against white women. As a result, the experiences of women of color have been frequently omitted from public policy and social movement discourse.[17] A similar analogy has been drawn between homophobia and racism within lesbian and gay movement discourse. By comparing gay rights with the civil rights movement and appealing to white politicians by demonstrating that "we are just like you," LGBT movement leaders have indirectly constructed people of color and lesbians and gay men as mutually exclusive groups.[18] Such strategies have built upon an imaginary "shared whiteness" to appeal for equal rights, helping to reinforce the enduring notion that being queer is "a white thing."

By the late 1970s, queer women of color, such as the members of the Black lesbian feminist group the Combahee River Collective, had already demonstrated that inequalities not explicitly identified, theorized, and opposed by a given social movement would become obstacles to the development of an intersectional movement identity, as well as obstacles to its operational success.[19] Feminists of color were at the forefront of the critical examination of single-identity movements, and the early 1980s marked the rise and proliferation of theory and activism focused on the intersections of identities and oppressions, now commonly referred to as intersectionality. Intersectional theory crystallized around the argument that race, class, and gender are not independent and additive forces, but multiplicative systems that define and support one another.[20] Noting the failure of identity movements in the United States to accomplish the inclusion and equality that they were themselves demanding, feminists of color forged a new multi-identity politics that was, according to the Combahee River Collective, "anti-racist, unlike those of white women, and anti-sexist, unlike those of Black and white men."[21]

Informed by early articulations of intersectional theory as well as the liberationist spirit of New Left politics more generally, many second-wave white feminists also attempted to forge multi-identity political projects, although they were not particularly successful. In the late 1970s, white lesbian separatists had envisioned a new culture that centered on "nonsexist, nonracist and nonclassist" values[22] and modeled "dyke nationalism" after Black nationalism.[23] White lesbian feminist Jill Johnston's dream of a separatist "Lesbian Nation" emphasized the need for a radical multi-issue agenda, yet one that still placed lesbian identity and "women-only space" at the center of political discourse and organization.[24] Not surprisingly, few women of color were drawn to lesbian separatism or to the notion that they should give up racial, cultural, and political alliances with men of color in order to build solidarity with white women.[25] The efforts of white lesbians to build a multi-issue movement only exacerbated the divide between themselves and lesbians of color. Ultimately, many white lesbian feminists focused their energies on exposing gender inequality in the gay liberation movement, resulting in the ironic effort to critique a single-identity movement (in this case, gay liberation) using what one might call a "single-identity critique."

The effort by white lesbians to build a lesbian-centered multi-issue movement is an early example of the way in which even multi-identity projects can be anchored in exclusive, single-identity frameworks. Recognizing this complexity, intersectional theory pointed to the importance of building multi-issue movements that are informed by the unique consciousness of women of color, a consciousness that develops from the simultaneous experience of race, gender, and class inequality.[26] Theories of multiple consciousness,[27] *mestiza* consciousness,[28] outsider consciousness,[29] and differential consciousness[30] each described gendered, racialized, and other multiple and contextual "ways of knowing" about how dominant cultures and institutions operate.[31] Moving beyond gender consciousness and race consciousness, intersectional theory placed *multiplicity* at the center of social justice discourse and promised an expanded understanding of how to engage in multi-identity activism.

Intersectional theory remains a vitally important framework for theorizing inequality within the social sciences. The intersectional approach includes several premises that have been summarized at length elsewhere,[32] but two arguments are particularly relevant to the evolution of multi-issue politics: First, intersectional theorists argue that all systems of domination shape and bolster one another, and for this reason, injustices cannot be separately analyzed or addressed. A clear illustration of the simultaneity of different forms of power and privilege comes from queer, Asian American activist Alice Hom, whom I've heard tell the story of her encounter with a white woman in a women's restroom. The white woman approached Hom, a butch lesbian, and with loud and clear overenunciation told Hom she was in the wrong bathroom. As Hom tells the story, the white woman imagined that she was male because she did not conform to feminine gender norms, but as the woman looked at Hom, she also saw an Asian male who was, therefore, a foreigner unable to read English or decipher the meaning of the sign on the bathroom door. As Hom explains, an analysis of race, gender, or sexuality alone could not fully account for her experience in the bathroom or for her subjectivity as a butch Asian American woman—the logics of racism, sexism, and homophobia each operate simultaneously and together to regulate her.

As Patricia Hill Collins and other intersectional theorists have argued, social justice work is further complicated by the fact that most activists simultaneously occupy the position of oppressor and oppressed.[33] Power is not solely distributed along lines of race, class, and gender, but also age, sexuality, religion, language, culture, physical ability, body size, immigration status, nationality, and countless other status distinctions. Thus, a second defining contribution of intersectional theory is its critique of the notion of universal identity categories, or the idea that resistance efforts can be organized around universal, singular identity claims. Instead, as discussed in the next section, intersectional theory dictates that resistance must be decentralized, local, and autonomous, with opportunities for the strategic formation of coalitions to address issues of common concern.

The Sociology of Intersectionality: Coalitions, Multi-Identity Movements, and "Success"

Because categories such as "people of color," "women," "Latinos," "lesbians," and "poor" are too broad to describe a uniform experience of inequality, intersectional theorists have argued that no single organization or project can effectively address the local and contextual issues of such broadly defined groups. Instead, smaller, local communities of people who share common interests (e.g., Korean garment workers, Chicana lesbians, residents of a specific neighborhood, etc.) can organize more effectively if they focus on the particular experiences and needs of their group.[34] Coalitions can then be forged across various communities and organizations, allowing diverse identity groups to come together for particular causes or protest events without requiring that a single organizational infrastructure meet the needs of all participants.[35] According to this model, a broader range of tactics emerges when people with different experiences of a given injustice combine their knowledge and skills.[36] Building from this understanding, intersectional theorists have emphasized that successful multi-identity activism should be decentralized, fragmented, and locally situated.[37] If intersectionality is the theory, then "coalition politics" is the practice.

Coalitions allow people of different backgrounds and experiences to create "partnerships for change,"[38] participate in "imagined communities" based on common struggle rather than common identity,[39] and ground their activism in a "politics of the flesh" that emphasizes the material realities of their daily lives.[40] Coalitions, particularly those organized around identities, are also examples of what Gayatri Spivak refers to as "strategic essentialism," or the strategic decision to identify with an oversimplified conceptualization of one's group in order to win or protect certain rights.[41] Coalitions are not about the experience of essential sameness, unity, and trust, but about the necessity of alliances to the survival of oppressed groups. Emphasizing that coalitions are not without their challenges and must not be romanticized, Bernice Reagon Johnson argues, "You don't go into a coalition because you just *like* it. The only reason you would consider trying to team up with somebody who could possibly kill you, is because that's the only way you can figure you can stay alive."[42]

Indeed, coalition work has become a common feature of social justice struggles and has gained the attention of sociologists interested in movement strategies and the construction of collective identity. Global justice movements, in particular, such as the World Social Forum movement, have built momentum through the development of local "affinity groups" ranging from university students and grassroots organizers to farmers and families. Such groups organize locally and develop an analysis of the ways in which global issues impact their local and national context, but they also converge for large-scale transnational meetings and actions.[43] Similarly, it could be argued that U.S. identity movements have begun to follow the coalition model. For instance, most large cities in the United States are home to dozens of special-interest LGBT organizations, including organizations that represent distinct gender, racial/ethnic, religious, and age groups (as well as gay parents, professionals, bowlers, motorcyclists, choir members, etc.). While many of these organizations have grown out of local conflicts and dissatisfaction with predecessor organizations, some scholars of social movements have argued that this fragmentation has strengthened the activist base of the lesbian and gay movement by expanding the range of ways to participate.[44]

Yet recent sociological research also indicates that the proliferation of local, autonomous movement organizations and the rise of coalition-based organizing have not eliminated "the single-identity problem," the tendency within even coalition-based movements to emphasize the goals and interests of the most privileged members. When it comes time for convergence, privileged groups may still attempt to control, lead, or otherwise take ownership of a given political struggle, particularly when they have greater access to traditional political power.[45] In his study of multicultural community organizations working together to fight AIDS, sociologist Brett Stockdill found that AIDS activists spent significant time and energy fighting racism and homophobia in their own and other HIV/AIDS organizations and were left with fewer resources for protesting against dominant institutions.[46] Other studies suggest that members of privileged groups shape the culture of activist projects by asserting their own gendered, racial/ethnic, religious, or class-based cultures and traditions (including food, music, style, modes of affect, and physical contact), which in turn define the look and feel of the movement.[47] For instance, activists of color have critiqued anticorporate, anti-globalization, and environmental coalitions for being primarily focused on the concerns of white communities, employing tactics that appeal more to whites than to people of color, or producing a mood and space that is most comfortable for whites.[48]

In particular, the persistence of "white culture" within progressive social movements has called for an examination of the cultural and psychological components of white liberalism. Building on intersectional theory, white scholars have begun to consider the contours of their own consciousness, their own culture, and the relationship of that consciousness and culture to their political decision making and activist involvements. Theorized primarily from the perspective of "the oppressed among the oppressed," early intersectional theory offered little guidance for understanding when, why, and how the "privileged among the oppressed" engage in multi-issue political struggles. How is political urgency developed regarding injustices that one neither sees nor experiences, when one's own concerns are immediate and visible? What factors motivate dominant groups to adopt and sustain an intersectional analysis of injustice?

In response to these questions, several white feminists have taken up the issue of privilege and power among white feminists involved in antiracist work.[49] In many cases, this research has exposed the failure of good intentions, diversity trainings, and antiracist discussion groups to effect long-term change or produce systems of white accountability in feminist organizations.[50] For example, in sociologist Ellen Scott's study of two feminist organizations, she contends that white antiracist discussion groups served as "an important symbolic indicator of the commitment of white women to fighting racism, and . . . convinced many women of color that [the organization] was worth their time and energy despite its legacy of 'white face.' "[51] Yet Scott adds that while the white women who attended antiracist discussion groups recognized the ideological and institutional foundations of racism, they nonetheless struggled to identify and talk about specific examples of their own racism and accountability.[52] Scott's work mirrors several other studies of whiteness that point to the gap between the antiracist values of white Americans and their inability or unwillingness to locate themselves within structures of inequality and accountability.[53]

Building upon these findings, social movements scholars have recently begun to evaluate multi-identity politics by examining not only *who* is involved (are we multicultural?) or whether issues of concern to multiple groups are being addressed (are we addressing homophobia *and* racism *and* sexism?), but also the more subtle social-psychological and cultural processes that enable dominant groups to assert their privilege and centrality, even in the midst of doing multi-identity work. Recognizing the need for a multi-pronged approach that could identify how "real" diversity is accomplished, recent sociological research has begun to shift attention away from analyzing failed attempts to produce inclusive activist organizations and, instead, has begun to map the necessary conditions for success. Such efforts emphasize the importance of multiple approaches, including interventions at the sociopolitical, organizational, and social-psychological levels. In particular, recent studies of have emphasized three factors: multi-identity strategies and tactics; organizational structure (i.e., leadership, formalization, coalition, and collaboration); and cultural and social-psychological factors, such as how to engage in consciousness-raising around multiple relations of power and privilege. I briefly summarize these three factors and return later to the hopeful directions they may, or may not, represent.

First, some accounts indicate that successful multi-identity politics must be measured by political *strategy*, or whether activists are making demands for multiple forms of justice. For instance, in her study of clerical unions, Sharon Kurtz argues that one way to assess multi-identity politics is to evaluate whether an identity movement employs a diversity of tactics that challenge the gendered and racialized injustices that constituents experience at the hands of the opposition, or the dominant institutions that the movement has named as enemy.[54] According to Kurtz, movement strategies and outcomes fall within a spectrum of "color/gender blind" and "color/gender conscious." Color/gender-blind strategies emphasize sameness and are organized around one social grouping or identity that everyone is believed to share in common. Color/gender-conscious strategies emphasize difference through activist organizing around the multiple and institutionally embedded injustices that affect constituents differently. For example, Kurtz argues that the labor activists she studied successfully challenged institutionalized racism and sexism by organizing multi-justice campaigns around issues that disproportionately affected women and people of color, such as affirmative action and child care. Exemplifying color/gender consciousness, this strategy worked to reformulate "labor issues" to include the needs of traditionally marginalized workers, such as women of color.

Other research on multi-identity politics has emphasized organizational structure, with focus on whether members of subordinate groups have access to positions of formal leadership. Some accounts demonstrate that when whites have held more power in movement organizations than people of color, they have protected their access to institutional resources, as well as prioritized their particular goals, values, and conceptual frameworks.[55] In such cases, dramatic restructuring and leadership by people of color has been posited as a necessary means of decentering whiteness and producing truly diverse organizations. In order for movement organizations to be successful at sustaining racial diversity, white members must not only commit to the idea of racial diversity and the recruitment of people of color, but also divest of power to ensure that a critical mass of people of color become decision makers.[56] Other structural factors, such as formalization, have also been linked to the sustainability of racial equality in movements. In contrast with the common progressive assumption that organizational formalization may alienate subordinate groups, bureaucracy and hierarchy can be used to distribute organizational control and regulate dominant groups, particularly if "the time and emotional investment required to make decisions collectively and consensually [has] the unintended consequence of excluding or marginalizing people of color and low-income people."[57] Creating hierarchies, and placing subordinate groups in charge, helps to circumvent the informal networks of power and decision making often controlled by dominant groups in collectivist organizations.

A third approach suggests not only the structural components of social movements reproduce inequality, but also the absence of necessary *social-psychological* work around issues of power and privilege. Successful multi-identity work requires that activists share what Brett Stockdill calls "multidimensional oppositional consciousness," or that they develop the ability to link one experience of inequality (e.g., racism) to that of another (e.g., homophobia).[58] Building a multidimensional consciousness requires that activists use their own experiences, culture, and emotions as a means of connecting to forms of oppression that they do not directly experience and from which they may benefit. Stockdill's study of AIDS activism examines how inequality at the community and movement level, in addition to inequality emanating from dominant institutions, is an obstacle to effective AIDS work. AIDS activists are less effective than they could be because "activists are so busy organizing to challenge intracommunity 'isms,' provide basic AIDS-related social services, and promote empowerment that they have less time . . . to protest against dominant institutions."[59] To combat this problem, Stockdill explains that AIDS activists drew from multiple sets of collective beliefs and oppositional cultures in order to challenge multiple inequalities within marginalized communities. Drawing heavily on intersectional theory, Stockdill concludes that the strategies that emerge from multiple oppositional consciousness are different from those typically used to challenge dominant institutions. Such strategies include, for example, the use of language and cultural symbols of particular communities to link one form of oppositional consciousness to another, such as using "racial oppositional consciousness within communities of color to promote pro-gay/pro-lesbian consciousness."[60]

A synthesis of these three multi-identity approaches—including attention to strategy, organizational structure, and consciousness—offers a promising and practical starting point from which to build diverse, inclusive movements. While the intersectional approach remained largely theoretical within sociology for nearly two decades, scholars of social movements have begun to operationalize the concept by developing a formula for engaging in multi-issue resistance efforts. According to this model, activists must recognize that inequalities are intersecting and complex and translate this awareness into new movement goals, organizational structures, and interpretive frames.

As I demonstrate in the following chapters, the queer organizations that are the subjects of this book had either accomplished each of these measures of successful multi-identity organizing or had made significant forward movement toward these goals. Yet I will also show that their efforts were highly professionalized, financially motivated, or competitive—reflecting the larger neoliberal project of putting diversity to work for institutional gain. As a result, queer activists who resisted the formalization and professionalization of diversity, or who did not constitute an easily representable or fundable target population, were further marginalized—ironically, in the name of diversity. In other words, even the above methods of undertaking multi-identity activism—strategic reformulations, multicultural leadership, and new forms of multi-issue consciousness-raising—can work to reinforce subtle and cultural forms of racial, economic, and gendered dominance.

Local and substantive forms of race and gender diversity are often achieved in queer politics; however, these victories have been used to render other forms of difference irrelevant, particularly those that cannot be easily professionalized or marketed (such as working-class queerness, butch dyke masculinities, and transgender subjectivities). For this reason, I expand upon current models for evaluating intersectional politics at the empirical level not only by looking at the instrumental functions of diversification projects focused on race and gender, but also by considering the limitations of identity politics more generally. The next section draws on queer and critical race theory to explore the ways in which identity claims themselves are vulnerable to institutional forms of discipline and containment. Even for those multicultural projects engaged in intersectional work, the reliance on institutionally recognized frameworks for representing identities, however multiple and intersecting, suggests a bleak future for identity movements.

Part 2. Diversity Culture, Queer Critique, and the Limits of Multi-Identity Politics

Though queer theory has made a profound impact among humanities scholars interested in the limitations of identity politics and the reproduction of social norms, its contribution is often overlooked in the social sciences, including within sociological research on social justice movements. Cross-disciplinary approaches have only recently begun to influence the sociology of social movements, such as a growing number of studies that draw on insights from queer theory to understand trends in gender and sexual politics.[61] Here I turn to queer theory to expand upon sociological approaches to the study of intersectionality and multi-identity activism.

As in queer studies, sociological research on identity has emphasized the social and historical processes through which identity categories are constructed. For instance, British sociologist Mary McIntosh's 1968 work on "the homosexual role" shifted attention away from medical and psychological models of deviance to the social function of labeling and stigmatizing homosexuality.[62] Predating Foucault's French publication of *The History of Sexuality* in 1976, which is often credited as the first account of the social construction of sexual identities, McIntosh and other sociologists helped lay the groundwork for viewing sexual identity not as a fixed or real aspect of the self, but as a new conceptual tool designed to maintain the boundary between normal and abnormal. Similarly, sociologists have also examined the origins and social construction of racial identities,[63] gender identities,[64] and class-based identities.[65]

However, many sociological analyses of inequality have deemphasized the processes of identity construction, focusing instead on the political and economic structures that constrain oppressed groups. In sociological accounts of inequality and resistance, emphasis has often been placed on how subordinate groups respond to oppression by bonding together in communities, embracing and reclaiming their shared identity, and building a common culture of resistance—in other words, the processes through which people make imposed identities meaningful and "real." From this perspective, when the structural consequences associated with identity categories are real, so too do identities become real to the individuals, groups, and cultures who inhabit them. Sociological research on lesbian and gay communities, for example, has focused on how lesbians and gay men manage discrimination, create communities, and challenge social stigma in families, workplaces, and social movements. Such research has produced knowledge vital to the project of improving the daily lives of lesbians and gay men; however, it has also had the effect of placing attention on the presumably shared characteristics and experiences of a generally stable, coherent, and fixed "gay community." Only recently has significant sociological attention has been paid to the invention and preservation of homosexual and heterosexual categories themselves.

Rooted in poststructuralist theory, queer theory's central point of departure from sociological approaches to lesbian and gay studies has been its claim that identities are necessarily unstable, or that there is no coherent, rational, unified subject or self that exists outside of, or previous to, relations of power.[66] The notion that individuals can claim rights based upon self-determined identities is, from this perspective, a distraction from the ways in which identities are given form by the social structures that name and discipline them. Queer theory challenges the notion that identity is the most radical or reliable source of personal or group knowledge and liberation. Instead, queer theorists such as Judith Butler are critical of the "identitarianism" that undergirds lesbian and gay politics and assert that we should be wary of clinging to identities without first understanding where they came from and what they accomplish.[67] Such critiques have given rise to new queer multi-identity frameworks that emphasize *dis*identification, postqueerness, antihomonormativity, and other ways of being "unpredictable" subjects, or what Norma Alarcon has termed "subject(s)-in-process."[68] In this framework, defiant subcultural practices and resistance to various forms of normativity and institutional control become the common ground of queerness, as opposed to a universal collective identity built around same-sex desire.

Similar critiques of universal identity categories are also at the heart of the feminist intersectional approach, particularly as it was originally theorized by feminists of color in the early 1980s. Mirroring the antiessentialist impulse within queer theory, feminists of color demonstrated that presumably natural and universal categories such as "woman," "Black," or "working class" are simply too broad to capture race, gender, class, sexual, and cultural differences. However, as intersectionality has become a widely used concept within sociology and women's studies, this underlying critique of the fixity of identity categories has often been replaced with a new "multi-identity" framework that views race, class, and gender (and other components of identity) as intersecting at a fixed point.

"Multi-identity politics" recognizes the complex relationship between the multiple identities people inhabit, while still generally taking for granted that these identities refer to knowable, unitary, and classifiable bodies and experiences. For instance, while intersectional theory has drawn attention to the racial, economic, and cultural differences among women, the intersectional approach has not challenged the gender binary itself or the systems that produce and protect the baseline requirements for recognition as a female or a male. According to queer scholars Robert Corber and Stephen Valocchi, intersectionality, "at least as a metaphor, implies fixity or stasis," whereas queer theory's emphasis on the mobility of sex, gender, and sexuality allows for an "even more complex understanding of the relationship between various categories of identity, one that does not see them as intersecting at a fixed point."[69]

In theory, the concept of intersectionality implies a rejection of "additive" conceptualizations of identity [race + gender + class + sexuality = self] in favor of a model in which multiple identities define and are defined by one another, and each location in the "matrix of domination" (e.g., working-class Latina lesbian) is experienced differently by those who inhabit it. However, in the *application* of intersectional theory, such as in diversity projects, intersectionality invokes the existence of fixed sites of intersection that give rise to shared—and therefore predictable and commodifiable—group experiences, political needs, and consumer preferences.

In light of these tensions and limitations, my analysis departs from the sociology of intersectionality by understanding the failure of mainstream diversity projects as not only a failure to include all of the relevant identities and issues, but as an indication of the ways in which even identity paradigms that allow for multiplicity can be subjected to discipline and co-optation. Numerous queer and critical race theorists have pointed to the ways in which identities themselves function as sites of discipline, or systems of categorization that neatly package similarities and differences in ways that enable dominant groups and institutions to control what counts as legitimate claims of knowledge or claims for rights. As George Lipsitz has argued, dominant groups have an investment in identity politics, and particularly the idea that members of oppressed groups share a stable and common knowledge base that is the source of resistance.[70] The logic of identity politics can be leveraged to diminish the political accountability of dominant groups (who, presumably, don't or can't understand oppression), as well as to name and control various forms of difference through the establishment of "multiculturalism" and other institutional frameworks.

In Foucault's well-known example, the notion that sexual practices constituted a kind of personhood or identity first circulated through a broad range of institutions in the late 1900s, including medical clinics, schools, religious institutions, and the media.[71] This mass circulation of sexual identity discourses provided the mechanism by which some people learned to identify and discipline their own sexual desires, ultimately *becoming* homosexuals who belonged to a stigmatized and now pride-based "community." Similarly, we might view diversity discourses as the way by which dominant institutions co-opt and circulate intersectionality, in a form repackaged for efficiency and control. As I will show in the next section, by managing and celebrating multiple identifications and differences, even complexity and multiplicity can be rendered stable and profitable. Just as in Foucault's analysis of sexuality, diversity offers a rubric for collective identification and the development of new systems and standards necessary to define what is "diverse." While diversity may be a collective identity rooted in difference, it is also one that simultaneously, and paradoxically, promotes identification and compliance with new institutional monocultures.

Diversity Culture's Disciplinary Effects

In *Mapping Multiculturalism*, Avery Gordon and Christopher Newfield explain that the rise of multiculturalism in the 1970s forced attention to racial differences and promoted the idea that shared aspirations for equality and diversity were to be the new foundation of national culture. Yet multiculturalism was also filled with contradictions. Multiculturalism enabled the development of coalitions of people of color, yet also became synonymous with managing race-based differences in the workplace. It was offered as the cultural foundation of political and structural change, but also functioned to reduce prejudice without changing the larger structures that inevitably create and sustain it. In sum, multiculturalism signaled the ways in which cross-cultural alliances "could evade the regulating effects of official procedure . . . at the same time [that] multiculturalism was another name for that regulation."[72]

Most accounts of multiculturalism focus on its use as a framework for promoting interaction across racial and ethnic groups. While the logic of multiculturalism is clearly interconnected with that of diversity, I focus my analysis on the more expansive concept of diversity in order to describe institutional responses to a broader range of differences and interactions than those related to race or ethnicity. As the attention of corporations and the media is drawn to a growing number of marketable identities, the language of diversity has replaced the language of multiculturalism in many institutional settings, and particularly within corporate discourse.

Diversity can be characterized as having two basic components—first, an instrumental frame that links multiple forms of equality and inclusion to other end results (usually productivity and profits), and, second, institutional programs that deflect attention away from one or more forms of inequality by promoting cross-cultural understanding and the celebration of multiple differences. Neoinstitutional scholars have traced institutional diversity discourses and practices back to the introduction of human resource management professionals trained to ensure corporate compliance with Title VII and other hard-won civil rights laws. Although civil rights compliance may have been the impetus for corporate departments such as affirmative action, Frank Dobbin and John Sutton argue that human resource professionals justified these departments and their professional roles by pointing to the rational, economic benefits of employee security and satisfaction.[73] By focusing on the ways in which increasing employee protections and benefits would also increase productivity and loyalty, HR professionals expanded their role beyond compliance and became experts in the broader and growing field of managing employees' gender, racial, and cultural differences in the service of profit. This development launched a thriving diversity management industry, complete with diversity departments, consultants, manuals, speakers' bureaus, books and videos, retreats, seminars, and trainings.

Thus, while activists and scholars in the 1980s and 1990s may have imagined themselves to be at the lonely forefront of multi-identity projects, this period also marked the beginning of a tremendous corporate undertaking focused on recognizing and appreciating multiple identity-based differences so that employees could reach their full potential as servants of the corporation.[74] According to Avery Gordon, corporate diversity management programs did in fact change the culture of corporations by linking antioppression values to corporate goals and mission. The corporate model emphasized the importance of leveraging diversity to better understand consumers and get the competitive edge on less diversity-savvy corporations. Above all else, and reflecting diversity culture more broadly, the corporate diversity philosophy gave legitimacy to the view that diversity is a necessary tool for the accomplishment of "something else." This something else is usually related to profit, but as I will show in the chapters that follow, the end goal can also be related to other ways of getting ahead, such as enhancing the public image, fundability, expert status, and social connections of individuals and groups.

Although its focus is on institutional ends, the diversity model simultaneously mirrors some of the principles of intersectionality and works to achieve many of the goals of multi-identity activism identified by sociologists of social movements. Corporations live up to many of the standards

that have been used within sociology to evaluate what counts as successful multi-identity activism, or what it looks like to transcend the "single-
identity problem"—including attention to more than one axis of difference,
focus on diversification of leadership from the top down, responsiveness to
the ways in which culture and identity influence group knowledge and action, and accountability to diversity-related outcomes. The Verizon Corporation, for instance, proudly asserts that diversity is not simply valued at the
lowest ranks of the company, but also "stems from the top of the business"
and is reflected in the company's leadership team.[75] Verizon also recognizes
that how people make meaning of the social world is strongly influenced
by cultural symbols and culturally specific knowledge. Demonstrating this,
Verizon's community-based program, "Realize Ambition: The Shot Caller
Showdown," "borrow[s] a popular hip-hop phrase used to describe a successful businessperson" to teach young Black students about business success.[76]
And, lastly, perhaps no institutional realm has perfected the art of measuring diversity-related outcomes better than corporations, in which standard
business practice includes donations to start and/or sustain community-
based organizations, employee resource groups for members of socially disadvantaged groups, nondiscrimination policies and domestic partner benefits, and various forms of diversity benchmarking.

On the one hand, some social movement research has focused on the
successes yielded by instrumentalist approaches to inclusion and equality.
Sociologist Nicole Raeburn has demonstrated that lesbian and gay employees learned to strategically employ the "ideology of profits"—including emphasis on employee loyalty, the practices of competitor companies, and the
buying power of the lesbian and gay market—in order to make the case
for domestic partner benefits and antidiscrimination policies.[77] In response
to this workplace activism, large corporations have taken the lead in extending domestic partnership benefits to lesbian and gay employees, even in
the midst of a hostile, antigay national political environment. On the other
hand, organizationally specific forms of equity, such as domestic partner
benefits, are frequently symbolic and underutilized, and do little to change
the larger systems that produce entrenched inequalities, such as hierarchy
and competition.[78]

The contradictions embedded in diversity culture are also reflected in
the mainstream media's engagement with diversity, and television tends to
go further than the corporate workplace in its exploration of the *intersections* of multiple differences. In recent decades, television has represented a
harmonious world in which cross-cultural friendships flourish with ease and
inequalities are either nonexistent or promoted only by a few immoral and

aberrant characters. For instance, this form of harmony was central to the appeal of the 1980s sitcom *The Cosby Show*, which depicted an upper-class African American family who appeared to be largely unaffected by the racist backlash of the time. According to media scholars, such representations of idealized multiculturalism helped contribute to the rise of complacency, racism-blindness, and concomitant forms of racial inequality in the 1980s.[79]

Today, the representation of presumably inconsequential cultural differences is no longer the primary approach to exploring identity politics on television. Recent studies point to the new media focus on diversity and injustice, including newsmagazine programs and television documentaries exposing institutionalized racism, sexism, and/or homophobia; comedy news programs that draw humor from pointed critiques of social inequalities in the United States; reality television shows in which "characters" discuss, enact, or resist various forms of identity-based oppression; and one-hour dramas in which the injustice itself is the drama.[80] Within the last category, my current favorite is the one-hour TV drama *Prison Break*, aired on the conservative Fox Network. In its first season, *Prison Break* exposed U.S. imperialism; military and government corruption; prisoner abuse; organized corporate violence; and the link between racism, unemployment, and the imprisonment of Black men. The protagonists of *Prison Break* are white, Latino, and Black men in prison; the villains are white women politicians and corporate executives and their white male CIA front men. More remarkable than the fact of the show's critical content is that *Prison Break*'s commercial breaks were filled with ads placed by sponsors of the show, including various corporate advertisements and a recruitment spot for the U.S. Air Force. In other words, the very people identified as the villains of the show are the same people paying for the show to be aired.

As I argued earlier in this chapter (recall the Washington Mutual example), this sort of seemingly contradictory maneuver—in which social justice critiques are funded or otherwise supported by the very targets of the critique—are characteristic of diversity culture. To the extent that self-critical political commentary is profitable, it has become a popular strategy for invoking social justice concepts while doing little to transform or destabilize institutionalized hierarchies themselves. As illustrated in the following chapters, this tactic has also been taken up by middle-class, white, and/or male queer activists who have learned to critique single-issue "gay politics" while simultaneously reinforcing their own political authority and leadership qualifications.

In a time in which critical discourses about injustice are circulating on television and in the country's most powerful private institutions, what role is to be played by identity movements in producing cultural change? Grass-roots organizing has arguably been the driving force behind consciousness-raising and cultural change with respect to racism, sexism, poverty, and homophobia. However, diversity culture has begun to decentralize these discourses or, perhaps more accurately, to recentralize them within mainstream culture. Will this development relegate grassroots movements to fundraising and social service functions, as people increasingly turn to the mainstream media for high-drama examples of injustice and easy-access social criticism?

Conclusion: The Paradox of Queer Diversity

On the one hand, the case studies presented here point to such a future by showing how queer organizations draw on diversity frames to de-queer their projects, or achieve normalcy in the eyes of donors, the media, and the general public. My findings resonate with other research focused on the business of social movements, or the ways in which activists strategically employ corporate discourses and practices, such as the adoption of profit and efficiency frames, in order to sell their demands.[81] As queer organizations grow and professionalize, "qualified" leaders are increasingly recruited from the private sector to ensure their sufficient experience in human resources management, their technological innovation, and their ability to spearhead financial growth (including long-term investments, endowments, capital campaigns, etc.). These leaders also bring to the movement an emphasis on better service delivery through diversification, and they approach diversity issues, or internal race and gender conflicts, from a public relations perspective (i.e., the management of "bad press"). This flow of human capital has enabled both financial and cultural exchange between corporations and queer organizations. Queer organizations provide corporations with access to a lesbian and gay market in exchange for grants and sponsorships, but they also provide corporations with queer symbols and the language of social justice in exchange for institutional framing techniques that normalize identity-based differences, such as diversity management.

On the other hand, I also show a hopeful alternative to this trend: a growing awareness among queer activists that there is an important distinction to be made between *diversity* as a material fact of difference, and *diversity politics* as an ideological project oriented toward normalizing and containing difference. In the introduction to this book, I posed the following questions: What happens when mainstream and respectable diversity politics come into conflict with a movement rooted in efforts to *defy* respectability? How do queer proponents of diversity respond when diversity is anything but unusual, defiant, or "queer"? Queer projects are a perfect site in which to explore the paradox embedded in the mainstreaming of difference, particularly if "queer" is to be understood as a challenge to the forces that normalize difference.

Performance theorist José Esteban Muñoz has argued that "disidentification" is a form of intersectional identity practice that distorts or parodies the dominant culture's representation of identities.[82] It is more than simply working within the dominant culture while critiquing it, which is often accomplished in diversity culture. Instead, it is also a refusal of any essentialist definition of one's group, produced either by mainstream culture, movement leaders, or others who police the boundaries of "community." Disidentification is not a concession or a strategy oriented toward legitimacy, but a campy and irreverent hybrid of mainstream culture and cultures of resistance that refuses fixity. Similarly, other queer scholarship retheorizes identity politics by pointing to subjectivities that resist commodification. Judith Halberstam has argued that "the butch dyke," unlike the figure of the gay man or the queen, has been remarkably difficult for film and television producers to sell to either audiences or corporate sponsors.[83] Even those characters intended to represent butch dykes on television shows such as *The L Word* are cast with actors barely identifiable to lesbian audiences as butch. Halberstam suggests that the butch dyke's media impenetrability, or her failure to allow "capital to run through her," represents one promising example of the subversive uses of identity.

Drawing on these and other emergent concepts within queer studies, the next three chapters examine, first, the extent to which three queer projects in Los Angeles internalize or disidentify with diversity culture and, second, the extent to which they enable collective identities that resist normalization and commodification. What impact does diversity awareness in the broader environment have on queer politics? What is the queer meaning of diversity? When and how do queers resist, distort, or manipulate diversity culture? In Chapter 6, I return to these questions by outlining the dimensions of what I call "queer intersectionality" and applying this framework to my analysis of queer projects in Los Angeles.

CHAPTER 3

Getting Skilled in Queer Diversity: Christopher Street West

The ability to understand, manage, and speak about diversity has become a highly marketable skill—or, to use French sociologist Pierre Bourdieu's term, a new form of "cultural capital"—in the U.S. workplace. Corporations, universities, and government organizations have paid billions of dollars to diversity trainers in order to eliminate workplace discrimination and harassment, with varying degrees of success.[1] When previous iterations of diversity management have failed to deliver the cross-cultural harmony they promised, new authorities have emerged to critique and redefine the field. A still-growing supply of books and certification programs provides business executives, managers, human resource specialists, consultants, entrepreneurs, and employees with the diversity skills necessary to get ahead in a changing global economy.[2] Yet an extraordinary irony of the growing workplace diversity movement is that the most disadvantaged workers—those holding the lowest-paid positions, the working poor, immigrant workers—are those least likely to be recognized as experts on the subject of diversity. Instead, the kind of diversity-related knowledge deemed worthy of placement on one's resume is typically that which is gained in college or as a manager or supervisor in the corporate workplace. The production of professional knowledge about diversity has helped to solidify class disparities rather than to challenge them.

As described in the next chapter, even grassroots queer organizations have been affected by the corporate diversity management movement and the professionalization of diversity. National and large local queer organizations often recruit leaders directly from the corporate sector, resulting in the influx of corporate-modeled diversity trainings, data-driven approaches to inclusion, and instrumental logics that emphasize productivity and public image over social justice. But how do queer activists, at a more individual level, determine what it means to be knowledgeable about diversity? Have ideas about what it means to be a qualified activist evolved in response to the growing emphasis on multi-issue politics in the queer movement, and the political environment generally?

Diversity skills—including the ability to speak publicly and articulately about the importance of diversity, to demonstrate one's commitment to different groups and their concerns, and to critique others' presumably deficient diversity skills—have currency not just within the business sector, but also within activist circles and community-based organizations. Diversity skills, as I will argue, are a core component of "activist capital," or the skills that provide some activists with moral authority and social and professional advantages at the movement level. Knowledge of, and commitment to, multi-issue politics *should* be of critical importance to queer activists, but my concern in this chapter is with the ways in which claims to diversity expertise (and correspondingly, criticisms of other activists' diversity-related incompetence) can work to mask class-based forms of difference or, more importantly, to marginalize working-class activists whose approach to diversity is framed as unprofessional.

In 2000, I began participant observation research at Christopher Street West (CSW), the organization that produces L.A.'s LGBT pride festival and parade. Unwittingly, I began studying CSW just before a series of press exposés and political interventions drew attention to the "incompetence" and poor social skills of the event organizers. In this chapter, I tell the story of conflicts between the working-class organizers of CSW's pride event, on the one hand, and lesbian and gay professionals, the gay press, and local gay politicians, on the other. Public criticisms of CSW came primarily from white gay men, who called for a "more professional" team of organizers— people who could ensure that the event better represented the race and gender diversity of the queer community. As I will show, these tensions point to the convergence of political values regarding the inclusion of multiple issues and differences, and upper-middle-class values that emphasize the importance of professionalism, visual aesthetics, and managerial skills. While some may view this convergence as a sign of progress, I point out what may be lost in this process: the contributions and representation of working-class activists, as well as alternative conceptualizations of diversity that foreground subculture, spontaneity, and vulgarity.

The Complexities of Class

Despite the significance of class in the reproduction of social hierarchies, class identity has often received less focused attention than race and gender within both mainstream diversity projects and progressive identity politics. In part this is due to the fact that many Americans view their race and gender identities as more salient, fixed, or definable than their class location, or see race and gender as the foundation upon which class identity is built. Referencing numerous accounts of the obstacles to building "class consciousness" in the United States, Stanley Aronowitz explains that "even the class-oriented left felt obliged to work through other identities—including race identities—because they believed these were . . . primary among those they sought to reach."[3] In the United States, race and gender tend to serve as the most visible markers of diversity and inclusion within visual culture, or as the categories of difference that are "written on the body." As in the case of CSW, groups and organizations that are particularly interested in the *visual display* of diversity may be likely to foreground race and gender in their diversity discourse and give limited attention to harder-to-represent forms of difference, such as diverse expressions of class identity and culture.

In part, the limited engagement with class in identity politics reflects the complexity of class identity itself. Class theorists have demonstrated that class status is not simply a reflection of one's wealth and income; it is also given form through differences in race, gender, education, geography, social connections, language skills, conceptual resources, and aesthetic tastes.[4] In the United States, class inequities are often hidden by ideologies of classlessness and meritocracy that either treat class inequalities as natural human differences, such as differences in intelligence, or make class distinctions invisible by providing no language with which to name them.[5] In an attempt to name the less visible and measurable components of class inequality, Bourdieu points out that class-based power is reproduced not only through the consolidation of economic capital, but also through disparities in the accumulation of social networks, professional skills, and ways of thinking (e.g., high personal expectations, a sense of entitlement to social advantages, hierarchical judgments of taste) that lead to success.[6] Disparities in cultural capital—including class-based judgments of taste and skill—are particularly resilient given the ongoing proliferation of new categories of distinction within elite consumer culture (new art forms, new foods, new social and intellectual trends).

What sorts of skills, networks, and ways of thinking are required to produce a queer pride festival? As social movement scholars have pointed out, changes in the sociopolitical environment can influence activists' expectations and their evaluations of movement successes and failures. The availability of new lifestyle options, identity discourses, and modes of representation may evolve into a set of rights or expectations around which identity movements reorganize, thereby transforming how activists think about the skills and qualifications of movement leaders.[7] Consequently, my focus is on the ways in which the professionalization of diversity, and the dissemination of diversity values in the broader culture, has worked to link matters of diversity with matters of quality and good taste. White middle-class activists know—just as white corporate executives know—that attention to race and gender diversity brings multiple rewards and advantages, including public perceptions of fairness, competence, and having one's finger on the pulse of "the community." Thus, in debates over L.A.'s pride festival, high-end and professional pride events have also been characterized as those in which race and gender diversity were clearly displayed on the parade route. This is certainly a step in the right direction. Yet, as I will argue, the proliferation of new, bigger, and "better" ways of producing diverse queer pride festivals— and concomitantly, new judgments about who is qualified to organize such events—has simultaneously worked to shift the ownership of pride from working-class to middle-class activists. In a movement focused on the visual representation of diversity, class diversity appears to have less value than other more visible forms of difference.

The Birth of Pride Celebrations and Christopher Street West

In 1970, Dudley,[8] a white gay activist in Los Angeles, received a letter from a friend in New York. Dudley's friend wrote to inform him that activists in New York were planning a gay and lesbian march to commemorate the rebellion that had happened at the Stonewall Inn the previous year and to inquire about what similar action Los Angeles activists might be planning. Inspired by efforts on the East Coast, Dudley and other gay liberationists founded both the Gay Liberation Front of Los Angeles (GLF) and Christopher Street West (CSW). While the GLF focused on projects such as a picket and boycott of Barney's Beanery, a West Hollywood restaurant that for over ten years had displayed a sign stating "Faggots—Stay Out!" the role of CSW was to promote pride in the community. With this task at hand, members of CSW began work to organize a parade down Hollywood

Boulevard, an effort that included a difficult court battle to obtain a permit from the City of Los Angeles and cooperation from the Los Angeles Police Department.

A festival was added to the Los Angeles Gay Pride Parade by 1974, and by 1978 the parade and festival had moved to their current location in West Hollywood. An unincorporated area in the center of Los Angeles County, yet outside of the jurisdiction of the L.A. County Police Department, West Hollywood had been a popular refuge for the gay community since the 1950s. By the mid-1980s, West Hollywood became known as "Boys Town," a name that spoke not only to the remarkable visibility of gay men on Santa Monica Boulevard (one of the city's main thoroughfares), but also to the growing number of West Hollywood businesses catering to the gay community. In 1984, residents in the area received national attention when they not only voted to make West Hollywood a city, but elected a gay majority to the city council. The cityhood campaign was envisioned by many residents as an opportunity to create a "gay Camelot" where the gay community would become, and remain, one of the largest and most politically powerful in the city. In 2000, white gay men held three of five seats on the West Hollywood City Council.

Although situated in West Hollywood, the CSW pride celebration had a statewide impact as the only pride celebration in Southern California. In its first decade, the CSW celebration not only expanded in size and numbers, but it achieved political significance as the center of pride for the gay and lesbian communities of Southern California at a time when simply being out together in the streets was a radical action. For many local residents and activists, the name Christopher Street West continues to be associated with highly emotional memories of hard-fought political victories, exciting coming-out experiences, and, in many cases, friends and revered community leaders who helped to build CSW before they died of AIDS. As a national leader among pride organizations, early CSW board members also provided resources and financial support to help start smaller pride festivals and other nationally prominent organizations such as the Los Angeles Gay & Lesbian Center (see Chapter 4) and AIDS Project Los Angeles.

Yet the central role played by CSW and its grassroots founders in Los Angeles' gay political scene did not go unchallenged, even during the height of the gay liberation movement. Conflicts over who should represent the movement were often framed in classed terms, and Dudley's unpolished, working-class presentation in particular caused resentment among wealthy gay men in the city.[9] While Dudley and other grassroots activists were planning pride parades and sit-ins, "wealthy and professionally successful gay men" were forming political action committees and holding "pool party" fundraising events with high-priced tickets.[10] Members of the all-gay, all-male Municipal Elections Committee of Los Angeles (MECLA), formed in 1977, were particularly concerned with Dudley's prominence in Los Angeles. Journalists Clendinen and Nagourney describe this tension:

> They [MECLA] were alienated by what there was of a gay movement in their city, and embarrassed by the people they saw quoted as their representatives. Why had the media decided that [Dudley]—a disheveled old man with thick glasses who boasted of taking a "vow of poverty," a man most of them would not even invite to their homes for a cocktail—was *their* leader?[11]

Here Clendinen and Nagourney not only emphasize financial resources ("vow of poverty") as a source of the alienation that gay professionals and grassroots activists felt from one another; differences in style and social connections were also particularly important to decisions about which gay men should be represented in the media. Ultimately, these conflicts did not suppress the power of grassroots gay and lesbian activism during the 1970s. They did, however, foreshadow trends within the movement that would later threaten CSW's survival.

While very little has been written about pride celebrations, these events now exist in every major city in the United Cities and in multiple cities throughout the world. California alone is home to twenty-five lesbian and gay pride festivals, ranging from weekend-long, multivenue events such as CSW's festival and parade, to intimate picnics and carnivals in smaller cities. As a result, several state, national, and international pride associations have developed and hold annual conferences in order to facilitate the interorganizational exchange of information about issues such as growth, safety, legal representation, public relations, and the future and meaning of pride events. Not surprisingly, the character of the events tends to reflect the character of the cities in which they are held. For example, as of 2001, CSW had never incorporated the contentious word "queer" into any of their event themes or organizational literature, while in San Francisco, known for producing a more "political" event complete with activist speakers and a parade that runs through the middle of the city's downtown, pride themes have included "Year of the Queer" and "Queeriffic!" Yet apart from local context, pride events also reflect ideological trends in the larger lesbian and gay movement. For example, early pride festivals, not far removed from the collective memory of the Stonewall Rebellion, were organized around themes that called for specific action, such as "coming out." Today, in the context of a mainstreamed equal rights agenda, festivals often make use of more abstract, party-oriented themes like "pride odyssey" or "pride . . . the next generation," disconnecting the original relationship between pride events and protest.[12]

The Antiprofessional Culture of CSW

I chose CSW as a research site at a time when I first imagined one of my projects to be a study of the state of political conflicts and alliances between gay men and lesbians in the "postfeminist" era. With the intention of examining gender dynamics in a queer organization with a local reputation for producing a male-dominated event, I called CSW to inquire about how to get involved. CSW's administrative assistant suggested that I attend the board meeting at the CSW office in West Hollywood that would take place the following month. CSW is owned and operated by a volunteer board of directors that holds public board meetings on the second Tuesday of every month. Seven men (five white men and two Black men) sat at the long board of directors table in a small room with walls covered by dozens of awards from national and local politicians, officials from the cities of Los Angeles and West Hollywood, and local businesses and nonprofit organizations. I joined eleven men who sat in the chairs designated for guests, and I addressed the board during public comment. I stated that I was surprised to see no women in the room and that I wanted to get involved by "helping to represent lesbian issues at the festival." One of CSW's copresidents thanked me for speaking and directed me to obtain an application from the executive Secretary to serve on the board of directors. Although surprised that I was already being considered as a prospective board member upon my first, and quite brief, introduction to such a well-known organization, I submitted the application and continued to attend the public meetings. Six weeks after my first visit to CSW, I was appointed to the board as the chair of the Volunteer Relations Committee.

Board members informed me that they were all relatively new to CSW and were the last remaining after more than ten board members, both men and women, had been voted off the board in response to suspicions about financial improprieties and interpersonal conflicts. Board members had fallen into multiple committee offices because there was no one else to fill them, and many expressed that there simply had not been time to recruit lesbians, or anyone else, to the organization. The predominance of gay men at CSW also had implications for the pride celebration itself and had not gone un-noticed by queer feminists in the Los Angeles area. During my initial re-search interviews and informal conversations, both local activists and staff in other lesbian and gay organizations declared that the CSW pride event had become simply a "gay men's disco" and that the interests and culture of lesbians and communities of color had not been represented.

A freelance reporter for the national publication *Lesbian News* told me that she was considering writing a story that would highlight the absence of any local women's bands at the festival, the lack of child care or a children's play area, and the fact that she saw "only two women during the first hour of the parade," with the exception of the small "dykes on bikes" contingent that traditionally leads the procession. A research contact from the L.A. Gay & Lesbian Center also reported that another lesbian newspaper was consid-ering calling a women's boycott of CSW after being "intentionally ignored" as an advertising source. Perhaps most contentious was the board's choice of fashion designer Mr. Blackwell and his partner Robert Spencer as celebrity grand marshals for the 2000 parade. Blackwell is most famous for his "Ten Worst Dressed Women" list and was described in CSW's 2000 *Pride Maga-zine* as "feared and revered." Many activists who paid attention to the pa-rade and were familiar with Blackwell's infamous list took the position that, as stated by one lesbian and former board president who had resigned in 1999, CSW was "celebrating and rewarding misogyny." Thus, unknowingly, I had joined the organization at a volatile time when rumors about sexism at CSW, and actions being planned in response these rumors, were brewing just beneath the surface.

Although the CSW mission statement asserts that the organization "educates and informs the straight community about our lives and rights," as part of my socialization as a new board member at CSW, copresidents Tom (white) and Charles (African American) informed me that CSW's fes-tival is not, and should not be, a political event. When I first inquired about whether we would be including speakers on the festival stages in addition to musical talent, Tom and Charles both suggested that the current board had not invited speakers because they themselves would find such an event "boring" and because the nearly thirty thousand people who attend the fes-tival would be bored as well. Tom told me, "L.A. Pride is not about being political. That is for San Francisco. Here, our motto is 'You pay, you drink, you fall down.' This is a celebration, it's not about being political." Charles concurred with this distinction between the role of CSW's pride event and that of San Francisco, "San Francisco pride is so boring because it is just hours and hours of speakers." The men at the meeting laughed and proclaimed: "The further south you go, the less political you get!" Despite this shared understanding that "L.A. is not about being political," board members and guests would occasionally make suggestions for the inclusion of people or presentations that would bring a political element to the festival. During a conversation about the possibility of displaying the AIDS Quilt at the event, Tom, a white gay man, derailed the idea by convincing the male board member who suggested it that, "it is too depressing. People come here to party and dance and get drunk and they don't want to see the names of their dead friends while they are doing it. And you know how it is, you get one crying and then they all start crying."

Although individual board members were conscious of the importance of representing their own cultures and communities, CSW as an organization and as a board of directors had not *institutionalized* a political discourse regarding gender, race, class, or even sexual identity. For example, Charles, a Black gay man, shared with me on the first night we met that one reason, among many, he decided to work with CSW was to reflect more racial diversity on the board, although this was not something he ever wanted to state publicly at board meetings. During my research, racial difference on the board was generally treated with color blindness and was rarely mentioned except in cases in which it seemed strategic to do so, such as when the board voted to remove Jesse, a Black male board member who was believed to have been charging personal items to CSW. CSW's attorney, a gay Latino man, asked that Charles speak to Jesse as one Black man to another, with the expectation that this would cut down on the potential for Jesse to experience his removal as racially motivated. While identity differences were acknowledged in instances such as these, addressing identity-based oppression was never articulated as part of the mission of the organization. During my six months serving on the initial board (the makeup of the board changed dramatically after six months), we never had a board-initiated discussion about the meaning of pride, our personal and political motivations, or how we envisioned CSW's contribution to queer politics. Instead, the desired mood at CSW was to be informal, crass, and "fun," and to avoid the ways that being "politically correct" or too process-oriented would distract us from the logistical work of the festival.

Ironically, time that might have been filled with overtly "political" dialogue about the mission of the organization was often filled with other sorts of emotional exchanges unrelated to festival logistics. Although a copy of *Robert's Rules of Order* (the widely used handbook for parliamentary procedure) sat in the boardroom, these rules were loosely followed, and teasing, flirting, arguing, and dramatic departures from the boardroom were common. For example, when Jesse, a Black board member, referred to Chris, a white board member and executive secretary, as "Mary," Chris dramatically exited the boardroom, leaving the meeting without its needed secretary. Board meetings regularly started late, lasted for five or six hours, and included hours of closed-session items ranging from lawsuits by past board members to discussions about missing documents, suspicions of sabotage of one board member by another, and accusations about board members and staff using CSW for personal financial benefit. In order for these matters to be discussed, other administrative items were frequently postponed, including the evaluations of frustrated staff members waiting for raises or information about the terms of their employment. According to Tom, however, the current board was functioning more effectively than the board he first joined. He told me that when he became president he had "to kick everybody off. It was chaos. Board members would bring forty-ounce beers and an eighth of liquor to the meetings, get in fistfights, and break our microphones. That's why our microphones don't work." When I asked Tom whether he thought we should try to recruit some "professionals" to the board, he responded, "professionals would never tolerate CSW. They'd get in here, see how things operate, and then leave." When I noted that there were also no "queeny" gay men on the board, Tom also asserted that CSW "used to have nelly types on the board, but they didn't get along with the bull dykes and the other board members."

While one previous board member that I spoke with disputed Tom's description of drunken, rowdy board meetings of the recent past, an important element of Tom's account was his assertion that CSW was not an organization run by professionals, nor would it be a comfortable or desirable place for them. At the time I began research, CSW's board was populated entirely with working-class, "straight-acting" gay men, a population of gay men dramatically underrepresented within lesbian and gay political organizations in West Hollywood. None of the men on the board held political office or positions of leadership in the West Hollywood community; none was a well-known activist or had ever served on a board of directors for another organization; none of the board members was employed in a lesbian and gay organization or did paid work related to the gay community; and none held a university degree. One board member sold bowling equipment with his father, one operated a small CB radio business out of the small house he lived in with his mother, one worked as an information systems specialist at an internet company, and another was unemployed and rumored to sleep in the office. CSW's board members seemed to have limited access to a radical, or even liberal, political discourse about gay liberation, multiculturalism, or feminism that most leaders of the LGBT movement are likely to have learned in college or as activists in lesbian and gay organizations. Instead, their work at CSW focused on producing a festival that they perceived as "fun" and "hot," and that they believed represented the kind of event that is wanted and expected by people who live in Los Angeles.

Given my strong feminist politics, the limited representation of lesbians on CSW's board, and external criticisms of male dominance at CSW, I was surprised to experience a growing sense of solidarity with the gay men at CSW and their decisions regarding the pride festival. While child care at the festival would increase the likelihood that lesbian and gay parents would attend the event, for instance, CSW's emphasis on partying over parenting and professionalism struck me as a form of queer resistance to what Lisa Duggan has identified as "homonormative" politics—or a lesbian and gay politics that promotes the image of monogamy, domesticity, and prosperity.[13]

Judith Halberstam has argued that in a time of increasing lesbian and gay assimilationism, "queer subjects" might be redefined as those who "live (deliberately, accidentally, or of necessity) during the hours when other sleep and in the spaces (physical, metaphysical, and economic) that others have abandoned," including, "ravers, club kids, HIV-positive barebackers, rent boys, sex workers, homeless people, drug dealers, and the unemployed."[14] Queer, in this model, is less about same-sex practices than about a way of life that defies the rules of normative, respectable adult citizenship.

Though CSW board members had not embraced the contentious term "queer," their crass style, working-class ethos, and refusal to replace public sex culture with more respectable forms of political engagement bespoke their queerness. And although they had eschewed the term "political," they nonetheless practiced what Rupp and Taylor refer to as a "politics of vulgarity"—in which brash sexuality and the refusal to be professional and appropriate challenge norms within both heterosexual and mainstream lesbian and gay culture.[15] In the midst of the standoff between the raunchy working-class gay men at CSW and the liberal feminist proponents of child care, I began to see the ways in which CSW board members represented an endangered form of queer resistance.

The Gay Press: Exposing the Incompetence at CSW

In 2000, the very decision to avoid being political and professional that board members believed they were making on behalf of the community became part of a media exposé consisting of multiple articles printed in six different local papers, each of which claimed to be representing community complaints. After the 2000 event, CSW was contacted by the first reporter, a white gay male columnist for the gay men's magazine *Frontiers*. The reporter requested interviews with CSW staff and board members and informed the board that concerns about diversity at the pride festival and rumors of a lesbian boycott had helped to set his investigations in motion. He explained that while the article would have the character of an exposé, the intention of the magazine was to stimulate a constructive public dialogue about the long-term best interests of CSW and the event. In light of the reporter's comments and the rumors of the boycott, board members prepared themselves to speak during the interviews about the importance of diversity in the lesbian and gay pride movement.

Indeed, the five articles about CSW that were printed in *Frontiers* did touch on some of the community-level debates regarding the meaning of pride and the political decisions of CSW's board. One article quoted Dudley, CSW's founder, charging the current CSW board with a "lack of vision and sincere commitment to the idea of gay liberation," and the mayor of West Hollywood stating that CSW had failed to produce a "celebration of our movement as a civil rights struggle, a political struggle, and a social movement" instead of a "big circuit party." In a follow-up article subtitled, "Reasons to Party: Activists Suggest Ways to Put Pride Back in the Parade and Festival," the reporter listed specific suggestions for making the event more inclusive and appealing. The suggestions, offered by four white gay men, ranged from the recommendation, made by Dudley, that " 'we' encourage Asian-Americans, American Indians, and Latinos to brighten our culture with their costumery," to erecting "the world's largest dance tent," to lasers and fireworks, and holding "round table and panel discussions on the most important issues we face today."

However, while community-level concerns about diversity at CSW provided the impetus for the articles, they also provided reporters with a politically justifiable ground upon which to depict CSW board members as unfit to manage such a profitable enterprise. In most of the articles, diversity issues took a backseat to details about various accusations of financial mismanagement, board resignations and removals, problems with festival entertainers, complaints about the parade being dull and poorly organized, and suspicions that CSW's grants and donations to the community were shrinking.[16]

As a reader, the most compelling element of the articles was not the list of CSW's recent failures, but the characterization of board members that centered, although implicitly, on power and class. According to one white male ex-board member quoted in a *Frontiers* article, "I got the impression that these guys are running the festival so they can feel powerful. There's this lack of skill on the board, they are afraid of people who have good minds and ideas." Providing support for this perception, the article focused on Tom, CSW's copresident, who was quoted asserting that he didn't read newspapers and remarking, in his off-the-cuff manner, that past board members were "lumps on logs" who needed to be "canned" or "flushed down the toilet." Indeed, the article reinforced a sentiment already widely felt by many lesbian and gay sponsors, city staff, and political leaders who had been observing the influx of unknown and unprofessional gay men to the CSW board. As one lesbian active on a City of West Hollywood advisory board expressed to me, "Everyone knows that [CSW board members] are better suited to work at 7–11 than to be on that board. It used to carry prestige, and now everyone knows it doesn't."

In response to *Frontiers*' successful depiction of a dangerous and embarrassing situation in which incompetent gay men had taken over CSW and were managing its annual million-dollar budget, several letters and email responses were sent to CSW from concerned readers, one of which stated, "Is [Tom] really as dumb as he sounds? Maybe you're [the board] all as dumb as dirt." After one resignation and one removal prior to the event in June, the board had dwindled to only five members: Tom and Charles as copresidents, Brian, Donna, and myself.[17] After the *Frontiers* article, Charles called a meeting with Brian, Donna, and me to discuss removing Tom from the board.[18] Suspecting this decision, Tom resigned in July.

The *Frontiers* articles set in motion a flurry of other articles that focused on the lack of skill and sophistication at CSW, as well as the City of West Hollywood's contingency plans that had been put in place to take over the event in the case that the CSW board fell apart. An article in *LA Weekly* highlighted several comments from Tom, now an ex-board member, including the statement that CSW board members attend "so-called fundraisers" only to "get a free dinner. . . . They are supposed to go there and network, but they don't." Similar articles appeared in the *Los Angeles Independent*, the *Hollywood Independent*, and the *West Hollywood Independent*.

Among those who were interviewed for the articles, there was a general consensus that the board had degenerated to the point that it consisted of people who were self-interested and hoping to gain power by being on the board. Implied as the moral or lesson of CSW's failure was that people without power in their personal lives or occupations will selfishly seek power in a nonprofit organization, while professionals will be more inclined to do the work of the organization for humanitarian, or selfless, reasons. By overlooking that one of the functions of community service for professionals is to establish personal and business contacts, the articles posited the material self-interests of the working class as less legitimate than the more abstract self-interests of lesbian and gay professionals.

While the five articles targeted at white, English-speaking readers focused on the incompetence of the CSW board, CSW's only piece of positive press after the festival came from *ADELANTE* magazine, the gay bilingual (Spanish-English) Latino magazine. *ADELANTE*'s article, which appeared after the 2000 event, commended CSW for its first annual "Calor Latino" dance area and de-emphasized West Hollywood by focusing on CSW's inclusion of Latinos living across Los Angeles, estimated now to be the largest segment of gays and lesbians in Los Angeles County.

What to Do with CSW?

While the media emphasized event mismanagement caused by an inexperienced and dysfunctional board of directors, activists such as Dudley and Rose (a well-known white lesbian elder and veteran activist) were prompted by the media reports to organize a discussion that focused on more long-range concerns about the political vision of CSW and the organization's role in the lesbian and gay movement. Dudley asked Rose to help facilitate the first meeting of a new, independent group called the "Committee to Revitalize Christopher Street West" and urged activists, board members, and other interested community members to join. Only two meetings of the Revitalization Committee were held before the group disintegrated, due largely to criticism from attendees that the committee had resulted in nothing more than an unproductive forum for complaint (e.g., a "bitch fest," as described by one white lesbian and past CSW executive director, to a reporter for the *LA Weekly*). Dudley's agenda included the recruitment of new board members, the creation of working committees, and the "identification of target populations" for outreach. However, these goals gave way to rounds of emotional debate and the airing of each attendee's particular grievances and proposals regarding CSW. The largely gay male group raised issues including, but not limited to, the possibility of moving the event to Los Angeles (and out of West Hollywood) to be more accessible to "*all* of the LGBT people of Los Angeles" and the need for better cross-cultural communication.

Shortly after the second meeting of the committee, Rose and two other professionals well-connected in the local lesbian and gay community, Richard and Linda, had begun conversations with one another about the need for an alternative structure to reform CSW: an action-oriented structure that would effect change at CSW and improve the organization's reputation rather than simply providing a space for an endless, albeit therapeutic, dialogue. While there was a consensus that changes needed to be made at CSW, the nature of these changes remained a matter of both public and private debate. In part, the confusion over what to do with CSW stemmed from the divergent concerns of the media and the members of the revitalization committee, the former primarily concerned with the incompetence of recent board members and the latter focused on the mission and diversity of CSW and its event.

Yet the story of CSW also illustrates an unsettling merging of concerns about race and gender diversity and concerns about professional competence and respectable behavior. As exemplified by the complaints linking lesbian inclusion to the need for child care at queer pride events, demands for gender and racial diversity are often leveraged by invoking a checklist of liberal values and expectations regarding what reasonable and fair-minded people should do to ensure that women and people of color feel welcome in a given space (e.g., child care, ethnic costumery, etc.). Of course, not all lesbians—including those with children—would view child care as a necessary, or even desirable, feature of queer pride events. For many queers, pride events function as the once-yearly "in your face" opportunity to transport raunchy queer sexual culture—our collective threat to family values and the sanctity of marriage—out of dark bars and into crowded public streets. The broader culture dedicates plenty of time to the celebration of children and the innocence, domesticity, and stability they represent. For many queers, pride events represent one of few remaining environments in which "family values" are inappropriate. Hence, at the same time that criticisms of CSW drew attention to issues of race and gender inclusion, they also raised issues of "class"—by which I mean both socioeconomic class and the kind of good taste and refinement that queerness resists. Indeed, queerness—including public sexuality, childlessness, gender nonconformity, refusals to be professional, and emphasis on the needs and desires of adults over those of children—has long been viewed as vulgar, tactless, and without class.

Gay Government Intervenes:
The West Hollywood City Council

While CSW board members were committed to hearing the concerns of the activists and community members who attended the Revitalization Committee meetings, it became evident soon after the meetings that the board needed to shift its attention from a community-based dialogue (e.g., the "town hall" structure of the committee meetings) to a behind-the-scenes political battle with the City of West Hollywood. In June, the board had begun to receive unofficial reports about CSW's relationship with the City of West Hollywood from Dean, a CSW volunteer and, as he described himself, "a friend to certain members of the West Hollywood City Council." In two reports provided to CSW, Dean, a white gay male management consultant, revealed that the city was planning a takeover of the festival by denying CSW an event permit and "soliciting RFPs [requests for proposals] from private organizations and companies to run next year's parade and festival . . . with the city as its beneficiary." According to the first of these unofficial reports, based on Dean's discussions with unnamed "decision-makers at the City" and complete with quotes from council members, CSW was suffering from an image problem in the eyes of the council and needed to "retain the services of an independent consultant 'who has his/her finger on the pulse of the community.'" The second report from Dean, a lengthy proposal listing his five-step plan to "repair relations with the City of West Hollywood and the community in general," urged the CSW board to hire him as consultant or interim executive director. In the proposal, with résumé attached, Dean highlighted the importance of connections and insider status to the survival of CSW: "I am willing to utilize my personal contacts within the city and the community at large to help the board orchestrate this effort of change. I am willing to put my own personal reputation on the line to make this happen." Echoing the words of other "informants" on the city staff, he indicated that the city council had little confidence in a board that they did not know personally and that lacked professional event-planning skills, both of which were problems that would be resolved if he were hired.

The possible hiring of Dean, although supported by some CSW board members who were eager to "move on," was strongly opposed by Revitalization Committee members who urged the CSW board not to pay for services (such as updating the bylaws and recruiting an executive director) that a skilled group of volunteers could perform for free. While the Revitalization Committee ultimately did not trust Dean's motivations and he withdrew from the revitalization effort, his early warning about an impending take-over by the city unless CSW made a concerted effort at professionalization was later confirmed by city staff. Thus, the board was forced to shift its attention away from consulting community members about "diversity issues" and focus instead on interpreting the concerns of an all-male, all-white, and largely gay city council.

It is not a simple task for a group of people who have been accused of being "incompetent," "unprofessional," and "better suited to work at 7–11" to figure out how to repackage themselves in a manner that will satisfy those who have deemed them unworthy to operate a grassroots queer pride organization. The board held emotional discussions about the "unfairness" of the council's judgments (e.g., "How can they judge us when they don't even know us?" or "How can they say we haven't worked hard?"), and, as a board member, I often found myself managing a dangerous balance between solidarity with the other board members and an understanding of the council's critique. As my identification with CSW solidified, I grew frustrated and embarrassed when CSW materials went out in the mail with typos, mis-spellings, grammatical errors, and informal phraseology that I never would have chosen. In the midst of the city's evaluation of CSW, I occasionally gave in to the city's logic about the importance of professional presentation by paternalistically offering to the other board members that I do some of the writing and public speaking for the organization, though such tasks were not my responsibility as the chair of Volunteer Relations. Fortunately, either the institutionalized democratic structure of the board or institution-alized sexism at CSW, or perhaps both, allowed the other board members to prevent me from speaking over them. This was fortunate not only because I realized that under such great scrutiny I likely couldn't perform better, but also because the larger issue at stake was the power-laden question of who was going to dictate how queer pride would be articulated in Los Angeles, and for what audience. I remembered that the queerness I cared about *was* messy, informal, and unprofessional, and intentionally so.

Yet the trouble facing CSW was that it was a messy, informal, working-class group performing for the organized, formal, and professional elites of West Hollywood. This situation had arisen from CSW's reliance on the city for its permit at a time when the city council was dominated by white gay men committed to professionalizing the look and feel of being lesbian and gay. CSW's awards banquet and annual fundraiser at the House of Blues was a perfect example of this tension, as the well-dressed guests, almost exclusively gay men who had paid $50 to attend (very inexpensive by West Hollywood standards), watched uncomfortably as the community awards were given away by nervous board members who spoke in monotone, got drunk, mixed up the awards schedule, spoke for too long, and confused the names of award recipients, the last of which was my personal faux pas. Later, a city council member described the banquet as "an embarrassment," while another research contact of mine, a manager at the L.A. Gay & Lesbian Center, proclaimed that he "heard it was pathetic." For gay men accustomed to lavish fundraisers organized by professional event planners, the awards banquet *was* pathetic and embarrassing. However, from the vantage point of the board members, the majority of whom do not themselves pay $50 to attend fundraisers, the important elements of such an event were in place. The venue was "fancy," the food was "fancy," the board "did our best" in presenting the awards—"What more do they want from us?" the board asked.

Saving the Day: Professionals Arrive at CSW

In early September 2000, Charles, an African American gay man who was now CSW's president, was approached by Richard, a gay white male event planner, about the development of a working commission to assist CSW in its efforts to address the concerns of the city council. Unlike the now-defunct CSW Revitalization Committee, Richard informed board members that the commission would be a small, volunteer group of skilled professionals and activists who could, for example, locate a suitable accountant for CSW, help to facilitate CSW's audit, assist with board development, and review and revise CSW's bylaws. In sum, the commission would help board members do the work that was necessary to reassure the city council that CSW was a viable organization, and would do so at no charge. In early September, the board was invited to meet with the members of the commission that Richard had organized. The mostly white and middle-class commission consisted of six members, including Richard: two white men, two white women, one African American woman, and one multiracial woman. Commission members were well-known and/or well-connected in the lesbian and gay political and professional communities of West Hollywood and Los Angeles—Linda and Diana held management-level positions at the L.A. Gay & Lesbian Center; Richard and his assistant Tina produced political and other nonprofit fundraisers (including an event hosting President Bill Clinton); Rose served on the West Hollywood Gay and Lesbian Advisory Board and was perhaps the most well-known name in lesbian-feminist activism in Los Angeles; and Barry was an event-planning consultant who contracted with, among others, the City of West Hollywood.

Following introductions, the meeting proceeded with a report from Richard about CSW's relationship with the City of West Hollywood. Richard confirmed, based on personal "late-night phone conversations with a council member," that the city council had directed their staff to research and advise them about the state of CSW's leadership, as well as to consider alternative producers for the festival and parade. A review of city staff's recommendations and an official vote as to whether to grant a permit to CSW would take place at an upcoming city council meeting. Because CSW needed only a majority vote, Richard asserted that the immediate goal of the commission was to lobby three of the five council members to "vote for CSW," and that lobbyists would need to be familiar to the council and skilled at "implementing message control." Lobbyists would need to speak about substantive improvements at CSW, and increasing the size and diversity of the board was one of the council's main concerns. Reiterating diversity-related concerns raised in the newspaper articles, Richard explained that CSW was no longer in touch with the diversity of the LGBT community and needed the assistance of people with public relations experience and "connections to diverse community leaders." After giving this report, Richard announced, "You have six new board members right here . . . if you want them." Commission members were offering to join the board of directors and to stay on the board through the production of the following year's festival.

Despite the agreement of the current board members that appointing well-known and well-connected professionals would improve CSW's image with the council, we also recognized that the balance of power would shift to the new board members who would now outnumber us.[19] Current board members articulated their reservations about adding the new group, focusing mainly on maintaining our positions of leadership within the organization and not being relegated to the role of "followers." While current board members did not frame their concerns in explicitly class-oriented terms, some asserted that it was important for everyone present to recognize that the current board was "just as capable and qualified" as the new group, despite not having the same connections with city officials. Frustrated by my sense that CSW's survival was now dependent upon the professional connections of the prospective board members, I focused my comments on how disappointed I was that we would need to "rely on gay and lesbian elites to save a grassroots organization."[20] Commission members responded by reassuring us that this wasn't about being "better than us" or "coming in to save the day." Instead, they explained, "we all have different skill sets," and they had the kind of skills that were required to inspire the confidence of the city council. During a break in which commission members left the room, board members came to a consensus that adding the new group was "best for CSW," a decision that would be ratified at the next board meeting.

A few days later, a follow-up meeting was called by the prospective board members. This meeting was also facilitated by Richard, who opened the discussion by stating that some members of the new group had been rethinking their offer to join the board in light of the concerns articulated by current board members at the last meeting. During a long and emotional dialogue, prospective board members argued that the current CSW board needed to take responsibility for the problems facing CSW, recognize that skilled people were needed to repair CSW, and stop "blaming everyone else" (i.e., the media, the city council, past board members) so that we could begin to "heal." One prospective board member clarified, "I said at our last meeting that this wasn't about us coming in to save the day, but the truth is, this is exactly what we are doing." Another member of the new group explained that the current board did not have the "skill set" or "what it takes" to handle the public relations challenge facing the organization, while another stated angrily, "You need to take personal responsibility for what happened [at the festival] last year!" In light of these assertions, prospective board members argued that the current board should not vote to add the new group unless we were truly comfortable with a shift in the balance of power, because, as one prospective board member stated, "It's going to be what *we* say for a while."

Yet prospective board members expressed the most visible anger as they explained that they had been inaccurately accused of elitism at the previous meeting. Current board members were told that we had "confused competence and experience with elitism" and that the new group was not going to "apologize for their hard work." Comments made by some prospective board members also suggested that the particular circumstances of their lives, such as years of activism, positioned them as beyond race, class, or gender critique. One white woman said, nearly in tears, "I won't have you lecturing me about sexism, racism, classism, because I have *lived* it"; another white woman passed out copies of her activist curriculum vitae and asserted, "I am *not* an elitist. I have never been one, I have never been accused of being one, and I won't tolerate being called one"; and a white gay man discussed being raised in poverty by a single mother and the hard work required to achieve his current success. Whether or not prospective board members had been accused of elitism per se, it was clear that they were not comfortable identifying as part of a gay and lesbian "elite," nor making explicit the class divisions that were now marked by the divide between the "new board" and "old board."[21] As prospective board members took turns stating why they were offended by the charge of elitism, they explained that their own marginalized identities as (white) lesbians and bisexual women, (white) gay men, or people raised in poor or working-class families did not resonate with identification as lesbian and gay elites.[22] At the same time, however, prospective board members reinforced their status vis-à-vis current board members by emphasizing their advanced political skills, connections with powerful officials, and professional reputations, the last of which some argued were being altruistically placed "at risk" by affiliation with CSW.

Despite these conflicts, the new group was elected to the board at the next public CSW board meeting. The weeks prior to the city council meeting provided a period of adjustment as new and old board members began to get to know one another, integrating the board with the understanding that, as suggested by Richard, "we don't need to like one another, we just need to respect each other." Yet in conversations among the original board members, some remained concerned about the kind of changes new board members might have planned for CSW, especially as new board members were elected to offices within the organization and began to hold the old board accountable for internal procedures that they deemed inappropriate. New board members discovered several procedures that they responded to with shock and disapproval, including that board members had charged CSW for hotel costs and per diem while on CSW business at pride conferences and events. Part of the "cleanup" at CSW, argued Richard, meant tight internal controls, particularly over board expenses during financial down times. CSW's income "doesn't belong to the board, it belongs to the community," he asserted, and a new policy was suggested that board members pay for their own hotel costs and per diem, with travel covered only in the form of vouchers provided to CSW by its sponsors. Two white women board members, including myself, contested the policy on the grounds that it would institutionalize a class bias in the organization by allowing only those who could afford these costs to represent CSW at important events. The board voted that this would be an interim policy until an official policy could be developed. Such structural changes were part of a period of monitoring the practices of old board members and correcting their "mistakes," a project that positioned the old board as, at best, financially careless and lacking good judgment, and, at worst, unethical and greedy. The prudence of new board members, on the other hand, justified their leadership in the overhaul and restructuring of the organization.

The expanded board went to work "diversifying" the organization and drew heavily upon Richard's connections with queer leaders throughout Los

Angeles and his experience (as an event planner) reaching out to people of color and white women in order to diversify white, gay-male events. The new board also worked to address community complaints that had sparked investigations at CSW. The following year's event marked the inauguration of CSW's "children's garden," some of CSW's awards were renamed after queer people of color, and board members began attending networking functions and fundraising events.

Who "Owns" Queer Pride?

Ultimately, the West Hollywood City Council voted four to one in favor of granting CSW its permit. Although CSW board members were pleased with the outcome, the remarks made by council members at the hearing revealed that board members had misunderstood the priorities of the city council. Under the impression that CSW needed to prove that it was a viable organization that represented the community and could work effectively with the city, board members who spoke at the meeting stressed the leadership skills and the gender and racial/ethnic diversity of the expanded board, as well as CSW's plans for outreach to women and people of color. Yet, city council members glossed over CSW's diversity and outreach plans and instead focused on the need for the festival to reflect positively upon, and benefit, the City of West Hollywood. The council member who voted against CSW was quoted in *Frontiers* stating, "Look, there is a very diverse crowd that attends the festival every year. But even I, a gay white male, don't feel comfortable at the festival, due to the unprofessionalism of it and the lack of activities. Diversity is the least of their problems." While diversity concerns had sparked investigations into CSW, the city council ultimately refocused the spotlight on the professional quality of the event.

The council agreed that CSW should be allowed to produce the event once more and be reevaluated the following year. Yet the suggestion that CSW's pride festival and parade would rest on the approval of government officials outraged some activists present at the meeting. According to Dudley, the City of West Hollywood would take the festival "over [his] dead body!" Dudley warned that allowing the city to produce the event was dangerous, asking, "What happens ten or twenty years from now when the city council has a Russian, heterosexual majority? What will pride look like then?"[23] Dudley added that the city's interest in the festival was only "ancillary" and that the event "truly belongs to Los Angeles" more broadly. *Frontiers* quoted Rose stating, "We must make the festival more welcoming to women and minorities. West Hollywood is Boys Town in the minds of many. The city itself isn't seen by these communities as a welcoming place for them; maybe a move to Los Angeles would remove that stigma." In the same article, the gay male mayor of West Hollywood disagreed, "We [the City of West Hollywood] do own it. We have significant resources, costs, and inconvenience invested in the festival."

What made the West Hollywood City Council, or any government or corporate body, feel entitled to take over the defining function of a historic, grassroots organization? In response to the activist argument that CSW owns the event as a result of its thirty-year history producing it, one council member replied, "What is special about CSW? History doesn't entitle them to run this. What about other organizations with history that could do a better, higher-end job, like AIDS Project Los Angeles [APLA] or Gay and Lesbian Alliance Against Defamation [GLAAD]?" Indeed, pride events are opportunities for tremendous revenue (approximately $1 million in large metropolitan cities), and, according to the logic of the council, these opportunities should go to the "best" organizations, through competition. Given the financial opportunity represented by pride events and the concomitant presumption that other organizations will gladly compete for such an opportunity, CSW's ownership of the event was reframed by the city council as a privilege earned through competition. From this perspective, CSW's failure to sufficiently take advantage of an opportunity to be a polished, "national leader in pride festivals" justified intervention, or at least healthy business competition.

The professionalization of pride events is also marked by the growing and enthusiastic presence of corporate sponsors (e.g., Budweiser, Washington Mutual, United Airlines, Showtime, Odwalla). Corporate sponsors receive vendor booths at pride events where they offer gifts and prizes, often combining same-sex erotic images with their corporate logo. As corporations become more skilled at packaging pride by queering their products and services, providing in-kind donations to the host organization, and helping to cover production costs, it stands to reason that the organization that simply "hosts" the event becomes less important. Vendors, exhibitors, performers, and parade participants generate the image of pride most visible to event attendees. As the work of producing such events becomes more logistical and professional, the more it appears that any organization with experience in event planning and corporate sponsorship *is* well suited to organize a pride event.

These dramatic changes in the political economy of pride events have helped to naturalize class-based evaluations of pride organizers. During Los

Angeles' first parade in 1970, participants pushed back surrounding police vehicles with a thirty-five-foot penis-shaped puppet in the style of a Chinese Dragon (which they referred to as "cock-a-pillar"). Today, CSW works hand-in-hand with the West Hollywood chief of police to contain and control the event. The growth and institutionalization of Los Angeles' pride event requires that organizers know how to work cooperatively with city officials, make deals with corporate sponsors, "implement message control," and reflect the diversity of the "community"—in sum, they must know how to run the event like a successful business. Even as some activists, such as Rose and Dudley, resisted the professionalization of pride by challenging the city's attempts to take over the event, little critical attention was given to the ways in which social connections and "professional skills sets" had become necessary to the production of queer pride in Los Angeles.

The Failure to Professionalize

A complex set of factors worked to position lesbian and gay professionals and well-known activists as more qualified to produce queer pride in Los Angeles than unknown, working-class activists. The most pronounced of these factors is the institutionalization and privatization of pride events generally, which has resulted in the need for pride festival organizers to work cooperatively with corporate sponsors, city officials, and the press. In contrast with the creative and critical thinking skills required to invent a thirty-five-foot phallic police barrier, professional skills and working relationships with authorities are now central to the production of pride events. However, the story of CSW illustrates that "bad press" regarding diversity can also suggest the need for a professional team of organizers—people with professional outreach experience who are in touch with the diversity of the lesbian and gay community. CSW's new board members brought these diversity skills to CSW. They had experience with diversification ("targeting" white women and people of color), speaking publicly about the importance of diversity, and making structural changes (such as the addition a "children's garden") that would signal their commitment to diversity.

The emphasis on diversity skills at CSW drew attention to middle-class forms of race and gender diversity, while stigmatizing the working-class culture of CSW's original board members. Toward the end of my research, Charles, CSW's working-class African American president, was convinced to "step back" so that Richard, a white gay man with strong diversity skills and connections, could lead the organization (though they later became equal copresidents). The case of CSW begs questions about *what kind* of diversity, then, is important to the production of queer pride events, and for whom. In debates over competence and professionalism at CSW, abstract diversity skills and visual symbols of inclusion—such as "ethnic costumery"—were given more value than embodying class differences that are less easily represented and, for that matter, may be less easily commodified. At the broader sociopolitical level, diversity culture in the United States has helped to facilitate this convergence of political values regarding inclusion and equality and upper-middle-class values regarding professionalism and good taste. At CSW, activists' concerns about the visual representation of women and people of color in the pride festival coexisted with concerns about the event's look and polish. Ethnic costumery, like fireworks, was framed as one way to make the event more visually interesting.

In Bourdieu's analysis of class identities and cultures, the working class is characterized by a taste for the practices and objects of necessity. "Necessity imposes a taste for necessity," or a taste associated with function over form, and with enjoyment that is "lower, course, vulgar, venal, servile—in a word, natural."[24] The taste of luxury, on the other hand, is associated with style, manner, representation; it is the taste of "those who can be satisfied with the sublimated, refined, disinterested, gratuitous, distinguished pleasures forever closed to the profane."[25] In the queer pride movement, and at CSW specifically, this tension between form and function is manifested in part by the competing goals and tastes of differently classed social groups. Working-class festival organizers prioritized embodied needs and desires (to party) over the tastes and desires of the gay press and government (to present a high-end event) and gay professionals and activists (to be professional, to be political).

As the queer movement transitions from urgency and survival to assimilation and "homonormativity," it stands to reason that the cultural capital of movement leaders will become increasingly important to evaluations of their effectiveness. However, I have attempted to show the link between the stigma associated with messy, do-it-yourself, unprofessional politics and the possible disappearance of working-class queerness and its contribution to queer resistance. While "diversity" marks one point of intersection between professionalism and social justice values, the politics of vulgarity marks the place in which classlessness and queerness meet. It is no small matter that working-class board members repeatedly failed at the project of professionalization. This failure represents a kind of organic resistance to the various normalizing forces within LGBT politics. It is a resistance characterized by a pathetic ruckus at the civilized fundraiser, or by the old board's persistent confusion about why the new board wanted to be "soooooo boring." Though perhaps not as subversive and performative as the deployment of a "cock-a-pillar" to push back the cops, their defense of dancing, music, drinking, and public sex at CSW continued in the tradition of defying the rules of respectable political expression. In this case, the antiprofessional voice of resistance did not ultimately win the battle over CSW's ownership, at least not the battle I witnessed. Yet in Chapter 6 I return to the story of CSW to consider what role antiprofessionalism might play in a queer response to the mainstreaming of diversity.

CHAPTER 4

Celebrating Queer Diversity:
The L.A. Gay & Lesbian Center

The words "diversity" and "inclusion" have been so overused in the language of lesbian and gay politics that one might expect the "queer community" to shine as an exemplar in multicultural representation, effortlessly integrating communities of color and their causes and concerns into the larger liberation struggle. Unfortunately, the politically correct rhetoric differs greatly from the incorrect reality.
> —Keith Boykin, past executive director of the National
> Black Gay and Lesbian Leadership Forum[1]

When you have a diverse workforce that reflects your clients, you are better able to serve your clients. And coming from the corporate environment, that is the feeling there. . . . You could have all the reasons to do good that you want, and in reality, you have a better product, you provide a better service, if you better understand your customer. So I think one of the reasons [the Gay & Lesbian Center] started Diversity Day was so that we can really look . . . at some of the ways that we are all alike and some of the ways that we may be different. Only through attempting to do that can you better your communications and your ability to work together towards your goal.
> —Robin, a white director at the L.A. Gay & Lesbian Center

As Keith Boykin's quote suggests above, queer activists aren't simply *interested* in diversity; rather, diversity is often the very centerpiece of queer political discourse. In part, the focus on diversity in queer politics is the result of long and hard-fought struggles for inclusion and visibility waged by working-class queers, queer people of color, and white lesbians. As sociologist Elizabeth Armstrong has pointed out, white leaders of the 1970s gay liberation movement responded to these challenges by defining gay politics as a "politics of difference"—but only as long as race, class, and gender differences took a backseat to the work of building a unified gay identity.[2] Accounts of more recent forms of queer organizing suggest that, after two decades of intersectional theorizing by feminists of color, queer activists (and activists generally) are becoming increasingly conscious of the intersectional nature of oppression and in response have developed new multi-issue political strategies.[3]

Yet, as explained in the second quote, queer activists have other, more instrumental reasons to be focused on diversity—reasons that are distinct from "doing good." As Robin learned from her previous experience in the corporate sector, understanding and celebrating multiple forms of difference also makes good business sense, even for queer organizations. This chapter illustrates that efforts to transcend the confines of single-issue gay politics aren't simply motivated by the expanded social justice commitments of queer activists. By emphasizing diversity, the leaders of queer organizations understand that they can also increase employee loyalty and productivity, broaden their range of supporters and funders, help repair a previously negative public image, and compete with other queer organizations already attuned to the value of the diversity. But these practical gains don't come without structural change. Achieving these outcomes requires more than simply "talking" about diversity; it often requires new levels of race, class, and gender inclusion, the development or expansion of multi-issue programs, and deliberate efforts to diversify organizational leadership. The L.A. Gay & Lesbian Center—the organization that is the subject of this chapter—has undertaken each of these efforts to diversify and restructure.

Most critics of diversity projects have focused on their failure to accomplish more than cultural appreciation or their failure to result in "real" inclusion and the redistribution of power. By such accounts, true diversity is measured by structural change, wherein organizations move beyond tokenism and are transformed by the inclusion of people of color, white women, queers, and the poor and working class. But structural change is not the end of the story about diversity. Even some forms of structural change are undertaken largely for instrumental reasons, and, as such, these forms of change may not have sustainable effects. What happens to inclusion and diversity efforts when they are no longer profitable or otherwise institutionally advantageous? If diversity benchmarks are met, does it also matter *how* or *why* diversity projects are undertaken?

The previous chapter illustrated how middle-class queer activists used the concept of diversity to assert their professional expertise and activist qualifications. In this chapter, I focus on the corporate-inspired practices used by queer "employee activists" to document and celebrate their own race and gender differences in the service of their employer organization. Other scholars have pointed to cases in which activists have turned to the business sector for organizing strategies and new techniques for framing their demands.[4] However, as Robin's quote makes clear, the corporate environment also provides a model for celebrating multiple differences in ways that enhance organizational effectiveness. At the L.A. Gay & Lesbian Center (the Center), strong ties to the corporate diversity model fueled the organization's growing interest in race, class, and gender diversity and its development of new multi-issue programs. Through various diversity initiatives, the Center's leaders also placed considerable attention on diversifying the organization's staff, leadership team, and board of directors. Yet as I will show, the Center's corporate-inspired approach to diversity—characterized by diversity trainings, diversity-related data gathering and benchmarking, and public relations efforts to improve the organization's image—also produced new tensions, and ultimately did little to change the "white culture" of the organization.

The story of the Center's racialized identity and culture is complex and subject to multiple interpretations. At the time I began my fieldwork at the Center, the organization had a national reputation for multiculturalism; a growing presence of people of color and white women in leadership; multiple programs addressing the intersections of racism, classism, and homophobia; and more than 50 percent people of color on staff. However, despite these indicators of racial and gender diversity, the Center also maintained a local reputation among queer people of color as the white LGBT organization in Los Angeles, a reputation that persisted regardless of the organization's efforts to change its public image and demonstrate its diversity to its local and internal critics.

In the spring of 2002, I was hired by a Center director and former research contact to write grant proposals and elicit corporate sponsorships in the Center's development department. During my interviews and participant observation at the Center, it became clear that making sense of the disparity between the Center's ongoing efforts to achieve a multiracial identity and its continued reputation for whiteness required looking closely at *how* the Center approached diversity. As I asked questions about race at the Center, my attention was drawn to the organization's own "diversity culture"— or the diversity-related repertoire of ideas, vocabularies, knowledge claims, modes of affect, and stylistic approaches that were given legitimacy at the Center.

As I will show, progressive whites at the Center explained that they felt reassured by the organization's professional and methodical approach to diversity, often arguing for more diversity-related data, expert guidance by diversity professionals, and thoughtful methods for hiring the "right" leaders of color. However, many (but not all) employees of color argued that this approach to diversity was a sign of the organization's need to "justify" diversity, as well as a sign of its cultural similarities to "corporate white America." Instead, they suggested a less discursive and instrumental diversity culture rooted in "just doing the right thing" and "doing it now."

In the discussion that follows, I illustrate that the Center's instrumental and excessive focus on declaring and promoting its own diversity—a strategy brought to the organization by leaders who drew on their previous corporate-sector experience with diversity management and public relations—became the very practice that some employees of color identified as evidence of the white culture of the organization. Ironically, the Center's diversity activities added to the burnout and turnover of many employees of color, and worked to slowly undo some of the gains that had been made to transform the organization.

White Normativity

As in many white-dominated organizations that have embarked upon diversification projects, the highest levels of the Center's leadership remained predominantly white even after multiple attempts to diversify. However, the Center's mostly white leadership only partially accounted for its ongoing reputation for whiteness. Also a key part of the picture was the organization's *culture*—a culture that several employees and external critics described as both white and corporate. Setting aside the matter of corporate culture for a moment, what does it mean to say that an organization has a white culture?

Critical race scholars argue that whiteness refers not only to individuals who are coded white and the social and economic privileges granted to them, but also to ways of thinking, knowing, and doing that naturalize whiteness and become embedded in social and institutional life.[5] According to this view, whiteness is not simply a structural location, but "a cultural disposition and ideology linked to specific political, social, and historical arrangements."[6] Queer scholars of color have begun to elaborate this position by pointing to the forces of white normativity, or the often unconscious and invisible ideas and practices that make whiteness appear natural and right.[7] This emphasis on white normativity as opposed to the notion of a fixed white culture highlights the ways in which evolving constructions of whiteness take form in and through institutions and become the standard by which "normal" people, ideas, and practices are measured.

Similar to the assertion of some feminist scholars that organizations are "gendered" in relation to, but also apart from, the gendered bodies that inhabit them, the concept of white normativity suggests that organizational practices may reflect the culture and interpretive frames of whites, regardless of the racial identities of organizational participants.[8] In the context of activist organizations, white-normative ways of thinking and doing may become central to how political work is understood and undertaken, especially if they are rewarded by funding agencies and other movement organizations. For instance, central concepts in the lesbian and gay movement, such as "unity," "coming out," and "diversity," are typically rooted in white American conceptualizations of the relationship between community, sexuality, and other axes of difference.[9] These concepts are integral to current constructions of lesbian and gay identity, making it difficult to sustain, fund, or promote lesbian and gay organizations that do not engage with them.[10] Queer political leaders, both whites and people of color, may experience pressure to engage in white-normative organizational practices that reflect white interpretive frames, may be hired and supported by whites for doing so, or may be unable to accomplish the work of the organization without doing so.

Understanding whiteness as a hegemonic cultural formation not only allows for examination of which racial groups have power in movement organizations (people of color or whites), but also avoids conflating the presence or leadership of people of color with automatic antiracism or multicultural success. More to the point of this chapter, it helps to flesh out the ways in which hegemonic whiteness is often *bolstered* by diversity projects or may persist despite leadership by people of color or the development of antiracist values among members.

Setting the Scene

A History of Exclusion

The Center's history is marked as much by dissension and fragmentation as it is by rapid growth and financial success. First named the Gay Community Services Center, the organization was founded in 1971 by gay male activists when the West Coast chapter of the political group Gay Liberation Front started to receive an extraordinary number of calls from gay men and lesbians in need of support services.[11] The Center opened in a dilapidated Victorian house not far from Hollywood, incorporated with the State of California, and declared its mission to "protect and serve, on a non-profit basis, the individuals, both male and female, of the homosexual community." Despite its stated mission to serve the female community, the Center immediately had a reputation for being largely gay male in focus and therefore drew very few lesbian staff or clients during its first few years of operation. In 1974, Center staff applied for and received a $1 million government grant to start the Alcoholism Center for Women (ACW), a new alcoholism recovery program for lesbians. With this addition, lesbian staff far outnumbered the gay male staff, yet were still not represented in positions of leadership, either on the board of directors or in the Center's management. In response, the director and staff of ACW broke off from the Center and began operating ACW as a new organization run by and for women.

Conflicts over structural inequalities and organizational identity positioned the Center as a springboard for several organizations in Los Angeles that were founded by disillusioned staff and volunteers. The most well-known of these were two offshoot organizations: ACW and a second lesbian organization named Connexxus, both of which developed as a result of the Center's decades-long struggle between lesbians and gay men.[12] AIDS Project Los Angeles, the country's second-largest AIDS service organization, also began as an offshoot telephone hotline program at the Center and developed into a multi-million-dollar AIDS organization under the leadership of previous Center employees who believed that the organization had not adequately prioritized the epidemic. Other large organizations, including those founded by and for people of color, such as Bienestar (see Chapter 5), began as committees or community action groups that met at the Center, benefited from the Center's resources, and remained at the Center only as long as was necessary to raise funds to rent office space in their home communities.

However, by the 1990s, the Center had a strong presence of women

leaders, including three consecutive lesbian executive directors—all white—
and several lesbians in senior management. This resulted in some complaints
from gay men who accused the Center of becoming a "lesbian organization,"
including the sexist suggestion made by a *Los Angeles Times* writer that the
series of lesbian executive directors "reflect[ed] the sad fact that women have
assumed more power in gay and lesbian organizations as AIDS has devas-
tated the ranks of gay men."[13]

Becoming "Gay Inc."

According to its 2001 Annual Report, the L.A. Gay & Lesbian Center was
the largest lesbian and gay social service organization in the world, with an
annual budget of $33 million, 250 staff members, 3,000 volunteers, and five
separate sites. The organization offered an impressive range of multi-issue
programs, most of which served predominantly low-income or homeless lesbians, gay men, and trans people of color—an immigration legal clinic, the
Pedro Zamora HIV-prevention program, homeless youth shelter, job placement and training program, and drop-in youth center (utilized primarily by
transgendered youth of color). In addition, the Center was also home to a
primary care facility, a cyber center, a cultural arts center, a clearinghouse
for HIV/AIDS literature, a full-service HIV clinic and pharmacy, a safe-
schools project, family services, and a same-gender domestic violence program. Situated in the middle of Hollywood, and in an area reporting one of
the highest concentrations of homeless queer youth, the Center's employees
and volunteers were trained to address a complex host of intersecting needs,
including homelessness, mental illness, violence, immigration status, HIV
status, unemployment, and lack of health insurance.

After years of providing these services, the Center's leadership in, and
expertise about, the LGBT community had become a taken-for-granted feature of Los Angeles' political and social scene. Reflected by its unparalleled
coverage in both the mainstream and gay press and its visits from national
and international heads of state (including then Vice President Al Gore), the
Center had become a model gay and lesbian community center and, not surprisingly given its location, a favorite cause among Los Angeles' lesbian and
gay elite. The Center's high-profile fundraising dinners, with tickets priced
at as much as $300 per plate, drew both celebrities and executives from cor-
porations that market to the lesbian and gay community. The Center's board
of directors, charged primarily with the task of recruiting new sustaining
donors, was comprised of entertainment industry executives, well-connected
business leaders, and the independently wealthy. Like many other LGBT

community centers, the Center's early growth was dependent, at least in part, on the financial support of wealthy, and sometimes closeted, gay donors living in the prestigious communities of Beverly Hills and Bel Air. By the 1990s, the majority of the Center's funding came in the form of HIV-related grants and support from corporations interested in targeting the gay market.

The Center had grown dramatically since its inception in 1971, and it had also developed strong corporate ties by recruiting its leadership team from the business sector and soliciting grants from wealthy donors and gay-friendly corporations. Claire, a white thirty-nine-year-old lesbian and the Center's then executive director, had been lesbian-identified for five years and had never worked for a lesbian and gay organization prior to leaving her career in management consulting in order to lead the Center. According to my supervisors in the development department, Claire was chosen over other candidates with decades of experience in LGBT organizing because the board of directors wanted a leader whose primary strengths were fundraising and financial management. In 1999, a *Los Angeles Times* article described Claire's "unsentimental" and "let's-get-busy manner," as well as the powerful, fast-paced, and prestigious nature of her work at the Center: "In the course of a day she might be giving Vice President Al Gore a tour of the Center, negotiating with union leaders about contracts for health care workers, then dining with prospective donors."[14] The article added that certain "buzzwords"—which likely had currency in both management consulting *and* queer political discourse—studded Claire's conversation: "empowerment, relevance, diversity."[15]

As I will show, the Center's reputation for whiteness cannot be understood apart from its corporate culture, and particularly its corporate-inspired approach to diversity. Joe, a gay Latino manager who was hired at the Center after working in a multibillion-dollar food distribution company, told me that he liked to call the Center "Gay Inc." According to Joe, "the CEO at [the food distribution company] had more time to say 'hello' to employees than Claire. . . . It's like she thinks she's the president of the United States." Beverly, an African American manager, explained, "I've always had a job in corporate white America. So I've always had to learn how to leave my Blackness at home and come to work. When I came to the Center, it was no different." A far cry from its early days in a dilapidated house run by a ragtag group of butch dykes and nelly queens, the Center's more recent iteration as "Gay Inc." reflected its new size, financial resources, location (now in what was once L.A.'s IRS building), and the new business skills and "corporate speak" presumably required of its leaders.

Though employees such as Joe and Beverly were critical of the Center's corporate culture, for many employees at the Center, particularly for Claire and others in management, being impersonal and professional and modeling a corporate environment were valued means of increasing the legitimacy of the lesbian and gay movement. The majority of the Center's executive management team, both whites and people of color, came to the organization after holding management positions in the private sector. They wore business suits to work, lunched with wealthy donors, and had offices on the administrative fourth floor of the Center's headquarters. Employees reported that it was difficult to get a meeting with Claire, who had gained a reputation for being unavailable and aloof. This was reflected in my own unsuccessful attempts to schedule an interview with her for this project; when I tried a third time to push Claire's assistant to schedule a meeting, I was finally told that she might be available "next year." On the other hand, the size and corporate culture of the Center also resulted in employee benefits often unavailable in smaller queer organizations. The Center had its own human resources department, and employees received health benefits, holiday bonuses, and various perks, especially for those who donated a portion of their salary back to the organization.[16] Also due to its size, the Center generally had more than a dozen job positions open at any given time and had become a popular place of employment for queer activists in Los Angeles.

Yet in addition to these characteristics, being "Gay Inc." also signaled the ways that the Center had embraced the corporate culture of diversity management. As sociologist Nicole Raeburn has illustrated, corporate diversity programs are generally couched in an "ideology of profits," in which understanding and promoting diversity is justified as a means of reaching diverse consumers, developing consumer loyalty, and enhancing public reputation.[17] Corporate diversity programs are also a means of nurturing a company's human resources, promoting satisfaction, unity, productivity, and efficiency among employees. The Center's leaders drew upon both of these logics but slightly transformed them for use in a queer context. Mirroring Robin's comment about having a "diverse workforce that reflects your clients," a comment that I return to below, the Center's leaders emphasized the ways in which understanding diversity helps people work together and leads to better delivery of queer services. Behind the scenes, and particularly in the development and public affairs departments, Center employees were also trained to be attentive to the financial and public relations benefits of highlighting race and gender differences among queer people. While I was working as a grant writer for the Center, two program directors expressed to me their belief that in Los Angeles' social service field, it was more difficult to find funding for gay and lesbian services than programs addressing racism or poverty—a point that was supported by my own grant prospecting research. As a result, the Center's development staff (including myself) were trained to emphasize the immigration clinic and homeless shelter, particularly when speaking to funders who might understand the urgency of racism and poverty more than the urgency of hate crimes against gay men. In one case, I was assigned to write a grant proposal for a Latino-specific grant from a large banking corporation, but asked not to use the words "gay and lesbian" and instead emphasize the organization's service to Latinos (not *gay and lesbian* Latinos—just Latinos!). The supervisor who assigned the task to me expressed strong discomfort with "closeting" the Center's programs but indicated that this was the request of a gay contact from the bank who was going to sneak the funding through to the Center.

In such instances, the Center's emphasis on racial or socioeconomic inequality brought legitimacy and funding to the organization, as well as enabled the Center compete with dozens of organizations run exclusively by and for people of color in Los Angeles. The "diversity of our [LGBT] community" was mentioned in nearly every public statement, program brochure, grant proposal, and report issued from the Center. Rarely intended as a reference to the diversity that queerness represents vis-à-vis heterosexuality, "diversity" was code for race and gender differences among LGBT people and had become a centerpiece of the Center's organizational discourse and identity.

A Multicultural Success Story?

In response to criticism from queer people of color, mainstream lesbian and gay organizations nationwide have begun efforts to diversify, and the Center is no exception. Urvashi Vaid, a nationally visible South Asian American lesbian activist and former executive director of the National Gay and Lesbian Task Force, has been one of the country's most vocal critics of racial inequality in lesbian and gay organizations. In her book *Virtual Equality: The Mainstreaming of the Lesbian and Gay Movement*, Vaid asserted that despite the movement's diversity rhetoric, "most gay and lesbian organizations have continued to operate as always. By embracing the myth of a united gay and lesbian community, monocultural organizations have been able to label themselves inclusive and representative simply by declaring it so."[18] Yet Vaid explained that dramatic change is also possible, and named a small group of organizations as exemplars. Among these was the Center, which Vaid described as follows:

> Under the leadership of progressive white gay organizer Eric Rofes,
> [the Center] embarked on major programs to transform their mission
> and composition in ways that would make groups more racially and
> gender diverse. Working with lesbians of color like Deborah Johnson-
> Rolan and Melinda Paras, Rofes succeeded in dramatically changing
> the organization, and in the process alienated many people who had
> philosophical or particular objections to the changes. . . . Conscious
> efforts like those . . . have been the exception, not the rule.[19]

The Center's reputation for multicultural transformation reflected a nationally visible history of queer people of color working with progressive
whites to diversify the organization's staff and improve its ability to serve its
racially diverse clients.

At the time of this study, more than two thirds of the Center's clients
were people of color, and 52 percent of the organization's employees were
people of color. Four members of the six-person executive management team
were white, and two were Black. Though the Center's leadership remained
predominantly white, the two Black executive managers held powerful and
highly visible positions in the organization, including the Center's managing
director (the second-in-command position) and director of education and
social services (the position that oversees all programs). Clearly, while the
number of people of color in leadership had grown consistently over the last
fifteen years, employees of color still remained underrepresented in positions
of leadership (32 percent of managers and directors were people of color according to the Center's 1998 data). Recognizing this disparity, the Center's
leaders again named racial diversification in leadership as one of the central
goals of the organization's 2001 strategic plan.

Diversity at the Center was marked not only by the racial identities of
the organization's staff, but also by programs that served predominantly or
exclusively poor communities of color. Like many lesbian and gay organizations in large urban centers, discussing the needs of clients of color, homeless clients, and transgendered clients—as well as understanding the complexities of multiple and intersecting forms of oppression—had become a
necessary component of the Center's work. Programs needed to address the
intersections of racism, homophobia, sexism, transphobia, and poverty in order to be effective, and by most accounts the Center succeeded in this effort.
Employees of color and whites worked together to develop techniques for
service delivery and advocacy based upon a structural analysis of how racism
affects their particular clients (e.g., How are sex workers of color treated differently by the police than their white counterparts? How does immigration

status affect domestic partnership issues? How can schools be made safer for queer youth of color who are targeted on the basis of both sexuality and race? etc.). The Center's multilingual advertising materials were designed to reach Los Angeles' broad range of racial/ethnic populations, and most of the Center's job postings announced that prospective employees must demonstrate their ability to assess and meet the needs of the "racially and socioeconomically diverse" queer communities of Los Angeles.

While the Center's programs reflected its growing commitment to a broad social justice agenda, new program developments at the Center (such as the inclusion of lesbian programs in the 1970s and 1980s) were also a response to external protest and available funding for growth, and not simply to the political or altruistic motivations of the organization's leaders.[20] To be clear, the programmatic structure of the Center was influenced by both the political commitments of dedicated employee-activists and by the changing sociopolitical environment of Los Angeles County. Increasingly, the survival of social service organizations in Los Angeles depends upon funding from agencies that give priority to programs serving low-income Latino clients—a logical and vitally important trend given that Latinos represent 45 percent of the county's population. Over the years, the Center's predominantly white leadership team has kept the organization competitive with respect to funding, in part by highlighting programs that tend to draw people of color (e.g., the HIV clinic, the drop-in center for homeless youth) over programs more likely to be utilized by whites (e.g., the cultural arts center, the seniors program, family services).

Yet as I learned in the Center's development department, the line between the organization's willingness to "chase funding" and the sincere political commitments of its leaders was often blurred. In some cases, promises were made to funders regarding race- and gender-specific client "contact numbers" (e.g. "30% of the people who use this program will be women of color") before program staff knew if they realistically had access to, or knowledge of, the population in question. For instance, Mark, a white male coordinator of a mental health services program, told me that he felt overwhelmed by all of the race-related questions that the granting agency's reporting forms required him to answer. Mark didn't know if he could find enough participants of color to satisfy the granting agency. He was going to need to "scramble to bring it all together."

Like other large cities in the United States, Los Angeles is now home to a number of organizations founded specifically by and for queer Latinos, Asian Americans, and African Americans. The existence of these organizations, some of which originally splintered off from the Center in response to conflicts over racial inequality, enabled the Center's multicultural staff and culture to be compared with the staff and culture of organizations exclusively serving queer people of color. For instance, according to Martin, the executive director of Bienestar, a queer Latino organization in Los Angeles, the Center "claims that it opens the door and welcomes [Latinos], but the music, the food, the everything, is not really welcome to Latinos." Such criticisms—commonly made by local queer activists in Los Angeles (both queers of color and progressive whites)—pointed to the gap between the Center's discursive emphasis on its own diversity and the realities of its unwelcoming *culture*.

Just Like Corporate America?
White Culture and Diversity Work

The Center's programs, its multicultural staff, and the growing attention of white employees to the need for more leaders of color signaled the organization's significant transformation from its early white gay male roots. Yet it was during the organization's efforts to formally document and celebrate this "success" that conflicts intensified regarding the Center's persistent whiteness. The Center's ongoing efforts to formally declare itself diverse, especially in response to competition with (and critique by) queer organizations of color in Los Angeles, reflected discursive strategies and conceptual frameworks that many of the Center's employees of color associated with whiteness. For the remainder of this chapter, I look closely at two of the Center's most prominent racial diversity projects: its annual "Diversity Day" event and the "Diversity Initiative" in its strategic plan. It was during the planning and activities surrounding these events that the Center's racial identity and culture were most frequently debated by the organization's staff and outside critics.

Celebrating the Hero in All of Us: Diversity Day

The Center's most regular and explicit diversity activity was its annual "Diversity Day." Diversity Day had taken several forms since it was instituted at the Center in the early 1990s. Most often a day of workshops designed to encourage employees to talk about race and other differences, it had also taken other forms, such a field trip to the Museum of Tolerance in 2000. Planning the event was the responsibility of the Center's "Employee Roundtable," a group of ten to fifteen staff members selected by the Center's executive managers. While this committee of employees was charged with designing Diversity Day each year, it was ultimately the Center's executive management team that had final authority over the event's design. In 2001, the year I attended Diversity Day, the event was a small outdoor multicultural festival, complete with a variety of ethnic foods and music, South Asian dancers, free time for socializing, and an (indoor) screening of a video in which several Center employees talked about their cultural backgrounds, experiences of oppression, and aspects of their identities that made them feel "proud."

Though the 2001 Diversity Day had the feeling of a celebration or party, it was a party that Center employees were *required* to attend. At a staff meeting held before the event, several employees groaned audibly when the date for Diversity Day was announced. Acknowledging the groans, Claire explained that Diversity Day would be improved this year and that employee feedback from surveys would be used to determine the format of the event. A slide show intended to encourage enthusiasm about the improved Diversity Day also implied a collective understanding that the event was an undesirable obligation by self-mockingly including phrases like "Not another Diversity Day!" and by announcing that the event had been renamed "We Can All Be Heroes Day." At the time of this staff meeting, the concept of "hero" had taken on new significance following the recent 9/11 World Trade Center attacks. During the meeting, Claire asked employees to participate in a moment of silence for those killed on 9/11 and then sing together the Woody Guthrie song, "This Land Is Your Land." At the 2001 event, the concept of diversity was linked to national pride, the police and firefighter heroes of 9/11, and the uncritical assertion that "this land was made for you and me." The new event name, "We Can All Be Heroes Day," communicated to employees that celebrating queer diversity was a form of *honoring* Americanism (e.g., American bravery, resilience, and power to "fight back")—rather than degrading it, as some conservatives might suggest, or critiquing it, as some queer radicals might hope for.

Diversity Day drew on familiar neoliberal values, including the notion that diversity was integral to both American identity and institutional prosperity. While the focus on heroism and patriotism was specific to the 2001 event, the notion that "we are all alike" insofar as we are all unique and different was a theme common to Diversity Day. As research on corporate diversity management culture has shown, this emphasis on the unique contribution that every individual and culture brings to the corporation is a common technique used to elide issues of power and privilege and instead emphasize employees' service to the institution.[21] While there was no profit to be made at the Center, the notion that diversity was a means to an institutional end was nonetheless explicit in the Center's discourse. When I asked Robin, a white lesbian director, about the history of Diversity Day, she explained the event was motivated by the same diversity goals that are now strived for and achieved within the corporate environment:

> The reason that they started Diversity Day is because . . . when you have a diverse workforce that reflects your clients, you are better able to serve your clients. And coming from the corporate environment, that is the feeling there. . . . You could have all the reasons to do good that you want, and in reality, you have a better product, you provide a better service, if you better understand your customer. So I think one of the reasons we started Diversity Day, was so that we can really look . . . at some of the ways that we are all alike and some of the ways that we may be different. Only through attempting to do that can you better your communications and your ability to work together towards your goal.

Robin's discussion of the motivations behind Diversity Day reflects three themes central to the corporate diversity management approach. First, diversity results in better service to clients, and is contingent upon the demographics of clients. A diverse workforce is necessary when an organization's client pool is similarly diverse. Second, serving the interests of the organization is the bottom line, the most legitimate justification for wanting diversity, and more important than other "reasons to do good." Third, diversity is as much, if not more, about the ways that people are the same than it is about the ways that people are different. According to Robin, Diversity Day allowed Center employees to simultaneously witness the ways that they were both different and the same, and this experience unified employees and strengthened their ability to work together.

On the one hand, the belief that the work of the Center could not be accomplished without formal attention to diversity marked an important change from its earliest iteration in the 1970s as a predominantly white gay male organization. On the other hand, this framing transformed diversity into a matter of business, an obligation of all employees, and a job duty. Staff attendance at Diversity Day was mandatory and the event had become an institutionalized feature of the Center designed to ensure that all employees viewed diversity—and particularly racial diversity—as critical to the Center's success. Because many of the Center's social service programs addressed multiple and intersecting inequalities in the course of their daily operation, it would be inaccurate to suggest that the Center's engagement with

diversity was isolated to a single day's event. However, the institutionalization of a compulsory diversity activity also suggested to employees that they
needed to be compelled to stop and think about racial diversity. As reflected
in the groans made at the staff meeting, many employees resented Diversity
Day for this reason, and as I discovered in the week leading up to the event,
sarcastic remarks about Diversity Day were a common part of the Center's
discursive culture.

While several of the Center's employees were critical of Diversity Day,
in many cases they disagreed along racial lines about how to define the
problems with the event. Building upon the Center's already strong focus on
professionalism, data gathering, and "best practices," progressive white employees generally focused on evaluating the structural elements of the event,
including the qualifications of event facilitators. Some argued that asking
employees to plan the event suggested a lack of commitment to the project
of diversification, a commitment that could only be demonstrated by hiring
experts and not relying on well-intentioned, but inexperienced, staff. Sheridan, a white male manager, explained:

> [Diversity Day] is not something that a group of well-intentioned
> junior-level employees can sit around and discuss how to do over
> the course of twenty hours. It's insulting to think that we can do it
> ourselves without the expertise of people who have been in this field
> for decades. It would be as if we attempted to call together a group of
> Center employees who didn't have management expertise and turned
> them loose with developing a strategic plan for fundraising.

Other progressive white employees agreed that to take diversity seriously
would mean hiring someone with "diversity skills" to facilitate the event.
According to Beth, a white manager, the event would be improved if Claire
"recognized that she has limited skills in talking about this subject. . . . Her
experience in this arena seems very, very limited." Though these kinds of
critiques were made most frequently by white employees, some employees
of color expressed similar concerns. According to Douglas, a Black gay
male manager, "developing a concept of diversity is something that people
study. It takes an expert skills set to be able to engage individuals in deep
dialogue."

In addition to concerns about the event's poor administration and the
need for diversity expertise, several progressive whites and some employees
of color complained that the event had not been confrontational enough
and had not gone "far enough" to confront white privilege. Such complaints

were first articulated in the mid-1990s, causing a group of employees to re-structure the 1998 Diversity Day so as to more directly confront multiple forms of power and inequality at the Center. Prior to the 1998 event, a memo was sent to all employees explaining that "what has been known as 'Diversity Training Day' is being put together very differently this year." The event itself included eleven different workshops cofacilitated by employees. Attendees were provided with an advance description of the workshops, some of which are abbreviated below:

> *Color, Culture, and Power*: This session will examine the distribution of power at the Gay & Lesbian Center by ethnicity and race and will ask how this distribution affects us as an organization and us as individuals. Participants in this session will explore some of the barriers to equitable racial and ethnic diversity at the various organizational "levels," and will push for finding new tools with which to address and assess these issues on an ongoing basis. Can the Gay & Lesbian Center do more than simply mirror a diverse and inequitable society?
>
> *Coexistence, Conflict, Change*: This session focuses on the subject of race and ethnicity and how they affect our relations to clients, co-workers, managers, and community members within our own identity groups and in others. This session will try to move beyond "coexistence" vs. "conflict" and into the terrain of how we can change and be changed by one another.
>
> *Can We Talk?*: This session will explore diversity-related barriers to effective communication at the *individual* level. Do race, class, gender, sexual orientation, regional differences, and other factors interfere with our interpersonal communication?
>
> *Class Notes*: How do difference in education, socioeconomic privilege, and job status express themselves at the Gay & Lesbian Center? Does the Gay & Lesbian Center have its own "class structure"?
>
> *E Pluribus Unum (For Many, One)*: Can we all assert our own uniqueness while respecting everyone else's at the same time? This look at the Gay & Lesbian Center's Diversity Philosophy will give participants the opportunity to answer this and other questions.

Employees who attended the workshops were also provided with eight pages of statistics on the Center's workforce, including gender and racial/ethnic demographics by department and job category, hires and promotions, and income level, as well as comparisons to the Los Angeles County workforce more broadly.

Some employees explained that the 1998 event was the most empowering Diversity Day they had attended, while others described it as a "complaint day" that resulted in little organizational change. Similar debates regarding the success or failure of Diversity Day occurred year after year; however, few employees seemed willing to abandon the event altogether, as it had become the symbol of the Center's commitment to engage multi-issue political questions and address its own structural hierarchies. Yet a small group of employees of color did offer deeper criticisms of the Center's emphasis on diversity by suggesting that there were inherent problems with turning diversity into an institutional practice of any kind. According to Beverly, a Black lesbian manager and one of my primary research contacts, the very notion of training in diversity was designed for whites and was not useful for people of color. She recalled a Diversity Day facilitated by a Latino professional diversity trainer brought to the Center from San Francisco:

> I don't even know what the purpose of [Diversity Day] is. . . . Why do you need people of color there? They've had to learn how to live and struggle in the white community, so it just doesn't make any sense. Now I could see if there are groups of people of color who don't get along, then maybe you can have some type of conflict resolution. But when we know that the white group is half the organization, what's the purpose? I sit there and it's just a joke. The first one I went to, they had this guy come up and part of his talk was about Blacks and Latinos. And he said, "Usually if you see a Black person in a meeting with their eyes closed, they're listening, but they just like to listen with their eyes closed." And I thought, well all be damned, here I am, if my eyes are closed, I'm asleep!

Beverly's comments exemplify the ways in which diversity projects often subtly validate the knowledge and experiences of whites, even in cases in which people of color play an active role in the discussions. As described in her example, diversity trainings commonly naturalize whiteness by teaching whites how to better understand the behaviors of people of color. They enable whites to make sense of the previously incomprehensible behaviors of people of color (listening with one's eyes closed); validate that such behaviors may appear strange, rude, or crazy to even the most reasonable white person; and translate these behaviors into codes that whites can understand. In theory, such a concrete and open discussion of racial differences would normalize these differences, build unity among employees, and improve organizational programs. From Beverly's perspective, however, Diversity Day *increased* racial tension by requiring that people of color look on while whites employees were provided with inaccurate generalizations and crass shortcuts for understanding and tolerating the differences of coworkers of color.

Employee disagreement about the meaning and effectiveness of Diversity Day reflected ideological and political tensions embedded in the event itself. On the one hand, the event provided an infrastructure that enabled employees to build the organization's multi-issue focus and engage in conversations about race, class, and gender privilege, such as occurred at the 1998 event. On the other hand, the Center's white-normative approach to diversity echoes broader dynamics in diversity culture, in which race, class, and gender diversity are encouraged while conceptual frameworks and organizational styles that normalize whiteness remain in place.

As explored in greater detail in the next section, the Center's diversity activities point to a primary characteristic of white-normative culture—the need for "rational," institutional, and often statistical justifications for racial inclusion. In contrast, some employees of color at the Center pointed to the intrinsic moral value of racial equality. Diversity, they argued, should need no justification, formalization, or one-day celebration.

Being Strategic about Diversity: The Diversity Initiative

The Center's leaders recognized that the activities of Diversity Day alone did little to address structural inequality in the organization. The Center's board of directors remained largely white, and employees of color continued to be overrepresented in the lowest-paid positions in the organization. To address these inequities, the Center's executive team developed a five-year strategic plan that named "commitment to diversity" as a central focus. The "commitment to diversity" goal in the strategic plan read as follows:

> Los Angles is the city of the 21st century with a diverse population and a rich variety of cultures and experiences. At the LA Gay & Lesbian Center, our clients represent the diversity of the city. At the staff level, we represent a range of racial and ethnic groups and embrace the importance of a diverse workforce to the services we provide. Because we value the benefits of racial and ethnic diversity at every level of the

organization—including senior management and the board—we want to increase our recruitment and retention efforts. Our commitment requires the cultivation of long-term relationships with people of color community leaders and opinion makers who will work with us to improve our outreach in communities of color. We plan to develop collaborations that ensure that these relationships provide benefits to all communities. We also will increase our involvement with people of color organizations and colleague organizations that provide services to people of color, and to speak out on policy and political issues of concern to communities of color. In the end, we hope that every community within our community will feel reflected and be represented in all aspects of the Gay & Lesbian Center, and that we will have expanded our collaborations with communities of color.

The diversity section of the Center's strategic plan declared that the organization's diversity efforts were to be focused on increasing the number of people of color in leadership, and improving relations with people of color organizations.

After developing the "commitment to diversity" goal, senior managers identified a group of employees (fourteen people of color, including several directors, and five whites, including myself) who they believed had "expertise in determining the measurements for this particular goal." They asked these employees to sit on a committee that would evaluate the objectives associated with the diversity goal. Senior management provided the implementation teams with two objectives for which to determine "measurements:" (a) increase the racial and ethnic diversity of senior staff and board, and (b) expand our involvement with communities and organizations of color. Implementation teams were given an instruction sheet listing questions that the team members should consider: "Are these the right strategies? What existing data, best practices, feasibility studies, past experiences are we drawing on? If these are the right strategies, how will they be accomplished and how much will be done [for] each in the next five years?" The sheet then instructed the teams to draft a narrative statement answering these questions and identifying measurements for each objective, including major budget amounts, and a chart listing the responsibilities associated with implementing the strategies, objectives, and goals.

During committee meetings, members generally agreed that the Center's diversity goals were extremely important and made several suggestions about how to increase the number of people of color in senior management (e.g., "we should advertise for leaders of color in more diverse publications") and how to build collaborations with queer organizations of color (e.g., "we should hold events in neighborhoods populated by people of color"). However, some members also diverged in their responses to the strategic plan, and particularly their assessments of the Center's current racial identity. Though disagreement did not break down along neatly divided racial lines, it was again a small group of employees of color (and no whites) who took issue with the premises of the diversity initiative. First, they argued, increasing the number of employees of color at the Center would not address the "culture of the Center," a culture exemplified by the organization's strategic and quantitative approach to racial inclusion. Second, they challenged the "us/them" dichotomy implicit in the suggestion that the Center should improve relations with "people of color organizations." "Isn't the Center itself is a people of color organization?" they asked.

Statistics and Other White Ways of Knowing

The instructions provided to the implementation committee by James, the Center's Black managing director, emphasized highly bureaucratic indicators of diversity, such as: "What existing data, best practices, feasibility studies, past experiences are we drawing on? If these are the right strategies, how will they be accomplished and how much will be done in each in the next five years?" Such questions were not only overwhelming, but they required committee members to discuss diversity in slow, quantifiable, and nonemotional terms that began to produce feelings of burnout and hopelessness. In response to this process, committee members of color argued that diversity "just needs to happen" and that the need for data suggested that the whole project was driven by a desire to "look good." According to Sabrina, a Latina manager, the strategic plan itself was less a sincere effort at bringing people of color into positions of power at the Center than it was a public relations effort designed to address the organization's poor reputation:

> I have some not good thoughts about the whole strategic plan anyway. The [diversity] portion of it I think is a continuation of lip service to satisfy a few persons out in the community. To try to make us look more liberal than we are when, organizations of color, why don't they come here? Because this is known as a white organization.

As I learned in the Center's development department, one reason that such bureaucratic questions about diversity "needed" to be answered is that they were asked on most of the organization's grant applications and reporting forms. Such requirements had ushered in a new era of bureaucratic race consciousness at the Center, in which obtaining funding depended upon the ability to provide data and best practices related to racial diversity and the racial demographics of Los Angeles. In this sense, the Center's approach to racial diversity—including data gathering, strategic planning, and the development of timelines—reflects the racial politics and identities of its leadership, but it also signals the ways in which counting and justifying various forms of diversity has become a necessity practice in most large nonprofit organizations.

Some employees of color argued that increasing the number of people of color in power would not be accomplished by planning and statistical analysis. According to Beverly, "counting" employees and engaging in a strategic planning process to achieve diversity were outdated measures designed by whites to convince other whites that diversity is valuable:

It's kind of hard to fight for change in an organization that does a strategic plan to figure out how to diversify or whether they need to. That's kind of the Stone Age times. A strategic plan scares me, because that means they're looking at numbers. It's not something that the organization believes needs to happen because it just needs to happen. You get tired of trying to fight for something that you know is right with people who are trying to convince themselves through their numbers and their strategic plans. You just get tired of trying to prove why you should be at the table, why you exist, why you're here. [The alternative is] you just go do it. . . . You just start doing it.

While several committee members remained focused on the link between "data" and diversification (How many people of color currently work at the Center? What positions do they hold? How much money do they make relative to whites? etc.), some employees of color denaturalized the white-normative assumption that such processes must be based on numerical indicators of equality and "fair" representation.

However, statistical justifications and other forms of counting were a central part of the Center's approach to identity work more generally. Counting and "outing" lesbians and gay men is a common strategy in white queer culture and activism, reflecting the notion that we can and should know how many people the movement "really" represents. Statistics—the basis of affirmative action approaches to social justice—have been a necessary yet limited component of civil rights strategy, one that may reflect what Patricia Hill Collins refers to as a "euro-masculinist" system of producing knowledge about, and making meaning of, the social world.[22] Some employees of color at the Center favored a "just do it" approach that prioritized common sense and direct action over data gathering, deliberation, and documentation of how equality serves the interests of something else (such as service delivery or maximizing profit).

The use of statistical measures to assess the Center's racial diversity not only privileged white ways of thinking and knowing about diversity, but also brought attention to conflicts between Black and Latino employees, conflicts that reflected trends in Los Angeles more broadly. The recently completed 2000 U.S. Census made counting a particularly relevant topic as it revealed that Latinos were the largest ethnic group in Los Angeles (45 percent), compared to a slowly shrinking Black population (10 percent). When a white employee suggested that the demographics of Los Angeles be used as a baseline to measure the Center's diversity, committee members of color pointed out that such a measure would set up Black and Latino employees for conflict and competition. To use the census data in this manner would indicate that while Latinos were strikingly underrepresented at the Center, Blacks were overrepresented. According to Sheridan, a white gay male director, white leaders at the Center had been more comfortable with Black colleagues than Latinos because the former were more "culturally similar," but also because the racial politics of the Center reflected the distribution of resources in Los Angeles more broadly:

> African Americans have been more acculturated in terms of the dominant white culture, and first-generation Latinos have cultures that are a lot less like the culture of the dominant white Gay & Lesbian Center group. I think it is not surprising that we have probably more success with African Americans in positions of leadership here than Latinos in positions of leadership. The flip side too is . . . if we're not welcoming, Latinos will form their own organizations. Whereas given the power structures and the resources in Los Angeles County, it's less likely that there will be the equivalent African American organizations, so we will attract African Americans who, of necessity, need to assimilate.

Similarly, others expressed that Latinos were more likely than Blacks to be uncomfortable and leave the Center, in part because Los Angeles is home to a number of queer Latino organizations to which they could belong, but also because Black employees had emerged as the dominant voice of people of color at the Center. In sum, counting employees of color not only centered white ways of conceptualizing and justifying racial diversity, but further reinforced the Center's white identity by naturalizing the culture and job security of whites (the standard against which diversity was measured) and by producing competition and instability for Blacks and Latinos.

During the strategic planning committee meetings, discussions about how to increase the number of people of color in leadership transformed into debates regarding racialized recruitment and hiring practices. As in most workplaces previously dominated by whites and in which racial diversification efforts have been instituted, white employees raised the question of whether "unqualified" people of color were being hired at the Center in a rush to diversify the staff. Representing the most conservative and explicitly racist view expressed during my interviews with Center employees, Sam, a white gay male director, employed the "reverse racism" argument to contend that race-based hiring had had a negative impact on the Center:

> We have hired people of color to be people of color and they tend
> to be really not qualified. Then because they are the only people
> of color around, we're stuck with them. I am a strong advocate of
> affirmative action, but to hire for color is wrong. It's racist, with like
> wom[e]n of color, they've all stayed way too long. They do damage
> to the programs. We tend to run with a pretty white board, and
> white directors, and when you do get the people of color in there,
> they could shoot somebody in the parking lot and they wouldn't be
> let go. I think the Center does not do a good job in . . . saying, "We
> need to find the right woman for the job." If it needs to be a woman
> of color, that's an important thing, but I think they make rash hires
> sometimes.

Using racist generalizations (i.e., "all women of color stay too long") and racist imagery (i.e., a parking-lot shooting) that most white employees at the Center would have found offensive, or would at least be unlikely to state so freely, Sam nonetheless expressed a common sentiment among white employees, namely that the Center has made rushed hiring decisions with its employees of color.

Progressive white employees, including some whites who identified strongly with antiracism, were also among those who emphasized the obstacles involved in hiring people of color. According to Russell, a white male and past executive manager at the Center:

Around the politics of racism, I really felt like I had the language down. I had always worked in predominantly communities of color my whole life, and here I was in this position to really make a difference in the workplace. [We] had this idea to diversify the staff . . . in all kinds of different ways, race being a very important one. . . . We [were] going to create a horizontal management. . . . I cannot tell you how many times we hired or promoted people with those politics, but once they got into the position, [they] turned into little dictator[s]. I think that's a product of racism. When people without power . . . are suddenly . . . in this position of power, what's the model that [they] have to draw from?

Russell blamed racism itself for the presumably poor leadership skills of people of color at the Center, arguing that people who have had less power in their lives will take advantage of the power that is given to them.

While white employees disagreed about the source of the "recruitment problem," they generally agreed that a recruitment problem existed, a problem that called for a slower and more deliberate hiring process. Employees of color responded by explaining that the suggestion that diversity recruitment had been dysfunctional was insulting to current employees of color, as this clearly implied that they were product of poor diversity recruitment efforts. The suggestion that hiring had been "too rushed" and should be slower and more deliberate, reminiscent of white responses to desegregation efforts more broadly, prompted employees of color to more strongly articulate their framing of the solution: "Just do it." All of the talking, data gathering, and boasting about diversity had highlighted the ways in which the Center had failed. Leticia, a Black lesbian manager, pointed to the contradiction between what was said and what was done:

What we need to do as an agency is that we need to either say that we are an agency that supports people of color and put them in power and do it, or say we are not and don't do it, and stand behind what we say. They wimp out and say shit that makes them look stupid, like there wasn't anybody qualified, which we know is not true.

"Just doing it" referred to the prefigurative project of recognizing that the Center, in its current iteration, was already a people of color organization, but it also referred to curtailing all of the diversity talk and simply putting more people of color in power.

Aren't We a People of Color Organization?

Employees of color at the Center resisted the idea that there was any single, quantifiable formula for achieving racial diversity. However, consensus was built on the implementation committee around the belief that the Center's first step should be to restructure by supporting and promoting the people of color already working within the organization. Yet equally important to promoting more people of color was the project of changing the white-normative discursive culture of the Center, including the bureaucratic approach to diversity that was standing in the way of "just *doing* it." Because people of color had achieved critical mass at the Center, discursive strategies were critically important to the project of making or unmaking the Center's white identity. The majority of employees of color I interviewed acknowledged that the Center had a local reputation as a white organization and that other organizations with more people of color in leadership had been more successful reaching various communities of color in Los Angeles. While the outcome of increased coalitions with people of color organizations was perceived as a positive one, many employees of color also argued that the means to this end was to recognize the Center itself as an organization operated by and for people of color. According to Douglas, a Black gay male director:

> At the Center, we [refer to] their community, the African American community, the Latino community, or the Asian community. What does it make us? Who are we? Are we all of those things? Evidently not, because it's an us and a they. And until the us and the they become we, we'll be stuck having the same conversation thirty years from now. At some point, something has to give. Either you are going to change, or you're not. If you're not going to change, then stop talking about it and go about your business.

When I asked if the Center is an "organization of color," Douglas replied, "No, it's not. I wish I could say that we were. And I definitely consider myself part of this organization, [but] the reality is, we are not. Because perception is reality."

According to Douglas, regardless of how many employees of color worked at the Center, being an organization of color was dependent upon both an internal and external change in perception. Douglas' emphasis on *perception* demonstrates that constructing a collective racial identity is a highly subjective, local, and contested process. Douglas explains that the Center would need to make more structural changes and change its understanding of diversity and itself, and these changes would need to be perceived as real by both members and outsiders. Several of the Center's employees of color already described the organization as racially diverse and were pleased with its diversity efforts. Others, like Beverly, argued that the Center was no different than corporate white America. In the absence of agreement about the Center's success or failure at achieving racial diversity, and given the looming possibility that the Center could reach racial parity in leadership and still "feel white," questions about what constitutes white culture and identity came to the fore.

Resisting White Normativity

The Center's direct-service programs were operated by a multiracial staff that worked together to challenge racism, homophobia, transphobia, poverty, and other inequalities faced by the Center's clients. Yet despite the Center's programmatic interventions, multiracial workforce, growing numbers of people of color in leadership, and national reputation for diversity, its white culture was reinforced in part by its mainstream and corporate approach to diversity. The Center's corporate-inspired diversity model compelled employees to talk about race and the racialized identity of the organization not only in instrumentalist terms focused on organizational effectiveness, but also in terms that privileged the knowledge and experiences of whites. The Center's diversity initiative in its strategic plan also whitened the organization by locating people of color outside of the organization and glossing over the contribution made by the organization's current employees of color. Lastly, while the Center's statistical approach to social justice was seemingly race-neutral, it functioned to document, justify, and track measures of racial diversity while ensuring job stability for whites.

All of these diversity strategies were designed to build and celebrate a multicultural collective identity at the Center, yet it was precisely the organization's formal efforts to declare its diversity that worked, internally, to reinforce the organization's white identity. While it could be argued that only white leaders, such as Claire, would produce the kind of diversity activities and organizational culture I have described in this chapter, I have attempted to illustrate that the Center's white culture is also a reflection of its mainstream, instrumentalist, and corporate approach to diversification—an approach that may well persist as the organization continues to diversify its leadership. Given the financial rewards and public relations benefits associated with formally "celebrating diversity," it may be difficult for leaders of color to sustain, fund, or promote large activists organizations without relying on the same instrumentalist frames that characterize diversity culture more broadly.

Of course it is also possible to resist mainstream diversity discourses and practices, as exemplified by some employees of color at the Center who drew upon different strategies ("Stop talking, just do it."), logics ("When my eyes are closed, I am sleeping."), and identity frames ("Aren't we a people of color organization?"). Their critiques denaturalized the framework that the Center's leaders borrowed from the corporate environment and exposed its reliance upon white-normative ways of thinking about and managing diversity. I revisit the broader significance of these strategies, and their contribution to queer politics, in Chapter 6.

CHAPTER 5

Funding Queer Diversity:
Bienestar

> When we talk about diversity, we are talking about the other,
> whatever that other might be.
> —Arturo Madrid[1]

As I have illustrated in the last two chapters, even activist uses of diversity often reinforce the line between what is normative and what is "other." Yet I have also tried to highlight the productive effects of diversity culture on queer activism, such as the increasing number of queer programs that address the devastating material conditions of being "othered" (e.g., poverty, homelessness, drug addiction, HIV/AIDS, etc.). The emphasis on diversity in queer social service organizations has helped to draw attention to the lived experiences of LGBT people who are the most underserved and the most at risk, to use the parlance of social service providers. This has been particularly true in queer HIV/AIDS organizations, where the life-and-death consequences of racial and economic inequalities among gay men have been especially pronounced. As Black gay activist and writer Essex Hemphill argued, AIDS—perhaps more than any other sociopolitical challenge facing LGBT people—"really manages to . . . clearly point out the cultural and economic differences between us."[2]

After more than two decades of AIDS activism, queer organizations now have access to millions of dollars in public funding to provide prevention and healthcare services to the people most affected by HIV/AIDS. As public health research continues to point to the elevated risk of HIV infection faced by gay men of color, an unprecedented number of grants now fund multi-issue programs that address the intersections of race, culture, class, gender, and sexuality. Organizations receiving these grants have made remarkable gains in their HIV-prevention efforts by developing programs that celebrate the sexual practices, desires, and subcultural experiences of gay men of color. By many measures, organizations run by and for gay men (and trans women) of color represent the forefront of multi-issue politics, skillfully weaving together antiracist interventions with queer and working-class cultures.[3]

Programs that strategically target specific at-risk identity groups, such as gay men of color, are often crucial to the work of reaching multiply marginalized communities. However, in this chapter I am concerned with the ways that some forms of otherness remain intact as activists work to justify their emphasis on narrowly defined "at-risk" identity groups. Ideas about risk, representation, and diversity have a tendency to become static, especially when funding streams and other institutional structures solidify around them. As I will show, identity-based funding has, in many cases, pushed queer organizations to assign diversity and "need" to fixed bodies and experiences, rather than enabling them to assess how emergent forms of representation often create new forms of risk and invisibility. As I argued in Chapters 3 and 4, professional diversity frameworks often accomplish some degree of multi-issue equity while failing to challenge the broader forces of white and middle-class normativity. In contrast, in this chapter I shift the analytic lens from professional diversity discourses emerging from within "white corporate culture" to public health discourses that have been heavily informed by grassroots HIV activism within communities of color. In a way similar to the contradictory politics within the corporate diversity management model, social service frameworks can also emphasize intersecting systems of inequality and, at the same time, be used to justify the marginal position of people and political issues that aren't legible to public funders.

To illustrate these developments, this chapter examines the politics of funding and representation at Bienestar, which began in the 1980s as a lesbian and gay Latino community organization but was later transformed into an HIV organization in response to the devastation of the AIDS epidemic and the concomitant funding available exclusively for gay men of color. As I will show, employees at Bienestar struggled to provide programs for Latina lesbians while meeting funding requirements focused on HIV (and gay males). Yet despite the organization's emphasis on the intersections of race, gender, class, culture, and sexuality, the dramatic influx of funding specifically for gay men of color worked to reinforce the notion that focusing on the needs of at-risk gay Latino men (over Latina lesbians) was the most powerful and logical means of expressing queer Latino unity and collective identity. On the one hand, community-based knowledge about HIV led

Bienestar's leaders to reject single-identity politics and instead place emphasis on multiplicity, sexual fluidity, grassroots leadership, and lesbian inclusion. On the other hand, the very same HIV-prevention models were used to justify the exclusion of lesbians from positions of leadership and full participation in the organization. In the face of overwhelming evidence about (and funding to address) gay Latinos' HIV risk, the risks faced by Latina lesbians were rendered invisible or irrelevant.

The Gender Politics of Risk, Representation, and HIV

Given the devastating number of AIDS-related deaths among gay men, the 1980s and 1990s witnessed new levels of unity between lesbians and gay men who came together to address the homophobic underpinnings of AIDS-related suffering, stigma, and public denial. Many scholars of lesbian and gay history have described this period as a time of solidarity during which sex debates and other political tensions between lesbians and gay men were either resolved or suspended so that activists could attend to the urgency of AIDS.[4] Some research indicates that lesbians across racial groups engaged in AIDS activism even while they perceived it as a distraction from their own health concerns.[5] What is clear of this period is that AIDS activism became a centerpiece of lesbian and gay organizing and gave rise to several direct-action organizations and projects that linked AIDS to queer visibility (e.g., ACT UP, Queer Nation). The phenomenal need for HIV-related services, combined with the need to distribute public and private funds to the organizations delivering these services, resulted in the development of a national AIDS infrastructure, including a network of AIDS service organizations, AIDS-related government bureaucracies, and a community of natural and social scientists studying the epidemic and the communities it affects.[6]

Yet this period was not without conflict among lesbian and gay activists, particularly regarding the extent to which "gay money" and resources should be redirected from gay liberation causes to AIDS-related projects.[7] Many activists argued not only that too much lesbian and gay funding was being diverted to AIDS but that the gay political agenda had also been swallowed by AIDS. For instance, Eric Rofes, a high-profile activist and former executive director of the L.A. Gay & Lesbian Center (see Chapter 4), publicly argued that gay activists had "sold out" by joining the AIDS bureaucracy and finding legitimacy in AIDS organizations where they could "de-gay" their agenda.[8]

On the surface, the "gay liberation vs. AIDS" debate was not about gen-

der or race politics; however, it certainly had gendered and racialized implications. By the late 1980s, government grants for lesbian and gay programs
appeared to be earmarked almost exclusively for HIV/AIDS, and many
lesbian and gay organizations shifted their attention to gay-male-focused
HIV programs in order to survive or grow.[9] Indeed, the extent to which
the AIDS infrastructure helped or hindered the struggle for queer visibility
and resources cannot be generalized, as it differently impacted lesbians and
gay men, queer whites and queer people of color. In most large cities in the
United States, the now widely accepted epidemiological contention that all
gay men are at high risk for HIV infection has translated into more and
better social services for all gay men, both HIV positive and HIV negative.
Public AIDS funding not only supports healthcare for HIV positive gay
men, but also supports countless HIV-prevention programs designed to encourage HIV-negative gay men, and particularly gay men of color who are
now understood to be at even higher risk than white gay men, to practice
safer sex.[10] Based on the principles of community and individual empowerment, many of these prevention programs address factors such as culture,
communication, and self-esteem through "fun," community-building activities that offer alternatives to high-risk behavior.

The availability of government funds for HIV services has also been a
particular catalyst for the growth of organizations established by and for
queer communities of color. Prior to the epidemic, white lesbian and gay
organizations were funded largely by wealthy, white gay men, while lesbian
and gay communities of color had fewer wealthy community members from
whom to solicit private funding and therefore maintained a greater reliance on government grants.[11] Thus, public grants for AIDS prevention programs—focused on reaching those most at risk—allowed for the proliferation of organizations that provided culturally sensitive services to "high-risk"
gay men of color. Yet the impact of the AIDS infrastructure on lesbians, and
specifically lesbians of color, suggests a different pattern. As I will show, the
link between HIV-prevention and empowerment programs for gay men is
relatively easy to draw by pointing to data on HIV infection rates. However
the use of AIDS money for lesbian programs, in light of their reportedly low
risk for HIV infection, has required that activists undertake some creative
grantwriting and complicated organizational restructuring, simply so that
lesbians can be served. Of course, lesbians remain at high risk for a number
of other dangers, such as sexual violence, suicide, depression, addiction, and
eating disorders.[12] Yet in many cases, these risks have been overshadowed by
the urgency and visibility of AIDS or have been only peripherally addressed
within programs that are operated using HIV-related grant money.

My aim in this chapter is not simply to point a finger at the resultant lack of funding for lesbian programs following the AIDS epidemic. Instead, I am more broadly concerned with the logic of "at-risk identities" itself, or the way that being able to demonstrate risk and fundability—and particularly risk comparable to that posed by HIV—has become a necessary task for lesbians wishing to lay claim to programs and resources within many queer organizations. This economy of risk, I argue, represents yet another form of diversity instrumentalism, in which full access and participation rests upon the ability of identity groups to embody a fundable social problem and articulate their belonging using prevailing—and often ill-fitting—discourses of risk and need. As I will show in my discussion of Bienestar, the centrality of HIV risk to the work and funding of queer organizations of color has required that lesbians of color articulate their right to inclusion using the language and metaphors of HIV prevention.

To the extent that white-run LGBT organizations receive more unrestricted funding from private donors, they also have more flexibility to offer lesbian-specific programs unrelated to HIV prevention. Yet, as other studies have illustrated, LGBT community centers, generally run by queer whites, are often unknown, located too far away, or too racist to be a realistic alternative for lesbians of color.[13] Comfortable community spaces and service providers for lesbians of color are limited, and few organizations provide an environment that is both queer and culturally familiar. Given these obstacles, the history of AIDS has also been a history of lesbians of color meeting, organizing, and receiving services and support within their racial/ethnic communities, including in AIDS organizations not particularly structured to receive lesbians, and run by and for Black, Asian, or Latino gay men.[14] In organizations such as Bienestar, lesbians of color find cultural solidarity in a queer environment, yet they also face an internal struggle with sexism, lesbian invisibility, and a dominant focus on HIV. As the story of Bienestar reveals, the instrumental emphasis on at-risk bodies and identities—and the steady stream of funding they ensure—has had a disproportionate affect on lesbians of color.

Bienestar: From Lesbian and Gay Organization to AIDS Service Organization

Bienestar began in 1989 as a health subcommittee of the East Los Angeles–based political and social group Gay and Lesbian Latinos Unidos (GLLU). According to Martin, the founding and current executive director of Bienestar at the time of my research, it was the lesbian leadership in GLLU that "forced the discussion about HIV in the Latino community" as early as 1985, while many of the male GLLU members wished not to discuss it. Similar to lesbian activists in other communities throughout the country, GLLU women led early efforts to develop an organizational infrastructure to address the epidemic.[15] Ana, a current Bienestar board member who had been involved with GLLU since 1985, agreed with Martin's account, adding that the lesbians in GLLU raised the start-up funds for the Health Committee and later did the manual labor required to open an office when the Health Committee became its own organization, named Bienestar:

> Yeah, the women ran GLLU. They *did*. The women were very strong. There were a few men that were strong, but the women always ran the organization. So we had a fundraiser, we had a couple of them. So, Bienestar was created, it had one employee and a little tiny office on Sanborn and Santa Monica. And Lydia did all of the construction herself and I wired the phones. Yeah, the women did all the work, and the guys watched.

According to Martin, the lack of male initiative in GLLU was due in part to "denial about AIDS," evidenced by the men's objection to the women's original proposal that the subcommittee be named the "AIDS Committee." Instead, at the men's prompting, GLLU members ultimately agreed upon the more ambiguous name of "Health Committee." Martin told me this story to demonstrate that Bienestar, which became its own nonprofit organization in 1989 under the GLLU umbrella, "always had a strong influence and leadership of women" and a regular majority of lesbians on the board of directors.

Although Bienestar was once part of GLLU and continued to maintain a lesbian presence on its board of directors, it was no longer a gay and lesbian organization. It was an HIV-focused "health" organization serving a diversity of Latino communities affected by AIDS in Los Angeles: primarily men who have sex with men, but also HIV-positive heterosexuals, "gang-affiliated" clients, monolingual Spanish-speaking clients, injection-drug users, and recent immigrants. In 1995, Bienestar became independent from GLLU as GLLU board members recognized that Bienestar had become a powerful agency in its own right, with a mission statement that no longer possessed a logical connection to the goals of GLLU. Ana explains that Bienestar grew quickly, especially as the broader (nongay) Latino community began to seek services.

[Bienestar] was doing advocacy for AIDS, and, at the time, [clients were] gay Latino men. But as more people were coming and needing services, as the different groups needed services, the organization had to evolve. And now people were starting to seek services of Bienestar [who] were not gay, and were having a problem, too, with the name "gay and lesbian" when they were not gay. . . . [Bienestar] was being stifled by Gay and Lesbian Latinos Unidos. It is serving the Latino community, but GLLU is gay and lesbian. Bienestar is services for Latinos. Health services.

Bienestar's mission statement made no mention of sexual identity and stated that it was established to "provid[e] social and support services to enhance the health and well-being of the [Latino] community" and was "dedicated to providing education to prevent HIV, STDs, TB, and drug and alcohol abuse; and providing direct services to people whose lives are affected by HIV and AIDS." Bienestar had been extremely successful in achieving these goals, and in 2000–2001, it was the largest Latino AIDS service organization in the United States. The organization had grown to approximately eighty staff members and six centers across Los Angeles (East L.A., La Casa in East L.A., Long Beach, Van Nuys, Hollywood, and Pomona), with its executive office in East Los Angeles. In the September 2000 issue of *Enfoque*, the organization's newsletter, Bienestar also proudly announced that it had received $1.5 million in Los Angeles County HIV Prevention and Education funds and had therefore been "awarded the most money from any applying agency" for that year.

Yet at the same time that Bienestar was not formally an LGBT organization, it was informally quite well-known for its LGBT programs and its leadership in the gay Latino community. Not only did gay men make up the vast majority of the staff and leadership at Bienestar, producing a dominant gay male culture in the organization, but the agency also dedicated one of its East Los Angeles centers, La Casa, exclusively to LGBT youth programs. Bienestar was a regular presence at LGBT community events as well, and widely advertised its services in the Los Angeles lesbian and gay press. One such advertisement that appeared in the popular lesbian magazine *Lesbian News* reads:

Bienestar is the place throughout L.A. County to meet, share experiences & interests with lesbian/gay/bisexual/transgender queer women & men in a fun, safe, and supportive environment. We offer services and social groups for women, men, youth & families. Our combination of cultural pride & self-empowerment create a space that is inviting and comfortable.

For lesbian and gay clients who were introduced to Bienestar by reading such advertisements or attending a social group at La Casa, it was likely that they would perceive Bienestar as an LGBT organization, rather than an AIDS service organization. For example, Monica, a queer female employee, was first introduced to Bienestar when La Casa outreach staff visited East Los Angeles College, where she was a student. Monica volunteered for La Casa for several months before she became aware that Bienestar had other centers and programs that did more than "just reach out to the gay community." During the time of my participant observation at Bienestar, lesbian staff produced at least four dance parties for queer women, a women's poetry night called Café con Leche, a queer women's daylong retreat, and several other social events designed to build a community of young, queer Latinas.

Programs at La Casa were operated using funds from HIV-prevention grants for "men who have sex with men" (or MSMs), as well as from a collapsed grant for queer youth that was used to support the queer youth program, QUE PASA, and its lesbian component, LUNA (Latinas Understanding the Need for Action). In 2000, the QUE PASA grant was the only funding source that named lesbians as a target population, and in 2001 the grant was terminated after its three-year term, leaving Bienestar to pull from its minimal unrestricted funds to continue services for queer women. While the QUE PASA grant allowed for support groups and social events for young lesbians, Bienestar's grant writers emphasized lesbian and bisexual women's HIV risk in order for queer women to be included in the contract. David, then director of QUE PASA, explained that this was done by highlighting the fluidity of queer youth sexuality, or, in other words, the possibility that young lesbians and gay men were having sex with one another. When I asked David whether the queer women's support groups focused specifically on HIV, he replied:

> No, they don't, and that's something that we have had issues with our funders in trying to explain to them. . . . HIV and AIDS continues not to be a major issue in the eyes of our funders for lesbian women. The only way that we are able to include lesbian women and bisexual women was . . . because the populations tend to congregate so closely at the younger populations, there was more of chance, you know,

people were still identifying with their sexuality, there was more fluidity in relation to them having sex with one another. And that was one of the theoretical things that we had to put into the proposal.

Bienestar had no funding for the lesbian-specific programs that it offered and advertised, and the past funding available for queer women was based, at least in part, on the premise that they were at risk of contracting HIV from gay men.

Yet lesbian staff told me that they rarely or never discussed HIV in the lesbian support groups they facilitated, and instead focused on topics of interest to their young clients, such as, "Where do you meet women and what do you do once you have met them?" They also complained that the gay male HIV-prevention focus at Bienestar was nevertheless evident in the "HIV risk assessment" forms that all lesbian clients were asked to complete. Lesbian staff were required to administer the assessments to their lesbian clients in order for the organization to meet the contact numbers specified in its contracts, however, the questions asked—or *not* asked—on the forms highlighted the fact that they were not intended for lesbians. Bienestar's standard risk assessment form asks respondents to identify as "gay," "bisexual," "heterosexual," or "transgender," prompting many lesbian clients to write in the word "lesbian" on their forms. A survey administered to all clients in the queer youth program, including lesbians, also focused heavily on condom use without any mention of dental dams, the safer-sex barrier that lesbian staff had occasionally discussed and distributed to their clients. These sorts of omissions provided some of the more subtle clues to lesbian staff and clients that there was a lack of resonance between the mission of the organization (HIV prevention) and the needs and desires that motivated young lesbian clients to come to the organization.

Why Bienestar?

When the coordinator of Bienestar's lesbian program left the organization in 2000, managers informed the one remaining lesbian employee that they did not have plans to refill the coordinator position. With only one employee and no funding, the lesbian component of Bienestar suffered by comparison to a thriving gay men's component that offered numerous support groups, held free weekend retreats and sporting events, and was staffed by approximately ten gay men across seven locations. In light of these disparities and the organization's primary identification as an HIV organization, why did Latina lesbians continue to view Bienestar as their home?

According to the organization's male leaders, Bienestar's lesbian component provided an exclusively Latina environment that fostered "*jota* pride," community building, and romantic relationships among Chicana/Latina lesbians. Martin, the executive director, explained that queer Latinas chose Bienestar not only because it produces events and programs rooted in Latino culture, but also because of the racism that Latinas experience in large gay and lesbian organizations with white leadership. As described in Chapter 4, LGBT community centers often appear to achieve racial/ethnic integration, but maintain a white-normative culture that is manifested in the look and feel of the organization and its approach to diversity. Exemplifying this point, Martin asserted that Latina lesbians needed Bienestar because LGBT organizations with predominantly white leadership will claim that they "open the door and welcome [Latinos]," but despite this ideological commitment, "the music, the food, the everything, is not really welcome to Latinos."

Both Martin and David explained that Latino culture and an environment free of racism were more important to Bienestar's lesbian clients than having a large and well-supported lesbian program. In response to my question about whether a lesbian program was appropriate in an AIDS organization managed by gay men, David responded:

> It is appropriate for the target population. . . . It's appropriate for the fact that it's not just about HIV and AIDS issues; it's about cultural sensitivity and cultural relevancy. And I have seen and heard stories from women that go to the agencies that do have lesbian-specific money, and because the women are only able to identify along a sexuality basis, they still have to deal with issues of racism at those agencies and may not feel comfortable. You know, it's amazing to me, even taking into consideration how small the women's program is here, the overwhelming response we get from the community is that it's needed at Bienestar.

Martin also expressed the belief that the supportive presence of Latinas in an organization run predominantly by and for Latino men was a reflection of a comfortable and natural gender division of labor in Latino culture. Lesbian board members, he argued, were invested in the success of Bienestar not only because of his personal "relationship with each of them" and because "there aren't opportunities for lesbian women to go and form their own organizations," but also because of the cultural role of Latinas as caretakers:

I think that in all of our family units, it is our mothers [and] our sisters that are primarily our caretakers, the ones who give us that support and even in an environment of machismo, it is always the women. And I think they feel comfortable, just keeping on that role in coming every month to the board meetings and doing the work because they are taking care of their brothers. Without really stopping and analyzing, I think it's just a very natural progression of our culture, why they are in that capacity.

For the gay Latino men in leadership at Bienestar, it was not surprising that Latina lesbians would seek services at their organization, regardless of whether the organization had made an explicit commitment to hiring lesbians or including service to lesbians in its mission.

In contrast, the lesbian staff at Bienestar offered a more nuanced explanation for the presence of young Latina lesbians in the organization. According to lesbian staff, it was the lack of an alternative, more woman-centered political and social organization for queer Latinas in Los Angeles that brought young Latinas to Bienestar. While some Latino/a gay and lesbian organizations, such as GLLU, were growing and active in the late 1970s and 1980s, the undeniable impact of the AIDS epidemic on gay Latino men, as well as the availability of AIDS-related funds, led many of these organizations to turn their attention to HIV/AIDS or to disband altogether. From this perspective, the most important factor that brought Latina lesbians to Bienestar was the lack of any other active lesbian and gay Latino/a organization in Los Angeles. Elena, a former lesbian staff member, stated that she might have become involved in an organization that was both culturally sensitive *and* gender sensitive had such an organization existed:

If I wanted to work for something that was more specific to being a *jota* and being queer-identified and female, all of that, I couldn't find that. . . . There was Lesbianas Unidas. They kind of have been defunct for a while. You can find things on college campuses. I don't know. I think there has been like a backlash as far as identity politics go. Lesbianas Unidas, who used to be around in the 80s and even up to the 90s . . . they were working off no budget, so anything that came to queer communities of color was in the form of AIDS and HIV moneys.

Similarly, Fatima, another lesbian staff member explained,

Bienestar is sexist, but if I leave, I'm afraid I'll never get to work with my community again. . . . I may be *pocha* and all that, but here there are other Mexican women who need me and respect me. And that's not going to be easy to find for a butch Mexican woman.

While Martin and David's comments implied that many of Bienestar's lesbian clients prioritized Latino unity over lesbian-specific programming offered in non-Latino organizations, Elena and Fatima emphasized that it was the limited choices for women of color in general and *within* the queer Latino community that led women to Bienestar.

A Gay Male-Dominated Organization

Lesbian staff at Bienestar described examples of tensions well documented in other studies of women working in male-dominated environments, including male coworkers' ignorance of male privilege and their entitlement to conversational and physical space. The management of physical space at Bienestar was a point of particular tension for lesbian staff who perceived that they and their clients had either been relegated to the least desirable space in organization's offices or were excluded from space that appeared designated for gay men. According to Elena, her supervisor's office was generally off-limits to her unless she was being reprimanded, but became an informal gathering place for her gay male coworkers. Elena pointed out that it was not being excluded from gay men's socializing that troubled her, but rather that this socializing took place in an office that she associated with power and authority.

Fatima, another lesbian staff member, recalled an incident about access to space in which her supervisor made explicit that the seniority of the gay men's support group justified its ownership of the most desirable meeting space. Fatima, who was holding a lesbian support group in a makeshift area of the office, asked her supervisor, Jorge, who was holding a gay men's support group at the same time in the "nice" group discussion room, whether he would be willing to alternate weeks in the better room. She recalled his response:

Just the fact that I was even asking him, he was a little offended. He was telling me, "I feel like you don't understand our history, you know. I've been facilitating this group with the same men for about two years and we worked hard to get this Hollywood center, and to get this nice group discussion room. And I feel, kind of like, for lack of a better word, *offended* that you are even asking me to share the room." And I was like, "You know, just think about how the women feel that the gay male group gets to have that nice room all of the time, with the TV, with the couches, with the nice lighting, with the Play Station, and the stereo. And we have to be outside with these portable walls, where the men come in and out when they are arriving late and we are trying to have a discussion session and we get all this interruption. What is so hard about sharing? It's not like I am taking something away from you, I'm asking you to *share* what we have together within the agency." And he had to think about it. He had to *think* about it!

Fatima also explained that the discussion that ensued around sharing the group meeting room signaled to her that her supervisor was lacking the ability to recognize male privilege or draw connections between systems of oppression.

I tried to use the issue of race. "How would you feel if a group of white people were using that nice discussion room all the time, while the people of color are having to . . . " And he was like, "No! I'm sorry, you can't be using that. I'm not going to go into that. No, I don't want you to use that example." I'm all, "It's a perfect example." Is it a lack of education? It's a lack of awareness, of how as a man, what his role is within the system. He has no clue. So that was just like one instance where I was like, "God, *where* am I working?"

Women staff explained that this kind of experience led them to believe that male coworkers could understand oppression only from the perspective of their own racial oppression, but not from the perspective of their gendered privileges.

Lesbian staff also described interactions with gay male supervisors and coworkers that they perceived as more "personal," designed to make them (or their work) appear unimportant in the broader context of the organization. Elena asserted that several months after she began work at Bienestar, the executive director was still referring to her by the wrong name, a practice that she believed was "purposefully done" because "he wanted [her] to feel unimportant, invalidated." Similarly, lesbian staff sometimes found that they were faced with choosing between invisibility or representation that was offensive. When Fatima found out that a group of gay male clients (and a Bienestar supervisor) would be singing a queer rendition of "The Twelve Days of Christmas" at the holiday talent show, and that the song included the line "five dykes a munchin'," she and another lesbian staff member confronted the supervisor who was participating. After explaining that the lyrics about lesbians were offensive in the context of a generally negative song about "tweakers" and STDs, the supervisor agreed that the line would be rewritten to reflect a more positive image of lesbians. At the actual performance, however, lesbian staff discovered that the line had been removed altogether, leading them to conclude that the men had trouble determining what to write that would not be offensive and so opted not to deal with the issue at all.

Many lesbian staff members had more or less expected to struggle with sexism at Bienestar based on the organization's reputation as well as their own understanding of sexism as an unavoidable structural problem, particularly in a gay male-dominated environment. Gender inequality at Bienestar was complicated, however, by the centrality of gay men to the organization's HIV-focused mission and the external legitimacy given to Bienestar's programmatic priorities given the urgency of the AIDS epidemic and the availability of funding for gay male programs. While lesbian staff could confidently point to examples of sexist comments, their complaints about policies and hiring practices were met with arguments about HIV risk that were difficult to refute. If Bienestar's mission was HIV prevention and most clients were gay men, on what grounds could lesbian staff demand an environment more sensitive to their needs? If there was no funding available for lesbian programs, how could Bienestar be expected to provide lesbians the same resources as gay men?

Lesbian Programs: Appropriate, but Not Necessary

The "Psychocultural Barriers" Model

Bienestar's leaders followed an HIV-prevention model that foregrounded the intersections of race, gender, sexuality, and culture. HIV-prevention services, the provision of which was the sole function of La Casa (and thus the lesbian program as well), were guided by the research findings of Rafael Miguel Diaz, a professor at the Center for AIDS Prevention Studies in San Francisco. Diaz's work on HIV risk reduction among gay and bisexual Latino men has focused on identifying psychocultural factors (*machismo, familismo,* and taboos about discussing sex) that are barriers to safer sex practices. According to this model, effective HIV prevention must move beyond sharing facts about transmission and instead provide culturally relevant interventions that address the host of racialized, gendered, and socioeconomic cofactors that contribute to unsafe sex.[16] At Bienestar, the application of Diaz's work meant providing support groups and social events for gay men that addressed an array of topics (sex, the body, masculinity, Latino culture, *joto* pride, etc.) in a fun, playful, and culturally familiar manner. For instance, one pamphlet produced by the gay men's program addressed the issue of male insecurity about penis size by referring to penises as chili peppers that were all different colors and sizes, but still "hot." Such efforts were designed to create a healthy, safe, and erotic space for gay Latino men to communicate with one another about sex and relationships. Because Bienestar's leaders understood healthy communication about sex to be the first step toward negotiating safer sex, they also made it clear to staff that it may not be necessary to mention HIV at all in order for a group meeting to be a successful part of the prevention effort.

Focusing on identity and empowerment—and downplaying HIV—was Bienestar's method of reaching at-risk Latino men, but it was also Martin and David's means of justifying the use of HIV-related funding for lesbian programs. David explained that Bienestar provided lesbian services because they approached HIV from an intersectional perspective that allowed staff to address more than one issue:

> Many people say . . . when a person comes in, I'm going to speak to you specifically on your biological risk to HIV and AIDS. Usually, it will tend to come from the original models that we have to do HIV prevention and education. Those models are not indigent [*sic*] to communities of color. In fact, the closest thing that we have for our community right now is a study by Dr. Diaz. It really speaks to the fact that when you are dealing with communities of color, there are many issues that you have to touch on, in relation to psychosocial, in relation to socioeconomic, in relation to quality of living, in relation to self-esteem. . . . And since we approach HIV through that lens, I find that for this particular agency, it is appropriate [to provide lesbian services] because we are not mandating, when a person comes in, that our conversations have to specifically be on one issue.

In theory, the psychocultural model justified the development of a lesbian program by de-emphasizing HIV and instead emphasizing issues that *were* of interest to young Latina lesbians (e.g., dating, sex, family, communication). However, in practice, lesbian employees were held accountable for collecting HIV-related data from lesbian clients, administering male-centered surveys to their clients, and helping the organization's grant writers make a case for lesbian inclusion by speculating about young lesbians having sex with gay men.[17] And, as I will discuss below, male staff could always turn to data on HIV infection rates to explain the greater significance and resources given to gay male programs at Bienestar.

One might ask: If lesbians were being served at Bienestar, then why should it matter who funded these services or with what intention? While Bienestar boasted that it was the only organization in Los Angeles that provided culturally relevant services to Latina lesbians, it did so without an ideological commitment to lesbian programs, lesbian staff, or lesbian clients. Bienestar had evolved out of a lesbian and gay community organization run primarily by lesbians (GLLU), yet lesbian organizing was no longer an end in and of itself, given the organization's new HIV-focused mission and its reliance on HIV funding. Although the use of the psychocultural model validated the importance of non-HIV-specific cofactors such as culture, family, self-esteem, and other issues that might be important to young Latina lesbians, it was based on accountability to funders and not Latina lesbians themselves.

Lesbian staff and clients at Bienestar were simultaneously grateful for the opportunity to be part of the only queer Latino organization that provided lesbian services, and also aware that their role in the organization was fragile and auxiliary. The lack of an ideological commitment to queer women's programming produced daily tensions for the lesbian staff charged with the development of these programs. According to Elena, her ability to use the same theoretical justification for social programming that gay male staff used neither compensated for other gender-related tensions at Bienestar nor resulted in equal support for the lesbian program:

> A lot of what was done at Bienestar was always under the guise of there [being] a multiplicity of factors of why people contract HIV, and the way you address those factors is not necessarily through direct education. It was in that vein that it was kind of addressed, you know, identity politics, sexuality, home, family, religion, for all the different populations. . . . We found creative ways of doing things, so I could always justify why I was doing a dance for queer women of color. I could justify [it], but it doesn't mean it was supported even though the men's groups would do the same thing. They can justify it along the way and link it back to HIV and AIDS. But the women's programming, it wasn't necessarily more difficult to justify, it just

wasn't received well because it was a lot of personal conflicts with me and the director. It was real, you know, head-to-head bunting because it was like very cut along the lines of gender.

Bienestar's identity as an AIDS organization also provided a logical rationale for queer women's marginalization (i.e., "there just isn't funding for your program") that made it difficult for lesbian staff to determine whether lack of support for their programs—and for themselves as employees—stemmed from a funding obstacle that the male leadership could do nothing about or from a more power-laden conflict between gay men and lesbians in the organization. That Bienestar had so few lesbian employees exacerbated this confusion by providing an insufficient network for women to organize, compare notes, and hold its leadership accountable to lesbian clients and staff rather than to funding agencies. Elena explained:

> Every time that I wanted to do a program that was women-specific or women-related, I had to go through two men before it could happen. . . . There weren't other women there who could advocate for [women's programs] happening as well. Funding didn't say it needed to happen, so there was no money. There were no stakes. And if it didn't happen, it didn't happen, there was no loss.

Similarly, Monica's explanation of why lesbian programs were not developed points to funding obstacles, but also emphasizes that these programs were threatening to gay male staff and not prioritized by Bienestar's leadership:

> In an agency that employs ninety plus employees, at any given time, they are only employing three queer women. Part of that I believe is because, as they say, the federal government does not provide funding to educate women on prevention. And so all the women who are brought in are brought in on non-gender-specific contracts. So, they have implemented a queer women's component, LUNA, . . . but [I think] every time that women try to push the program out there, they are stopped, because of funding, they're stopped because of the reality that these men feel that the women are taking over the space when they come in. . . . I think that the morale of the women is very low.

Lesbian staff were aware that limited funding to support lesbian youth programs was a real obstacle, most likely faced by organizations other than

Bienestar. Yet the constant attention to HIV/AIDS funding as a means to explain all disparities between gay men and lesbians in the organization begged other questions for lesbian staff, questions that focused on inequalities between gay and lesbian employees and that they argued had little or nothing to do with external funding for lesbian programs. Why weren't more queer women being hired at Bienestar? Why weren't current lesbian employees being promoted?

"We Are the Population We Serve": Hiring and Promotions at Bienestar

While lesbian employees viewed tensions around promotions and hiring as evidence of sexism at Bienestar, the organization's male leadership turned to HIV/AIDS data, both prevention models and case numbers, to explain inequalities in pay and promotions between lesbians and gay men. Committed to the notion that staff members should represent the population they serve, Bienestar's leaders emphasized the importance of "peer-led" programs in which the identities of employees closely matched those of their clients. On one hand, the ability to represent a disadvantaged community was a point of pride at Bienestar, as staff judged the quality of their services according to their ability to relate to, and to remember being in the position of, their clients. According to Elena:

> I know that, as a program, we were always proud to say that, [David] was always proud to say that: "We are the population that we serve. We are the ones who have been here before, in a sense." I know [David] was really proud of that. He had his bisexual, his transgender, he had the gay man, he had the queen, he had the dyke, he had the *chingona* femme.

Yet Elena also points out that this same philosophy was used to justify the absence of lesbians in leadership positions, and in the organization in general. For instance, she described an argument she had with David about the lack of women at Bienestar, precipitated by her request for a performance evaluation:

> "Well, can I get my evaluation?" "Too busy for it. No time for it."
> That was always their excuse. So, we got into this match, and it was
> back and forth about how we didn't do enough, we didn't get enough

women. . . . And then he said, to put a stop to it, "Well, the staff here represents and reflects the number of AIDS cases in L.A." And that was supposed to justify everything in that statement, so that was really the mentality. The ten to two [staff] ratio reflected AIDS cases, or reported AIDS cases.

The number of AIDS cases and other statistics about lesbians and HIV were used at Bienestar to justify and naturalize the predominance of gay men in leadership positions and the glass ceiling, or "sticky floor," that lesbian staff experienced.

During our interview, Martin stated that peer leadership was important in the "actual delivery of service" but "not in the management." However, only one lesbian, Blanca, held a management position at Bienestar. The absence of lesbians as center supervisors (the managers to whom the lesbian staff I interviewed had to report) was particularly frustrating to frontline lesbian employees who watched these positions be filled by young gay men they perceived as less experienced and qualified. According to Monica, who was forty-three years old and a mother of several children, being a young and attractive gay man was sufficient qualification to be in management at Bienestar:

I have noticed that if you are a young homosexual, between the ages of eighteen and twenty-four, with or without a bachelor's degree, you have all of the criteria that it takes to move up the ladder within this agency. If you go within the agency, in every single center, with the exception of one . . . all of the supervisors are young, handsome homosexual males. The one in Van Nuys has a woman, and she has no feminist politics whatsoever.

Lesbian employees such as Monica, who hoped to make a career of her work at Bienestar, pointed out that peer leadership was not only code for gay male leadership, but for an organizational culture that rendered feminist politics irrelevant.

While the psychocultural model was used to explain why a lesbian program was *appropriate* at Bienestar, the number of AIDS cases was used to explain why developing the program, and, concomitantly, hiring and promoting more lesbian staff, was not *necessary*. Together these logics produced among lesbian staff the sense that a lesbian presence at Bienestar was a privilege or luxury, a sense to be contrasted with the feeling of entitlement that they perceived in gay men. Tina, a transgender Latina who coordinated

Bienestar's male-to-female (MTF) transgender program, asserted that it is "the way lesbians have sex" that made them third in the hierarchy at Bienestar. When I asked Tina to compare and contrast the experience of the transgendered women and (nontrans) lesbians at Bienestar, she replied:

> We are in the same situation for funding. We are both fighting for funding because we're both such invisible communities when it comes to HIV prevention because of the way we have sex, or we're just underreported. . . . But one big difference is that [trans women] are like a notch up in the chain of things. Because it's gay men [who] get all the attention because of the way they have intercourse, anal sex, and [MTFs] are after them because we also have anal sex. And the [lesbian] women are at the bottom of the chain because the way they have sex is not as risky supposedly.

At Bienestar, the good news of being theoretically at low risk for HIV infection became bad news for lesbians who hoped for job advancement in an organization in which the staff makeup was expected to reflect AIDS demographics.

Tina argued that lesbians at Bienestar were not only evaluated according to the kind of sex they were presumed to have and its corresponding risk level, but based upon well-worn, sexist ideas about women being weak and overly emotional:

> It's obvious sexism is a problem at Bienestar because if you look at management, or any department at all, men outweigh women. If you ask about salary, same situation. You see, gay men, or any male[s], get paid more. . . . And I think one of the reasons is because they think women are weaker and, I guess, more stupid. They say like, "Women are so emotional. They can't handle this job so they get tired and they just quit." And, there has been a high turnover of women, and I think the reason is because they hire so little women and they give them so much to do, and they don't pay you the same amount as somebody else doing the same work you're doing.

Notions about women as weak and unstable workers who "get tired and just quit" produced a type of self-fulfilling prophecy at Bienestar. While gay men in leadership often expressed a strong emotional attachment to the *organization*, lesbian staff were more likely to express emotional attachment to their *clients*. For example, Bienestar employees were occasionally urged to "volunteer" work to the organization above their forty-hour workweek, reportedly because Bienestar did not have the money to offer overtime pay. Fatima, a lesbian health educator who was running the lesbian component alone after two other lesbians had quit, described a staff meeting in which Jorge, her supervisor, began to cry while expressing his frustration that some staff members "complain about being asked to volunteer" and "won't stay after hours." Jorge went on to explain that he had just found out that one of his clients had been practicing unsafe sex and, reminded of Bienestar's importance, was reinspired by the mission of the organization and the importance of being dedicated to the Bienestar "familia."

Lesbian employees, on the other hand, had similar emotional experiences with clients, but were more likely to work extra hours with clients *outside* of Bienestar (such as at lesbian films, plays, drag king rehearsals), and to have such experiences remind them of their own individual importance as one of few lesbians in a male-dominated organization. Indeed, lesbian employees were less inclined to work volunteer hours at Bienestar, to socialize with managers on their off time, or to feel a strong sense of commitment to the Bienestar family. In this sense, they were *not* "ideal" employees; they were less likely to demonstrate the kind of extra effort and dedication that was visible to the male leadership. However, Elena shifted accountability for these dynamics to the men at Bienestar by emphasizing that attachment to the organization was not *fostered* in lesbian staff or clients. She argued that some lesbian clients had positive, but brief, experiences with the organization, while other women in the community avoided the organization because of its reputation for being sexist:

> [Some lesbian clients] got what they needed, and they moved on. That's great. They may not have developed a personal attachment to the organization or felt that they didn't want to leave it. You know what I mean, when you have a certain devotion to it to come back and work? None of that has been really fostered in the women. . . . Because the [Latina] community will say, when you go out into the community, that the organization all along has really been known for sexism. I think that when I left there was a lot of transition that happened as well. A lot of the women that went there when I was there didn't go back because of the leadership.

In the absence of a mission that held intrinsic value for lesbian staff and clients, lesbians could identify few incentives for remaining loyal to the organization.

Resisting Hierarchies of Fundability:
The Town Hall Meetings

Some lesbian employees suggested that they had an initial honeymoon period in which it was exciting, and a relief, to work in a queer Latino space.
However, most of these women explained that they had a change in consciousness about Bienestar within the first year of their employment. Committed to their clients and fearful of being unable to find another queer Latino work environment, each of the queer women I interviewed described a
period in which they stayed at Bienestar despite burnout and during which
they strategized to accept or improve their working conditions. Some lesbian employees highlighted the importance of developing personal coping
strategies—such as placating male supervisors or drawing clearer boundaries
at work—for accepting that the organization would never change. Others
devised plans to organize women clients and staff and eventually confront
the agency's male leadership. While placating or complimenting male supervisors sometimes improved daily working conditions for lesbian staff, this
strategy offered little hope as a long-term solution to their subordinate position at Bienestar. In July 2000, only two queer women, Fatima and Blanca,
remained in the organization. Under these circumstances Fatima and Blanca
decided to hold a town hall meeting at a local café and invite women clients,
past lesbian staff members, and other Latina lesbians in Los Angeles. The
town hall meeting was intended to inform the women in attendance about
the structural deterioration of the queer women's program and the lack of
emotional and financial support being given to lesbian staff. Fatima argued
that planning the town hall meeting was about encouraging queer Latinas
to "take the matter into [their] own hands":

> I was feeling desperate. I don't feel supported by the agency at all. The
> town hall meeting was born out of lack of support, lack of recognition,
> lack of services. I was feeling very radical at that moment. I felt, I have
> begun to build a community, a following of women within my groups.
> They are not aware of the kind of problems that exist within the
> agency structure if you are an employee, but it's going to affect them in
> some way. So, I wanted to build, kind of like, a council, that involved
> not just the women that came to my groups at Bienestar, but women
> that wanted to join us in just planning, and seeking out the funds on
> our own. . . . I'm like, "Screw this, we've got to take the matter into
> our own hands."

While men were not invited to attend the women's town hall meeting and it was held outside of Bienestar, Fatima and Blanca contend that Bienestar's leadership had seen the announcements and were aware that the meeting was scheduled to take place. One week before the women's town hall meeting, however, Blanca received an e-mail message from Martin, Bienestar's executive director, announcing a general town hall meeting for the entire Bienestar community—staff, clients, and interested community members. Blanca described this general town hall meeting, scheduled one week before the women's meeting, as a "buzzkill for [the women's] town hall event." During a dinner meeting at which I was present, Fatima and Blanca also expressed their belief that queer women clients and staff were clearly not being encouraged to attend the general town hall meeting since it had been scheduled at the same day and time as the regularly scheduled queer women's support group and since neither Blanca nor Fatima had received the e-mail announcement until the day before the meeting.

Fatima used the general town hall meeting as an opportunity for Bienestar's leadership to hear directly from young lesbian clients by calling each of her group members and asking them to attend the meeting instead of the regularly scheduled women's support group. As a result, twenty-five women (and forty-five men) attended the general town hall meeting and several lesbian clients came prepared with questions to ask of the facilitators. The meeting, facilitated by two gay Latino men (one Bienestar administrator and one employee from Llego, a second gay Latino organization), had an open format in which attendees were asked to raise their hands and express their concerns, which would then be written on a flip chart. Concerns about lesbian representation, articulated by clients, staff, and other lesbians from the community, nearly dominated the discussion. The comments of women attendees produced a long list of needs—retreats for women; services for FTM clients; more lesbian magazines in the Bienestar centers; research on, and funding for, Latina lesbians; more lesbian employees and employment opportunities at Bienestar; flyers and others visual materials produced by Bienestar that include images of queer women; services for lesbians with children (e.g., retreats that include child care); a Latina lesbian health task force; and more lesbians in management to ensure that funding went to the women's component. One lesbian in the audience, the partner of a past Bienestar employee, addressed gender inequality directly by arguing that there was a double standard at Bienestar:

> There needs to be more sensitivity to women's issues. Women help the men with their outreach, but they are responsible for their own

[outreach] and the men don't help. This is a double standard. Women need to feel more welcome, but we don't. We have one foot in, one foot out. The women's component needs to be allowed to *grow*!

In response to this comment and the growing momentum of the dialogue focused on lesbians at Bienestar, the facilitator from Llego remarked, "This town hall has been kindly sponsored by Bienestar, but other organizations are here. So let's focus not on a specific program or organization so that this is useful for everyone." Visibly angry, the woman who had made the comment about "the double standard" got up and left the meeting.

In response, lesbian clients expressed to the facilitators that they focused on Bienestar because it was the organization to which they had access. One lesbian client, in her early twenties, explained, "I don't mean to point at Bienestar, but it is the only place in East L.A. It is the only place I know in L.A., that's why I talk about it." After a break, the meeting continued with a strategy session, guided by the question "¿Y ahora qué?" (What now?). Participants were asked to offer ideas about how to address the five general areas of concern that had been touched upon during the previous session of the meeting, one of which was called "lesbian issues." While a few participants expressed gratitude for Bienestar's willingness to host such a meeting, the tone of the second half of the meeting became increasingly tense as both women and men in the audience communicated their suspicion that the strategy session would result in few "real changes." One gay man asked, "What will come of this meeting? Is this just a list or will something actually be done?" Another gay man suggested that the meeting should have been held outside of Bienestar in a neutral, or "safe," space.

The facilitator from Bienestar, later described by the lesbian staff as "totally defensive," responded by shifting accountability to the staff and clients in the audience. "You have all been asked a thousand times what your needs are," he explained, and later, when a gay man suggested that Bienestar should have domestic violence services, he asked in response, "Have you asked for that? We aren't telepathic. We don't know what the issues are." Similarly, when a lesbian in the room delivered a passionate speech about the "triple oppression from racism, sexism, and homophobia" faced by lesbians of color, and added that lesbians are not encouraged to feel entitled to Bienestar's services, the facilitator again requested that lesbians themselves account for how to improve these problems. Gesturing to a cluster of young lesbian clients sitting together in one section of the room, he inquired, "What are *you* doing to better the program?" One teenage lesbian client responded with frustration, "Well, I am going to the groups. We are willing to be educated so we can educate others, but that is why we are *here*!" As tension escalated between the audience and the Bienestar facilitator, the second facilitator announced that he wanted to acknowledge that both facilitators, because they were male, were limited in their ability to understand lesbian concerns. After the meeting, I spoke briefly with Martin, who had been silent during both sessions. "We just don't have the funding. It is good to hear these concerns, but we just don't have the funding," he explained with resignation.

The following week, thirty-eight lesbians and bisexual women attended the town hall event facilitated by Fatima and Blanca, including several of the women clients who had attended the general meeting. The women's town hall meeting had a six-point agenda listed on a handout that was distributed to the attendees: (1) empowerment (women clients and staff read their poetry), (2) what is Bienestar?, (3) purpose of the meeting, (4) "our voice"/open forum, (5) plan of action, and (6) networking. Open only to women and held in a café owned by a "queer-friendly" Latina, the meeting produced a markedly more candid discussion than the meeting held at Bienestar. The women asked a series of questions, many of which highlighted their distrust of Bienestar and its leadership: Will funds we raise for the women's component actually go to women? How can we raise money for the women's component but keep it independent of Bienestar's control? If we get the funds, will that do anything to change the lack of respect lesbians receive at Bienestar? How can we develop workshops to teach women to speak about sexism? Do we want to break off from Bienestar altogether?/ Why don't we start our own program? How can we "use" Bienestar to our advantage since it is already established? How can we make use of the talent and skills of the women present at this meeting? Will "taking to the streets" and publicizing these concerns make Bienestar accountable to women? Why aren't we holding other organizations more accountable for not having *any* programs for queer Latinas?

Some women clients also appeared to feel more comfortable expressing vulnerability and sadness at the women's town hall meeting. For example, Carla and Rosie, a young lesbian couple who had been regularly attending the lesbian support group in East L.A., made a poignant emotional appeal to the group. "I never went [to Bienestar] because I heard it was for men," Rosie asserted. She began to cry and continued, "There is no place for me." Carla added, "Rosie was *so* in need for services. . . . Women are always there for men; it's not *fair* that they aren't there for us." When Rosie tried to speak again but was prevented by her own tears and shaking, Monica attempted to validate that the situation was very upsetting and that Rosie was courageous by explaining, "If I were as young as you, and they treated me like that, like they did at the [general town hall] meeting, I wouldn't have come back." According to Monica, the youth and vulnerability of the women clients, paired with the insensitivity of the male staff, meant that many women "do not come back:"

> When you say you are creating a safe space for women, but you have men present, and you have men who are hostile towards women, maybe not intentionally, these women are going to shut down when these men are there. These men are loud, these men are rambunctious, and they're offensive if you are a young girl trying to come out. So you come into this agency looking for a safe space, and you're going to be shut down immediately. You're going to keep coming back, because there is nothing else. But there are very few women who keep coming back. Women who have any type of political consciousness whatsoever do not come back to the agency.

Approximately one month after the town hall meetings, Carla and Rosie stopped attending groups. Although they were frequently called by lesbian staff, they did not come back.

A few months later and toward the end of my fieldwork, a second women's town hall meeting occurred and drew a smaller group of women, including some local college students who indicated that they were working on a lesbian health survey project that they hoped would produce data that might be useful to Bienestar's women's component. While all of the women who attended the two meetings appeared enthusiastic about effecting change at Bienestar, no one emerged as a leader and no plan was developed to begin the significant work necessary to raise money for the women's component or a new queer women's center. Women staff explained that they were too financially vulnerable to risk losing their jobs by organizing a movement that would expose Bienestar.

Rethinking Risk

On the surface, the story of Bienestar is a familiar one: women struggling with sexism in a male-dominated workplace. Yet I have also shown that gender inequality at Bienestar was not simply a reflection of the sexist attitudes of gay male employees, though this was clearly an important factor. The subordinate role of lesbians was also given legitimacy by the very same ideas about fluidity, intersectionality, and community empowerment that were used to explain the original need for lesbian programs at Bienestar. Similar to the contradictory deployment of "diversity" described in Chapters 3 and 4, Bienestar's male leaders drew upon seemingly progressive ideas about multiplicity and representation in order to welcome lesbians into the organization. However, the feminist potential of this approach was undermined by the hegemony of HIV prevention, concomitantly narrow conceptualizations of queer risk, and instrumental accountability to funding agencies instead of political accountability to lesbian clients themselves. Of course, the centrality of HIV to queer understandings of embodied risk is not specific to Bienestar or other social service organizations run by and for queer people of color. Yet to the extent that queer of color organizations experience greater reliance upon AIDS funding to remain in operation, HIV infection rates and other data about HIV risk are likely to play a large role in determining the goals and programmatic structure of these organizations. This suggests that the needs and interests of lesbians of color, more so than those of white lesbians, are often erased, even in the context of multi-issue AIDS organizing and social service delivery.

To be clear, I am taking the perhaps controversial position that HIV is not the most urgent social, physical, or mental health concern facing most lesbians, including lesbian clients at Bienestar. According to a Centers for Disease Control 2006 online report, "To date, there are no confirmed cases of female-to-female sexual transmission of HIV in the United States database. Through December 2004 . . . of the 534 (HIV infected) women who were reported to have had sex only with women, 91% also had another risk factor—typically, injection drug use."[18] On the other hand, many lesbian AIDS activists have protested against the paucity of research on HIV infection among lesbians and have pointed to growing rates of HIV infection among incarcerated women and female injection drug users who have sex with women.[19] Others have demanded that it is time for the LGBT movement to give due and equal attention to lesbian breast cancer, particularly in light of the tremendous activism and care work done by lesbians to address the impact of AIDS on gay men. Yet, given that less than 5 percent of all (heterosexual and lesbian) women in the United States die of breast cancer (heart disease and other health risks carry a far higher mortality rate), the discourse on lesbian breast cancer strikes me as one example of the ways in which lesbians have been compelled to frame their issues and demands in terms already set forth within the AIDS bureaucracy, and by gay men. Of course this is not to suggest that lesbians don't face disease risks, but rather to suggest that lesbian-specific community outreach and prevention efforts might be just as likely to emphasize other, more immediate concerns: the lack of lesbian public space, sexual harassment and violence at school, body image problems, negotiating butch/femme/trans border wars, limited useful information about lesbian sex and relationships, and (most importantly, in many cases) challenging the misogyny of gay men.

However, rather than replace lesbian HIV risk with this or another fixed set of risks, it may be more productive to move away from economies of risk altogether, at least as the grounds upon which claims for power and visibility are made. In fact, we might even view the emphasis on eliminating all risk from queer life as a normalizing and disciplinary force within lesbian and gay politics. For instance, Judith Halberstam has argued that queer subjectivity is expressed in part through a departure from normative conceptualizations of risk and safety:

> For some queer subjects, time and space are limned by the risks they are willing to take: the transgender person who risks his life by passing in a small town, the subcultural musicians who risk their livelihoods by immersing themselves in non-lucrative practices, the queer performers who destabilize the normative values that make everyone else feel safe and secure . . . [20]

Halberstam reconsiders queer risk as a site of pleasure and danger, choice and necessity. Her analysis also hints at the limitations of exceptionalizing some forms of risk as pure victimization—or beyond the influence of desire and agency (e.g., HIV risk, at-risk youth, etc.)—while other forms of risk (e.g., lesbian invisibility, sexism within queer culture) are coded as less urgent matters of cultural or political debate.

As the story of Bienestar reveals, institutional categories of risk—based on institutional conceptualizations of difference—are often hierarchical, static, and too narrowly defined to respond to the evolving complexities of queer multi-identity politics. At Bienestar, gay Latino men were understood to be the most at risk and the most in need, and therefore they also became the most recognizable and fundable figures of queer Latino culture in Los Angeles. Compared to the threat of AIDS, Latina lesbian politics appeared trivial and selfish, despite the growing sense of crisis that lesbian staff and clients experienced regarding the deterioration of the lesbian program. I revisit this outcome, and the way in which it reflects trends in multi-identity politics more broadly, in the next chapter.

CHAPTER 6

Defying "Diversity as Usual": Queering Intersectionality

As noted in the preceding chapters, scholars of neoliberalism have demonstrated that promoting racial, gender, and sexual diversity is no longer inconsistent with the political-economic aspirations of corporations and the state. In fact, emphasizing diversity has, in many cases, been reframed as a *necessary* path to corporate profits. Understanding and representing racial, gender, and sexual diversity has helped corporations expand their consumer base, enhance consumer and employee loyalty, and demonstrate to investors that they are keeping up with emergent business trends (i.e., diversity management, targeted marketing, etc.). Yet throughout this book I have shown that such instrumental approaches to diversity are not isolated to institutions, like corporations, that we typically associate with power and injustice. Even queer activist organizations have been subject to the influences of diversity culture, especially those organizations that have recruited leaders from the corporate sector or otherwise set their sights on professionalizing and commodifying queer diversity. In the preceding chapters, I have pointed to expanding efforts within queer organizations to leverage racial and gender diversity in order to garner funding and legitimacy, or to get a competitive edge in an increasingly diversity-interested, neoliberal world.

My central assertion in this book has been that diversity projects are ultimately at odds with social justice efforts when they are aimed toward instrumental outcomes. Though each of the case studies has told a different story about how queer diversity is articulated and by whom, each has also revealed that formally celebrating the race, class, and gender diversity of "the queer community" can function to stifle forms of difference that are not easily professionalized, funded, or used for other institutional or financial gains.

This development is certainly racialized, classed, and gendered, yet not in clearly predictable ways. As I have attempted to make clear, the instrumentalism embedded in diversity politics is the source of the danger, and not necessarily the race, class, or gender identities of the people who promote or benefit from the focus on diversity in a given local context. In fact, diversity is powerful as an institutional device because it has been so widely embraced by people across political and demographic lines. This may be precisely because the language of diversity can be used to garner both moral *and* professional/financial authority at the same time. From major corporations to queer community organizations, the emphasis on diversity has helped conservatives and liberals alike make movement toward greater acceptance on multiple fronts, yet without changing the way Americans think about diversity's bottom line.

But what is the bottom line? As I have argued, diversity culture reinscribes the fundamental importance of professionalism, attention to public image/respectability, and the pursuit of financial prosperity—end goals that justify, and exceed the value of, diversity itself. This is accomplished by emphasizing the way that dominant business practices and cultural values are upheld, rather than challenged, by diversification. Each of the case studies in this book has illustrated this convergence of diversity values with normative, professional, and upper-middle-class forms of political organization. At Christopher Street West, the pride organization, a racially diverse group of lesbian and gay professionals asserted their professional diversity skills and diverse connections in order to "rescue" the organization from an equally racially diverse, but working-class, group of activists they perceived as unprofessional, unconnected, and incompetent. At the L.A. Gay & Lesbian Center, the organization's formal and public emphasis on race and gender diversity was praised by many activists (both people of color and whites, women and men), while others argued that the Center's overly discursive focus on its own diversity was one of the greatest indicators of its white corporate culture and its lack of sincere commitment to employees of color. And, at Bienestar, gay Latino men drew on ideas about diversity, fluidity, and intersectionality to describe the importance of programs for gay Latinos but also used these concepts to explain why Latina lesbian programs were less urgent and more difficult to fund than those for gay men.

Leaders in each of these organizations drew on the language of difference, equality, multiplicity, and even intersectionality to keep racialized, gendered, and (especially) classed forms of normativity intact. As I have shown, even as the organizations diversified and engaged in multi-identity activism, their emphasis on the institutional functions of diversity helped to preserve middle-class, male-centered, or white-normative ways of "doing

difference." Yet it is not clear to what extent shifting the balance of power—
or changing the race, class, or gender identities of leaders—can completely
eliminate these forms of normativity or resolve the problem of diversity's
misuse. Many analyses of racial, gender, and sexual discrimination in organizations have critiqued the practice of tokenization and suggested that
identity-based restructuring is the solution (i.e., restructuring so that people
of color, queers, and white women form a new critical mass at the leadership
level). However, studies of neoliberal political formation reveal that traditional identity-based hierarchies are being transformed such that more and
greater access to power is available for the most assimilated, culturally normative, and politically mainstream representatives of diversity. With time,
the scale of these changes may reveal that tokenism is no longer at the crux
of the matter. Instead, the logic of "diversity as good business" highlights
the consequential divide between those forms of racial, gender, sexual, and
class diversity that are profitable and those that are not.

My analysis in this book has been heavily informed by queer critiques
of normativity, or "conventional forms of association, belonging, and identification."[1] Such critiques have helped to highlight the limitations of identity
politics, including the ways that identity activism can work to sustain hegemonic ideas about gender, sexuality, race, and class—even as activists make
successful strides toward equality at the local level. However, some social
movement scholars remind us that activists' deployment of normative logics
may also be *strategic*, or intentionally put to work for the good of the larger
struggle. For instance, in his study of LGBT activists in gay-straight alliances, sociologist Daniel Cortese argues that queer activists placed strategic
emphasis on the beliefs and experiences of their straight supporters in order
to normalize and universalize their cause, as well as to tap into straight social networks and organizational resources.[2] Viewing such efforts as "strategic" focuses our attention on how activists, drawing on their own agency,
define their local and contextual successes (i.e., Did they in fact produce
more resources and legitimacy for LGBT people in their area? If so: strategic
success.)

Yet when we invoke strategy, it is important to determine whether
activists are achieving greater visibility and access to resources by undermining normativity or by uncritically colluding with it. In the context of
LGBT politics, Lisa Duggan refers to the latter response as "the new homonormativity," or "a politics that does not contest dominant heteronormative
assumptions and institutions, but upholds and sustains them, while promising the possibility of a demobilized gay constituency and privatized, de-
politicized gay culture anchored in domesticity and consumption."[3] This re-

packaging of queerness (and racial difference) as normative and profitable is particularly evident in the story of the L.A. Gay & Lesbian Center, where the organization's leaders drew on corporate diversity discourses (e.g., "diversity is good for business"), without any critique of these frameworks or aspirations for undoing them. In such examples, the deployment of normative logics in the service of LGBT visibility and resources results in a transaction in which the subversive possibilities offered by racially diverse and multigendered queerness are exchanged for the broader possibilities offered by "diversity."

This transaction—perhaps comparable to the exchange of European ethnicity for the privileges of whiteness—results in some immediate gains. As I have shown, queer diversity projects that draw on mainstream identity frameworks have nonetheless helped to produce multi-identity, multi-issue LGBT organizations. At the L.A. Gay & Lesbian Center, corporate diversity management concepts were used to explain the need for a racially diverse staff that could meet the needs of the organization's similarly diverse clients. At Christopher Street West, public attention to whether the pride festival was welcoming to the diverse queer communities of Los Angeles resulted in the addition of new festival areas—such as a children's garden—that, in the eyes of many participants, made the pride event more lesbian-friendly. And, at Bienestar, gay Latino men extended HIV-prevention models in ways that made lesbian inclusion possible. These examples show that challenges to single-identity (or gay-only) politics have transformed LGBT organizing in many productive ways. LGBT organizations across the country have indeed become more racially and gender diverse, and organizations established by and for queer people of color, in particular, have become common.

However, in light of increasing movement by LGBT activists toward instrumental diversity frameworks and homonormative politics, my goal in this concluding chapter is to distinguish these forms of multi-identity organizing from what might be termed "queer intersectionality." The concept of intersectionality is now commonly used within the social sciences to refer to interlocking systems of oppression—particularly race, class, gender, and sexuality. In particular, a growing body of research on social movements has applied intersectional theory to identify models of multi-identity activism emerging within contemporary movements. Such studies document how many activists have transcended singular and self-interested understandings of their cause and have instead worked to promote more diverse movement leadership and expanded forms of social change. Yet, as outlined in Chapter 2, these accounts often fail to consider the relationship between grassroots multi-identity activism and the widespread attention to diversity and equality now characteristic of corporate, pop-cultural, and political realms. In contrast, this book has taken on the arguably discouraging task of pointing out that activist or community-based diversity discourses often look remarkably similar to those found within corporations and on television. Perhaps even more unsettling, I have focused on the personal, professional, and financial rewards that often motivate people to enthusiastically pursue and celebrate diversity. Given these complexities and the contradictions of neoliberalism, we remain without a clear sociological understanding of what intersectional resistance looks like in an increasingly diversity-obsessed world.

Yet despite this bad news, the activists whose stories are told in this book have also pointed the way toward new and queer ways of thinking about intersectionality. In each case, some activists recognized that the focus on diversity in their respective organizations was not delivering its intended or stated effects. These activists resisted instrumental and professionalized approaches to diversity, in each case asserting new critical discourses that, I will argue, have a particularly queer flavor. In the next section, I suggest that their critiques reflect an emerging voice of queer intersectionality, or an intersectional politics that struggles for racial, gender, class, and sexual diversity while resisting the institutional forces that seek to contain and normalize differences or reduce them to their use value. In the last section of this chapter, I conclude by broadening this discussion to propose a theory of queer intersectionality that views antinormativity as necessary to dismantling interlocking systems of oppression. If defiance against normativity and mainstreaming is a queer impulse, as queer theorists have argued, I suggest that a queer political frame may be necessary to *all* forms of intersectional resistance.

Emergent Activisms: Voices of Queer Intersectionality

While it can certainly be argued that the circulation of diversity concepts in the LGBT movement has been a sign of progress, many LGBT activists have been critical of this trend by pointing to the gap between the movement's diversity rhetoric and persistent inequalities at the leadership level. Such criticisms point out that diversity discourses often fail to tell the truth about what's really happening in the movement (i.e., who is the most visible, who has the most power and resources, etc.).

However, a close look at diversity-related conflicts within three LGBT organizations in Los Angeles has revealed that some queer activists interrogate the normative logics that have become embedded in the concept of diversity itself, or at least in its deployment as an institutional device. In each organization, lesbians, working-class queers, and/or queer people of color challenged the way that their differences were being put to institutional use. To do this, they drew upon three primary modes of resistance: *antiprofessionalism, antidiscursivity,* and *anticommodification.* These strategies reinforced the crucial importance of multi-identity activism; however, they also formed a defiant response to mainstream diversity politics.

1. Antiprofessionalism: Resisting Homonormative Diversity Politics

Each of the case studies has shown how invoking diversity can be used to enhance professional authority while simultaneously marking a personal or group commitment to race and gender inclusion. As I demonstrated in Chapter 4, the L.A. Gay & Lesbian Center's adoption of corporate "diversity speak" and diversity management practices helped diminish the stigma associated with being a lesbian and gay organization. Far from an oppositional strategy, the Center's focus on race and gender diversity indicated that it was just like other large professional organizations (universities, corporations) where the focus on diversity was a central part of doing good business.

Yet it was at Christopher Street West where the link between diversity and professionalism was most pronounced. Critics of CSW's working-class board of directors argued that the organization needed to be run by skilled professionals and high-profile activists. They explained that people with professional diversity skills had their fingers on the pulse of the lesbian and gay community and would know how to inspire the confidence of local officials and other important festival stakeholders. Lesbian and gay professionals would be able to "implement message control" and remake CSW's public image so that it reflected the race and gender diversity that the lesbian and gay community wanted to see on the parade route. Professionals, they argued, would be able to accomplish a checklist of diversity-related tasks that would help ensure that people of color and white women felt welcome at the festival and parade. Perhaps, some argued, they would create a "children's area" at the pride festival to stimulate lesbian attendance, and they would encourage parade participants to wear "ethnic costumery" to demonstrate racial/ethnic diversity and enliven the parade.

However, CSW's working-class board refused to be professional or political by these standards—a stance that I argue represents a vital mode of resistance to the professionalization of diversity or to the mainstreaming of multi-identity politics. As working-class activists at CSW moved forward with less overtly political forms of diversification—such as producing a Latino dance venue complete with Latino music and go-go dancers, which was praised by Los Angeles' gay Latino press—they also poked fun at predictable forms of political engagement (such as public speakers) and heteronormative symbols of inclusion (such as "family-friendly" activities). They were loud, crass, sex focused, and uninterested in gaining the approval of gay professionals or being granted legitimacy by heterosexual onlookers. They refused the term "political," yet they spent literally hundreds of unpaid hours working to keep lesbian and gay public sex culture alive in Los Angeles. And though there were few lesbians among their ranks, their commitment to living on the edge of respectability opened space for my own sense of queer alliance with them, one that ultimately resonated with my queer feminist sensibilities far more than the call for child care (even as the latter was framed as a women's issue). In sum, working-class board members were uninterested in the "diversity as usual" approach of West Hollywood's growing lesbian and gay professional elite. Instead, they practiced a queer "politics of vulgarity," in which drama, camp, sexuality, and the disavowal of professionalism functioned as a preservation of queer *and* working-class cultures. In a political climate in which only the most managed and visible markers of diversity politics (i.e., race and gender) seemed to matter, CSW board members gave voice to the less frequently noted intersections of class and sexuality through their refusal to be professionalized.

On the one hand, the celebration of diversity within the LGBT movement has helped to normalize and contain queer differences by (a) circulating of a rigid set of professional diversity rules and skills (a kind of bourgeois "diversity etiquette"), (b) privileging the most visible and ostensibly "knowable" or predictable forms of difference, and (c) marking the boundaries between respectable and unrespectable forms of identity activism. These developments arguably reflect a broader project in which multi-identity activism is becoming increasingly subsumed within a professionalized and streamlined diversity industry. On the other hand, the story of CSW also illustrates that the mainstreaming of diversity is being met with challenge at the grassroots level. Though lesbian and gay professionals emerged to help "save" CSW with the moral force of diversity on their side, the issue of class diversity came to the fore as working-class activists at CSW repeatedly refused to internalize accounts of their failure or incompetence.

As this and other studies have shown, invoking professional skills and standards is one method for dominant groups and institutions to co-opt multi-identity discourses and reproduce their control and expertise when confronted with difference. In light of this, I argue that activist critiques of liberal professionalism are, now more than ever, a vital source of fuel for the project of deepening intersectional politics. Drawing upon critiques that emerged at CSW, some concrete examples of queer intersectional politics might include the following: making an explicitly nonprofessional background an important qualification for some activist leaders; building a parody of dominant culture (and its sad attempts at co-opting diversity) into activists' tactical repertoires; and expanding the range of activities that are understood to be political, including sexualized (or otherwise subcultural, undignified, and embodied) forms of rebellion against professional norms.

2. Antidiscursivity: Resisting the Incitement to Discourse on Diversity

As we know from Foucault's examination of sexuality, increased public attention to human behaviors and identities does not always or only have liberatory effects. Instead, the "incitement to discourse" about sexuality marked the birth of new tools of discipline and a new means of binding people to fixed identity categories. Extending Foucault's view in the psychoanalytic direction, "sexual liberation" itself can be understood as a kind of cultural fetish object, one that masks sexualized forms of violence by promising pleasure and individual freedom. Similarly, my claim that we are living in a "diversity-obsessed" culture is intended to describe the somewhat fetishistic quality of diversity discourses, or the way that the ubiquitous focus on diversity masks persistent forms of dominance as it helps to sublimate liberal guilt. Like sexuality, the concept of diversity has given rise to new opportunities for political coalition and resistance to identity-based oppression (or counterdiscourses, to use Foucault's term). However, it has also become a discursive tool that affords individuals and groups an opportunity to uncritically disavow inequality in general, and their own gender, racial, and economic privileges, in particular.

The L.A. Gay & Lesbian Center offers an empirical example of these tensions. As I argued in Chapter 4, the Center's strategic emphasis on racial (and gender) diversity ultimately helped to remake the organization into a vital resource for multi-issue social service and advocacy in Los Angeles. Yet this transformation from the Center's white gay male roots was accomplished by embarking on various diversity projects that some employees, particularly employees of color, described as too slow, too bureaucratic, and overly discursive: The Center's leaders gathered demographic statistics and other data to justify the diversification effort; they developed diversity initiatives and working committees to figure out how to recruit more people of color into leadership positions; they required that employees attend an annual "Diversity Day" where they explained why and how diversity was important to the work of the Center; they spoke at length about the Center's diversity goals in their public remarks and organizational materials; and they strategized about how to improve their reputation among "people of color organizations." In addition, many of the Center's employees were asked to serve on committees charged with brainstorming about how to augment the organization's racial diversity, resulting in dozens of employee-generated plans, memos, reports, and presentations on diversity.

At one level, this list of the Center's diversification efforts reads like a step-by-step plan for how to successfully transform a predominantly white organization into one that is racially diverse. Indeed, many of the Center's diversity-related goals came to fruition and led to structural changes in the organization. Yet *talking* about racial diversity also happened so frequently at the Center that it became not only mundane but a symptom of the Center's enduring white culture. In the face of the Center's enthusiastic focus on celebrating and enhancing its own diversity, some employees wondered if the Center doth protest too much about diversity's importance. Employees of color, in particular, argued that the Center's leaders needed to stop talking about diversity and "just *do* it." Too much talk about diversity signaled that the organization had something to prove, that it was all about image management, and that the Center must not *already* be a "people of color organization." Instead, critical employees argued that diversity should happen more organically, should stem from common sense, and should be accomplished by direct and immediate actions rather than data gathering, deliberation, and documentation of how and why diversity should be undertaken.

By some accounts, the history of the Center is a success story about white lesbian and gay activists working to transcend single-issue gay politics in favor of a new multi-issue diversity politics. Yet the organization's internal critics asserted that *how* diversity is achieved—and not simply *whether* it is achieved—is also vitally important, as it is one of the constitutive elements of an organization's culture. As one African American employee argued, the Center's culture was very similar to what she had experienced in "white corporate America." As in the corporate environment, diversification had indeed taken place at the Center, yet "diversity" (the word and the idea) had also become a normalizing force in the organization. It had become overused, empty, and "white."

In part, this emptiness stems from the overly discursive or rhetorical

quality of diversity. In an era in which countless books, trainings, certification programs, and consultants have "elevated" diversity to a smart business practice, we might consider that critical nonparticipation in diversity
rhetoric represents another important mode of resistance to the mainstreaming of multi-identity politics. Drawing upon critiques that emerged at the
Center, some concrete examples of queer intersectional politics might also
include containing "diversity talk" until deeds are done (e.g., for every action of speech, an action of practice?); abandoning the compulsion to collect
data and engage in justificatory discourses; building a stronger foundation
of support for forms of diversity that are already in place instead of invoking
the diversity that exists elsewhere; and being willing to "look bad" through
the difficult, trial-and-error process of creating a multi-issue movement.

3. Anticommodification:
Resisting Hierarchies of Fundability

A number of studies have examined how oppressed groups are commodified
through market processes, including exploitative labor practices, the cultivation of identity-based target markets, and the manufacturing of demand for
stereotypical representations of race, gender, and sexuality in popular culture. However, limited attention has been given to the commodification of
identities in nonprofit and/or social-justice realms, where identities and their
structural consequences must be explained—in fact pitched and sold—to
prospective funders. Anyone who has ever participated in a fundraising effort probably knows that even the best of causes are difficult to fund, precisely because individual donors and granting agencies have (or feel that
they have) scarce time and resources compared to the number of requests
they receive. As a result, my own experience in fundraising often led to the
discouraging sense that finding money to operate even the most necessary of
direct-service programs—for instance, food banks, homeless shelters, HIV
services—required an approach that was aggressive and competitive (i.e.,
"Now that I have your attention, I'm going to tell you in less than five minutes why you should fund *our* organization and not all those others. . . .").
In some cases, "closing the deal" required invoking hierarchies of need and
urgency (e.g., "Here's why queer homeless people need beds even more than
straight homeless people. . . .") or involved vastly oversimplified or stereotypical descriptions of the problems being addressed ("Homophobia is experienced even more harshly by LGBT people of color because communities
of color can be . . . well . . . very homophobic."). For me, LGBT fundraising

often felt like entertainment-industry deal-making, a bizarre similarity that was especially evident while I was living in Hollywood (the Center's location) and surrounded by a sea of people pitching their important ideas.

In activist organizations, the commodification of identities also refers to the ways in which some identities and inequalities become more or less fundable than others. In response to this outcome, social movement organizations may respond with new programs or discourses, such as Bienestar's transformation from a lesbian and gay organization to a gay-male-focused HIV/AIDS organization. Hierarchies of fundability reflect donors' beliefs about which groups or issues demonstrate greater urgency than others, yet they may also reflect the ways in which funding infrastructures make some injustices more visible or easier to fund. As I have shown, both of these factors were in operation at Bienestar, where readily fundable HIV-prevention programs for "at-risk" gay Latino men flourished and, conversely, difficult-to-fund programs for presumably less "at-risk" Latina lesbians were devalued and marginalized.

The story of Bienestar reveals that in the still HIV-focused world of LGBT community organizations, lesbian-specific programs are often ancillary or restructured so that they can be operated with HIV-prevention funding (or other funds designated for gay men). At Bienestar, this meant not only that the lesbian program was small and under-resourced, but also that gay male staff members could draw on epidemiological data regarding HIV infection rates and gay male risk to justify their view that lesbian employees' demands for more resources were trivial and selfish. The taken-for-granted urgency of HIV risk, particularly for gay men of color, positioned men at Bienestar as the quintessential embodiment of both queer Latino oppression and pride. But the abundance of funding available for at-risk gay men also provided the institutional rationale for investing in gay men's programs (with money, space, and promotional materials), while lesbian programs were regularly ignored or diminished.

In response, lesbian employees and clients resisted Bienestar's HIV-funding hierarchy by organizing town hall meetings that shifted attention to the risks faced by lesbians, including the misogyny they experienced at the hands of gay men. In some cases, and I think more valuably, they refused to engage in economies of risk altogether by suggesting that community accountability and reciprocity, rather than data on risk, should determine how gay men at Bienestar interacted with lesbian coworkers and clients. As one client (and a partner of a lesbian employee) said, "Women help the men with their outreach, but they are responsible for their own [outreach] and the men don't help. This is a double standard. Women need to feel more welcome, but we don't. . . . The women's component needs to be allowed to *grow!*" Arguments such as this also speak to a broader historical context in which both the physical and affective labor of lesbians has been necessary to build and sustain organizations such as Bienestar. Lesbian programs must be encouraged to grow because they are vital to the history and survival of LGBT communities generally, regardless of whether the outside world recognizes them as worthy of funding.

Too often marginalized groups—or the representatives of diversity—are able to achieve inclusion, access, and representation only after demonstrating, in one way or another, that they bring profit or funding to the table. In contrast, asserting entitlement to political space and resources despite being unfundable represents a third mode of resistance to the mainstreaming of multi-identity politics. Analysis of conflicts at Bienestar yields more concrete examples of how to "queer" intersectional activism, such as training employee-activists to de-link fundability from assessments of political urgency; developing strategic fundraising strategies that involve the democratic distribution of risk/identity-based funding to all participants; and engaging in consciousness-raising aimed at teaching activists to celebrate the rare occasions in which racial and gender subjectivities resist or circumvent commodification.

Queering Intersectional Theory

While I have highlighted emergent forms of resistance to the mainstreaming of intersectionality, what may not yet be evident is what makes these challenges *queer*, apart from being articulated or enacted by LGBT activists. To be clear, I use the term "queer" not as a means of privileging sexuality or sexual identity within multi-identity politics but as "a political metaphor without a fixed referent"—a metaphor that describes various modes of challenge to the institutional and state forces that normalize and commodify difference.[4] Anchored from the beginning in a broad critique of the mechanisms that tie people to fixed identity categories, queer analysis offers a timely intervention into neoliberal identity politics and the institutionalization of diversity. Though few sociologists engaged in intersectional analyses have taken up queer theory, my hope is to have pointed to its usefulness—in fact its necessity—to sociological considerations of identity and social movements. As David Eng, Judith Halberstam, and José Esteban Muñoz have argued:

It is crucial to insist yet again on the capacity of queer studies to mobilize a broad social critique of race, gender, class, nationality, and religion, as well as sexuality. Such a theoretical project demands that queer epistemologies not only rethink the relationship between intersectionality and normalization from multiple points of view, but also, and equally important, consider how gay and lesbian rights are being reconstituted as a type of reactionary (identity) politics of national and global consequence.[5]

While intersectional analysis has often been used within the social sciences to examine how dominant groups produce singular constructions of justice, adding a queer lens to intersectionality also directs critical attention to the "relationship between intersectionality and normalization"—exemplified by the increasing deployment of multiplicity and diversity rhetoric in the service of state power. A queer approach extends intersectional critiques of singularity and looks also to the proliferation of multi-identity projects—including the focus on race and gender diversity within mainstream lesbian and gay politics—as the potentially expanding ground of co-optation and social control. Wary of identity politics generally, queer critique begs the question: *Can multi-identity politics be rescued from co-optation and commodification?*

I have shown how current conflicts among queer activists can be understood as one battleground upon which the struggle between the mainstreaming of diversity, on the one hand, and the preservation of critical intersectionality, on the other, is taking place. Yet it is important to note that these grassroots challenges also mirror efforts by queer scholars to grapple with the above question by synthesizing queer and intersectional theory. By way of conclusion, I briefly review some of these innovative theoretical developments and link them to the empirical findings of this study.

Subjects-in-Process and the Politics of "Not Yet"

While diversity culture has worked to catalog differences and render them more manageable, predictable, and profitable, queer feminist theorists of color have pointed to the value of a far more groundless and unpredictable identity politics. Drawing on Norma Alarcon's critique of multiculturalism, Juana Maria Rodriguez explains that "no single term or construct can fully inscribe the historically marginalized subject":

Instead, [Alarcon] states that many feminists of color are engaged in a politics of "not yet" as a response to the multiple attempts to determine their subjectivity. . . . Alarcon's own term, "subject-in-process" . . . does not insinuate a progressional, unidirectional development; instead the process is often spastic and unpredictable, continually unfolding without origin or end, an act of becoming that never ceases.[6]

Such accounts suggest that intersectional politics must not only enable multiple and interlocking identifications, but must be the site of opposition in which identities are understood to be spastic, unpredictable, and in-process—and perhaps, by extension, unprofessional, unmanageable, and unfundable. It strikes me that such a project is fundamentally at odds with the instrumentalist approaches to multi-identity politics that seek inclusion and diversification as a means to achieve organizational growth, legitimacy, and efficiency. For instance, at the L.A. Gay & Lesbian Center, where events such as Diversity Day were designed to make queer race and gender differences more central to organizational functioning, some employees responded with their own form of Alarcon's "not yet / that's not it" position by asserting that the organization's persistent emphasis on diversity had still failed to represent their needs and experiences.[7] Instead, they argued for less talk and deliberation about diversity and more immediate action, despite the "risks" that some white employees perceived would follow from "rushed" (spastic) action.

Just as "not yet" refers to an identity politics that resists fixity, it also refers to the way in which the "practical solutions" to the problem of mainstreaming and normativity are not yet clear or categorical (I note here that practical solutions are frequently of concern to sociologists). Yet this need not be discouraging, given the power of intersectional critique itself to continually demand "that's not it" and to invite new "tactical subjectivities."[8]

Disidentification and Parody

Performance theorist José Esteban Muñoz suggests that "dissing identity"—or *disidentification*—is one such identity tactic that poses challenge to the mainstreaming of difference. While diversity projects tend to strengthen ties to fixed identity categories and encourage identification with predictable markers of cultural difference, disidentification is a "strategy that works on and against dominant ideology." Muñoz explains: "Instead of buckling under the pressures of dominant ideology (identification, assimilation) or attempting to break free of its escapable sphere (counteridentification, utopianism), this 'working on and against' is a strategy that tries to transform a cultural logic from within."[9]

Muñoz draws on the work of queer performance artists of color to describe disidentification in practice: It is simultaneously a parody of racist, misogynistic, and homophobic ideologies (enacted through "white face," drag, and other cross-embodiments) and a campy reappropriation of often shameful stereotypes, which are reconfigured to highlight what is dramatic, pleasurable, erotic, or even glamorous within them. Like gay male camp works to transform the disgraceful stereotype of the nelly queen into an "act" that is playful, critical, and desirable, disidentification takes form as a kind of *intersectional* camp, in which mainstream representations of race, gender, class, and sexuality are all simultaneously fodder for satire and transformation.

Today's most visible gender, racial, class, and homophobic stereotypes are typically far less violent than those that circulated in the public sphere prior to the New Left movements of the 1970s. Instead, it is often the "facts" about cross-cultural diversity (e.g., "Blacks listen with their eyes closed," "lesbians want child care at pride festivals," "Latina lesbians have always enjoyed caretaking for gay men," etc.) that currently do the work of constraining intersectional subjectivity or alerting us that even diversity-interested parties haven't "gotten" it yet. In other words, they too elicit a strong response of "that's not it." According to Muñoz, even critical counterdiscourses, such as the call to "celebrate diversity" within LGBT politics, "can fluctuate for different ideological ends, and a politicized agent must have the ability to adapt and shift as quickly as power does within discourse."[10]

Here I am arguing that within the context of multi-identity activism, this kind of adaptability entails a *disidentification with mainstream diversity discourses*, or a critical—and perhaps campy and parodic—relationship to the normative logics that sustain diversity culture. On the one hand, many LGBT activists have invested in mainstream approaches to diversity, particularly by emphasizing the skills, resources, and normalcy ("we're just like you!") that diverse LGBT employees and consumers bring to the both the movement and the marketplace. On the other hand, and as I have shown, other LGBT activists disidentify with, poke fun at, and critically reframe the professional norms that have transformed diversity into a competitive and often hierarchical institutional practice. By renaming the L.A. Gay & Lesbian Center "Gay Inc." or defiantly asserting "we're not about being professional," some activists have created critical distance between themselves and the increasingly homonormative lesbian and gay movement in which they are situated and implicated.

Though in this book I have illustrated how this form of resistance manifests at a somewhat individual level, I also want to highlight the possibility that activist organizations (and not simply individual activists) could actively cultivate disidentification with mainstream diversity culture. Most LGBT organizations are to some extent dependent upon the funding or other resources they receive from mainstream institutions (large foundations, corporate entities, local and state government); however, this form of dependency need not require a direct identification with the liberal diversity politics of these institutions. While this may seem a basic point, it is one that appears to have been lost in the race for queer legitimacy at both local and national levels. Thus, the challenge for queer intersectional politics lies in how to take what is desired and needed (from lesbian public space to livable wages) while still creating ideological distance from—or critically interrogating—the logics that are used to distribute these resources. To use Muñoz's words, the challenge is to produce a "disidentification that enables politics."[11]

Queer Ethics: Do the Right Thing

Other recent theoretical developments within queer studies indicate that creating ideological distance from normativity and state power is not unrelated to the project of forming a queer ethics or giving renewed attention to the mobilizing power of "doing the right thing." Yet within the realm of sociological research on social movements, this seems a truly a queer idea. The suggestion that activists might invoke *ethics* as the basis for their demands— or as a new ground for building multi-issue coalitions across difference— stands in contrast to the focus on successful outcome-oriented strategies, especially those that deliver policy change or other legal victories. As sociologist Nicole Raeburn found in her study of lesbian and gay workplace activism, "arguments about 'doing the right thing' carry little weight in the profit-driven corporate world."[12] As a result, lesbian and gay activists learned to make their demands for equal treatment, inclusion, and visibility by downplaying the "ideology of ethics" and instead emphasizing the "ideology of profits." The ethical questions involved in queer politics are overshadowed by the logic of capital.

That queer activists have increasingly framed their demands for inclusion and visibility in profit-oriented terms comes as little surprise given early theoretical insights on the relationship between capitalism and gay identity.

As historian D'Emilio argued in 1983, while capitalism produced new means of sexual regulation and social control, it also provided the conditions for the emergence of gay identity by enabling individuals to circulate and organize outside of the nuclear family.[13] In addition to the ways in which the demands of queer activists are converging with the corporate bottom line, recent representations of "queer" as a consumer market and lifestyle (e.g., *Queer Eye for the Straight Guy*) suggest that capitalism was not only necessary to the *emergence* of gay identity, but for its ongoing maintenance as well.

Yet theorists such as Janet Jakobsen have posed an ethical challenge to the link between queer politics, consumer individualism, and the marketplace. Jakobsen contends that the values of freedom and individualism—which are rooted in the Protestant Reformation and manifest primarily through freedom to marry and consume—undergird single-issue lesbian and gay cultural politics in the United States.[14] As they are currently understood and articulated, freedom and individualism have failed to produce widespread challenges to single-issue identity-based movements. Hence, Jakobsen concludes that reconfiguring these values (or creating new ones) is necessary to intersectional politics. Thus, *ethics*—in addition to, but perhaps more so than strategic identities and shared material interests—become a new foundation for building intersectional political movements.

I take up queer ethics because they were arguably the subtext of conflicts that emerged in the organizations I examined. For instance, in the face of persuasive and seemingly logical arguments about the lack of funding and resources to develop lesbian programs at Bienestar, lesbians nonetheless made appeals for equity by invoking the values of empathy, reciprocity, and justice (e.g., "Just think about how the women feel." "How would you feel if white people had the nice discussion room all of the time?" "Women help the men, but the men don't help."). Similarly, at the L.A. Gay & Lesbian Center, critical employees called for the organization's leaders to stop producing bureaucratic justifications for diversity and "just do it." As Beverly said: "You get tired of trying to fight for something that you know is right with people who are trying to convince themselves through their numbers and their strategic plans. . . . [The alternative is] you just go do it. . . . You just start doing it." In both of these cases, activists disavowed instrumentalist strategies to make their claims for equity and instead drew upon a common-sense, intersectional, social-justice epistemology that communicated: "We belong because it's right . . . and you should know that by now."

Studies of multi-identity movements have emphasized the crucial importance of education and consciousness-raising to the project of building effective coalitions across difference. However, given that opportunities for multicultural education are increasingly abundant and that intersectionality has become a centerpiece of liberal arts curriculum, one thing that diversity culture reveals quite clearly is that the social change impact of education is not without its limits. The activist voices I have focused on point to these limits (e.g., the limited usefulness of "numbers and strategic plans") and instead highlight the significance of affective and ethical alignments ("Think about how we feel." "Do it because, at some level, you must know it's right."). Precisely because such appeals read as naive or radically optimistic vis-à-vis the ideology of profits, I suggest that they may represent vital efforts to undertake what Jakobsen calls "the reconfiguration of values" within the context of neoliberal diversity politics. While formulating a queer intersectional ethics is beyond the scope of this project, I hope to have made clear that the mainstreaming of intersectionality is in part accomplished by conceptualizing radical ethics as irrational and ineffective and, conversely, by conceptualizing instrumentalist approaches to equality and diversity as strategic and success oriented. In the face of these developments, a movement-based return to ethics is in order.

Disavowing Diversity

While many view the broad circulation of diversity concepts as a measure of progress, I have argued that instrumental approaches to diversity are not worth their temporary gains. To make my case, I have drawn a distinction between instrumental diversity strategies oriented toward institutional legitimacy and hybrid multi-identity practices rooted in deeper forms of resistance and critique. Admittedly, this project has offered only preliminary speculation about how the latter approach may take form in practice, but I am also optimistic that the some of the principles of queer intersectionality I have described here—antiprofessionalism, antidiscursivity, anticommodification—represent new measures to be used in our evaluations of what counts as successful multi-identity politics.

In the introduction to this book, I posed the question: What, if anything, is still "queer" about queer approaches to difference? With regard to the management of LGBT organizations, the unfortunate answer is "very little." An inside look into three organizations in Los Angeles has revealed a narrowing gap between LGBT approaches to difference and those emerging from inside corporations and other mainstream institutions. Activists in queer organizations, like Americans in a variety of organizational settings, are fast at work leveraging diversity in the service of personal and institutional gain. Yet there are also queer activists resisting this trend from inside the LGBT movement. Not only is this resistance underway, it is fueled by a promising synthesis of queer and intersectional modes of critique. As I have shown, challenges to essentialist and instrumental diversity politics cut across the problems of white normativity, middle-class professionalism, misogyny, and homophobia. In an era in which normativity and mainstreaming function as primary means of disabling identity movements generally, queer defiance offers a vital contribution to intersectional politics and a weapon against the co-optation of diversity.

Notes

Chapter 1

1. Walter Benn Michaels, *The Trouble with Diversity: How We Learned to Love Identity and Ignore Inequality* (New York: Metropolitan Books, 2006), inside flap.
2. See, for instance, Lisa Duggan, *The Twilight of Equality? Neoliberalism, Cultural Politics, and the Attack on Democracy* (Boston: Beacon, 2003); Henry Giroux, *The Terror of Neoliberalism: Authoritarianism and the Eclipse of Democracy* (Boulder: Paradigm, 2004); Avery Gordon and Christopher Newfield, eds., *Mapping Multiculturalism* (Minneapolis: University of Minnesota Press, 1996).
3. See Giroux, *The Terror of Neoliberalism*.
4. Judith Halberstam, *In a Queer Time and Place: Transgender Bodies, Subcultural Lives* (New York: New York University Press, 2005), 4.
5. See Robert Corber and Stephen Valocchi, "Introduction," in *Queer Studies: An Interdisciplinary Reader*, ed. Robert J. Corber and Stephen Valocchi (New York: Blackwell, 2003), 1–20.
6. David Eng, Judith Halberstam, and José Esteban Muñoz, "Introduction: What's Queer about Queer Studies Now?" *Social Text* 84–85, vol. 23, nos. 3–4 (2005): 1.
7. Urvashi Vaid, *Virtual Equality: The Mainstreaming of Gay and Lesbian Liberation* (New York: Anchor Books, 1995), 106.
8. See Keith Boykin, "Where Rhetoric Meets Reality: The Role of Black Lesbians and Gays in 'Queer' Politics," in *The Politics of Gay Rights*, ed. Craig Rimmerman, Kenneth Wald, and Clyde Wilcox (Chicago: University of Chicago Press, 2000), especially 79.
9. Elizabeth Armstrong, *Forging Gay Identities: Organizing Sexuality in San Francisco, 1950–1994* (Chicago: University of Chicago Press, 2002), 3.

10. David Harvey, *A Brief History of Neoliberalism* (Oxford: Oxford University Press, 2005), 2.

11. See Giroux, *The Terror of Neoliberalism*.

12. Duggan, *The Twilight of Equality*.

13. See Len Artz and Bren Ortega Murphy, *Cultural Hegemony in the United States* (Thousand Oaks, CA: Sage, 2000); Gordon and Newfield, "Introduction," in Gordon and Newfield, eds., *Mapping Multiculturalism*; Eduardo Bonilla-Silva, *Racism without Racists: Color-Blind Racism and the Persistence of Racial Inequality in the United States* (New York: Rowman and Littlefield, 2003); Nicole Raeburn, *Changing Corporate America from the Inside Out: Lesbian and Gay Workplace Rights* (Minneapolis: University of Minnesota Press, 2004).

14. See Gordon and Newfield, "Introduction."

15. See Bonilla-Silva, *Racism without Racists*.

16. See Herman Gray, *Cultural Moves: African Americans and the Politics of Representation* (Berkeley: University of California Press, 2005).

17. Avery Gordon, "The Work of Corporate Culture: Diversity Management." *Social Text* 44, vol. 13, no. 3 (1995): 3–30; Raeburn, *Changing Corporate America*.

18. Bonilla-Silva, *Racism without Racists*.

19. See Gray, *Cultural Moves*.

20. See Viki Coppock, *The Illusions of Post-Feminism* (London: Taylor & Francis, 1995).

21. See Niki Cousino, Julie Wyman, and Sarah Lewison, et al., producers, *Sisterhood: Hyping the Female Market*, video (New York: Paper Tiger Television, 1993).

22. See Jennifer Cotter, "Martha Stewart: Global Capitalist Behinds the Domestic Label," *Red Critique* 5 (July/August 2002).

23. For instance, Ariel Levy, *Female Chauvinist Pigs: Women and the Rise of Raunch Culture* (New York: Free Press, 2005).

24. See Suzanna Danuta Walters, *All the Rage: The Story of Gay Visibility in America* (Chicago: University of Chicago Press, 2003).

25. See Gregory Herek, "Gender Gaps in Public Opinion about Lesbians and Gay Men," *Public Opinion Quarterly* 66 (2002): 40–66; Raeburn, *Changing Corporate America*; Walters, *All the Rage*.

26. Vaid, *Virtual Equality*, 247.

27. See Joshua Gamson, *Freaks Talk Back: Tabloid Talk Shows and Sexual Nonconformity* (Chicago: University of Chicago Press, 1998).

28. John D'Emilio, "Capitalism and Gay Identity," in *Powers of Desire: The Politics of Sexuality*, ed. Ann Snitow, 100–13 (New York: Monthly Review Press, 1983).

29. Alexandra Chasin, *Selling Out: The Gay and Lesbian Movement Goes to Market* (New York: Palgrave, 2000), 25–26.

30. Katherine Sender, *Business, Not Politics: The Making of the Gay Market* (New York: Columbia University Press, 2004).

31. Duggan, *The Twilight of Equality*, 65.
32. Dylan Rodriguez, "The Political Logic of the Non-Profit Industrial Complex," in *The Revolution Will Not Be Funded: Beyond the Non-Profit Industrial Complex*, ed. Incite! Women of Color Against Violence, 21–40 (Cambridge, MA: South End, 2007).
33. See Smith, "Introduction: The Revolution Will Not Be Funded," in Incite!, ed., *The Revolution Will Not Be Funded*, for an extended discussion of these effects.
34. See, for instance, Darrel Yates Rist, "The Deadly Costs of an Obsession," *Nation*, 13 February 1989; Eric Rofes, "Gay Lib vs. AIDS: Averting Civil War in the 1990s" *OUT/LOOK* 2, no. 4 (1990).
35. See Watney, "The Spectacle of AIDS," in *The Lesbian and Gay Studies Reader*, ed. Henry Abelove, Michele Barale, and David Halperin (New York: Routledge, 1993).
36. See Raeburn, *Changing Corporate America*.
37. See Sharon Kurtz, *Workplace Justice: Organizing Multi-Identity Movements* (Minneapolis: University of Minnesota Press, 2002).
38. See, for instance, Patricia Baker, "Doing Fieldwork in a Canadian Bank: Issues of Gender and Power," *Resources for Feminist Research* 16, no. 4 (1987): 45–47; Kathleen J. Ferraro, "Negotiating Trouble in a Battered Women's Shelter," *Journal of Contemporary Ethnography* 12, no. 3 (1983): 287–306; and Judy Wajcman, *Women in Control: Dilemmas of a Workers Co-operative* (New York: St. Martin's Press, 1983).
39. I note here that this is a controversial method, one that has raised concern for some readers of this work. For similar examples of research involving an intimate partner, see Evelyn Blackwood and Saskia Weiringa, *Female Desires: Same-sex Relations and Transgender Practices across Cultures* (New York: Columbia University Press, 1999).
40. For an extended discussion of grounded theory, see Barney Glaser and Anselm Strauss, *The Discovery of Grounded Theory* (Edison, NJ: Aldine Transaction, 1967).
41. See Mitchell Duneier, *Sidewalk* (New York: Farrar, Straus, and Giroux, 1999).
42. I conducted a total of thirty-one interviews; however, two interviewees served as informants for more than one research site and have been counted twice here.
43. I received IRB approval for my dissertation project while taking a graduate ethnography seminar at UC Santa Barbara. Because this study did not involve sensitive or at-risk populations, and because subjects' identities have been kept confidential, this study qualified for UCSB's abbreviated and expedited Human Subjects protocol. Though the study evolved over time, the salient IRB issues did not change and therefore I did not reapply or apply for a separate protocol for each case study.
44. France Winddance Twine, "Racial Ideologies and Racial Methodologies," in

Racing Research, Researching Race: Methodological Dilemmas in Critical Race Studies, ed. France Winddance Twine and Jonathan W. Warren, 1–34 (New York: New York University Press, 2000).

45. See Martyn Hammersley and Paul Atkinson, *Ethnography: Principles in Practice* (New York: Routledge, 1995), for a summary of these principles.

46. See, for instance, Laura Grindstaff, *The Money Shot: Trash, Class, and the Making of TV Talk Shows* (Chicago: University of Chicago, 2002), 275–88; Twine, "Racial Ideologies and Racial Methodologies"; and Esther Newton, "My Best Informant's Dress: The Erotic Equation in Fieldwork," in *Margaret Mead Made Me Gay: Personal Essays, Public Ideas*, ed. Esther Newton, 243–58 (Durham: Duke University Press, 2000).

47. See Martin F. Manalanson, *Global Divas: Filipino Gay Men in the Diaspora* (Durham: Duke University Press, 2003).

48. See Juana Maria Rodriguez, *Queer Latinidad: Identity Practices, Discursive Spaces* (New York: New York University Press, 2003), 114–52.

49. See Betsy Lucal, "What It Means to Be Gendered Me: Life on the Boundaries of a Dichotomous Gender System," *Gender & Society* 13, no. 6 (1999): 781–97.

50. See, for instance, Newton, "My Best Informant's Dress"; Blackwood and Weiringa, *Female Desires*; see also Ellen Lewin and William Leep, *Out in the Field: Reflections of Lesbian and Gay Anthropologists* (Chicago: University of Illinois Press, 1996), for a general discussion of queer methodologies.

51. Leila Rupp and Verta Taylor, *Drag Queens at the 801 Cabaret* (Chicago: University of Chicago Press, 2003).

Chapter 2

1. See David S. Meyer and Suzanne Staggenborg, "Movements, Countermovements, and the Structure of Political Opportunity," *American Journal of Sociology* 101 (1996): 1628–60.

2. For examples, see Bonilla-Silva, *Racism without Racists*; Coppock, *The Illusions of Post-Feminism*; Duggan, *The Twilight of Equality*; Gordon and Newfield, *Mapping Multiculturalism*; Michaels, *The Trouble with Diversity*.

3. For examples, see Hank Johnston and Bert Klandermans, eds., *Social Movements and Culture* (Minneapolis: University of Minnesota Press, 1995); Jane Mansbridge and Aldon Morris, *Oppositional Consciousness: The Subjective Roots of Social Protest* (Chicago: University of Chicago Press, 2001).

4. See, for instance, Arlene Davila, *Latinos Inc.: The Marketing and Making of a People* (Berkeley: University of California Press, 2001); Walters, *All the Rage*.

5. Duggan, *The Twilight of Equality*; Giroux, *The Terror of Neoliberalism*; see also Harvey, *A Brief History of Neoliberalism*.

6. Duggan, *The Twilight of Equality*, 43.

7. Gray, *Cultural Moves*.

8.   Gray, *Cultural Moves*; See also Bakari Kitwana, *Why White Kids Love Hip Hop: Wangstas, Wiggers, Wannabes, and the New Reality of Race in America* (New York: Basic Civitas Books, 2005).

9.   Gamson, *Freaks Talk Back*.

10. Kurtz, *Workplace Justice,* 36.

11. "Diversity at Verizon," *Verizon*, http://multimedia.verizon.com/diversity/.

12. Kurtz, *Workplace Justice*.

13. See Combahee River Collective, "A Black Feminist Statement," in *Social Perspectives in Lesbian and Gay Studies: A Reader*, ed. Peter M. Nardi and Beth E. Schneider (New York: Routledge, 1998), 521–26; Belinda Robnett, *How Long? How Long? African American Women in the Struggle for Civil Rights* (New York: Oxford University Press, 1997).

14. See bell hooks, *Ain't I a Woman?: Black Women and Feminism* (Boston: South End, 1981); Deborah King, "Multiple Jeopardy," *Signs* 14, no. 11 (1988): 88–111.

15. For this history, see King, "Multiple Jeopardy."

16. King, "Multiple Jeopardy," 45.

17. See Kimberlé Crenshaw, "Mapping the Margins: Intersectionality, Identity Politics, and Violence against Women of Color," *Stanford Law Review*, 43, no. 6 (1991): 1241–99.

18. Allan Berube, "How Gay Stays White and What Kind of White It Stays," in *The Making and Unmaking of Whiteness*, ed. Birgit Rasmussen, Eric Klinenberg, Irene Nexica, and Matt Wray (Durham: Duke University Press, 2001), 234–65.

19. Combahee River Collective, "A Black Feminist Statement."

20. See Patricia Hill Collins, *Black Feminist Thought: Knowledge, Consciousness, and the Politics of Empowerment* (Boston: Unwin Hyman, 1990).

21. Combahee River Collective, "A Black Feminist Statement," 522.

22. Lillian Faderman, *Odd Girls and Twilight Lovers: A History of Lesbian Life in Twentieth-Century America* (New York: Penguin, 1991), 216.

23. See Jill Johnston, *Admission Accomplished: The Lesbian Nation Years (1970–1975)* (London: Serpent's Tail, 1998).

24. Faderman, *Odd Girls and Twilight Lovers*; Johnston, *Admission Accomplished*.

25. Faderman, *Odd Girls and Twilight Lovers*.

26. See, for instance, Angela Davis, *Women, Race, and Class* (New York: Vintage Books, 1983); hooks, *Ain't I a Woman*; Gloria Hull, Patricia Bell Scott, and Barbara Smith, eds., *All the Women Are White, All the Blacks Are Men, Some of Us Are Brave* (Old Westbury, NY: Feminist Press, 1982); Barbara Smith, ed., *Home Girls: A Black Feminist Anthology* (New York: Kitchen Table Women of Color Press, 1983).

27. King, "Multiple Jeopardy."

28. Gloria Anzaldúa, *Borderlands La Frontera: The New Mestiza* (San Francisco: Aunt Lute Books, 1987).

29. Maria Lugones, "Playfulness, 'World'-Traveling, and Loving Perception," in

Making Face, Making Soul/Haciendo Caras: Creative and Critical Perspectives by Feminists of Color, ed. Gloria Anzaldúa (San Francisco: Aunt Lute Books, 1990), 390.

30. Chela Sandoval, "U.S. Third World Feminism: The Theory and Method of Oppositional Consciousness in the Postmodern World," *Genders* 10 (1991): 1–24.

31. Collins, *Black Feminist Thought*.

32. Kurtz, *Workplace Justice*.

33. Patricia Hill Collins, "Toward a New Vision: Race, Class, and Gender as Categories of Analysis and Connection," *Race, Gender & Class* 1, no. 1 (1993): 25–45; Maxine Baca Zinn and Bonnie Thorton Dill, "Theorizing Difference from Multiracial Feminism," *Feminist Studies* 22, no. 2 (1996): 321–31.

34. See Nancy Naples, ed., *Community Activism and Feminist Politics: Organizing across Race, Class, and Gender* (New York: Routledge, 1998).

35. See Myra Marx Ferree and Frederick Miller, "Mobilization and Meaning: Toward an Integration of Social Psychological and Resource Perspectives on Social Movements," *Sociological Inquiry* 55 (1985): 38–6; see also Kurtz, *Workplace Justice*.

36. See Sohera Syeda and Becky Thompson, "Coalition Politics in Organizing for Mumia Abu Jamal," in *Feminism and Antiracism: International Struggles for Justice*, ed. France Winddance Twine and Kathleen Blee (New York: New York University Press, 2001), 193–219.

37. See, for instance, Sandoval, "U.S. Third World Feminism."

38. June Jordan, "Report from the Bahamas," in *Moving towards Home: Political Essays* (London: Virago, 1989), 137ñ46.

39. Chandra Mohanty, " Cartographies of Struggle: Introduction to Third World Women and the Politics of Feminism," in *Third World Women and the Politics of Feminism*, ed. Chandra Talpade Mohanty, Ann Russo, and Lourdes Torres (Bloomington: Indiana University Press, 1991), 1–47.

40. Cherrie Moraga and Gloria Anzaldúa, eds., *This Bridge Called My Back: Writings by Radical Women of Color* (New York: Kitchen Table Women of Color Press, 1981).

41. Gayatri Chakravorty Spivak, "Subaltern Studies: Deconstructing Historiography," in *The Spivak Reader: Selected Works of Gayatri Chakravorty Spivak*, ed. Donna Landry and Gerald Maclean (New York: Routledge, 1996), especially 214–16.

42. Bernice Reagon Johnson, "Coalition Politics: Turning the Century," in *Home Girls: A Black Feminist Anthology*, ed. Barbara Smith (New York: Kitchen Table Women of Color Press, 1983), 356–57.

43. For examples, see Amory Starr, *Naming the Enemy: Anti-Corporate Movements Confront Globalization* (New York: Zed Books, 2000).

44. See Armstrong, *Forging Gay Identities*.

45. Carolyn Howe, "Gender, Race, and Community Activism: Competing Strategies in the Struggle for Public Education," in *Community Activism and Feminist Politics: Organizing across Race, Class, and Gender*, ed. Nancy Naples (New York: Routledge, 1998).

46. Brett Stockdill, "Forging a Multidimensional Oppositional Consciousness: Lessons from Community-Based AIDS Activism," in *Oppositional Consciousness: The Subjective Roots of Social Protest*, ed. Jane Mansbridge and Aldon Morris (Chicago: University of Chicago Press, 2001).

47. See, for instance, Robnett, *How Long? How Long?*; Taylor, "Emotions and Identity in Women's Self-Help Movements," in *Self, Identity, and Social Movements*, ed. Timothy Owens, Sheldon Stryker, and Robert White (Minneapolis: University of Minnesota Press, 2000); Silke Roth, "Developing Working Class Feminism: A Biographical Approach to Social Movement Participation," in Owens, Stryker, and White, eds., *Self, Identity, and Social Movements*; Stockdill, "Forging a Multidimensional Oppositional Consciousness."

48. For examples, see John A. Adams, "The Mainstream Environmental Movement: Predominantly White Memberships Are Not Defensible," *EPA Journal* 18, no. 1 (1992): 25–27; Dana Alston, ed., *We Speak for Ourselves: Social Justice, Race, and Environment* (Washington: Panos Institute, 1990); Amory Starr, "Is the North American Anti-Globalization Movement Racist? Critical Reflections," in *Fighting Identities: Race, Religion, and Nationalism—Socialist Register*, ed. Leo Panitch and Colin Leys (New York: Monthly Review Press, 2003).

49. See, for instance, Nancie Caraway, *Segregated Sisterhood: Racism and the Politics of American Feminism* (Knoxville: University of Tennessee Press, 1991); Ruth Frankenberg, *White Women, Race Matters: The Social Construction of Whiteness* (Minneapolis: University of Minnesota Press, 1993); Peggy McIntosh. "White Privilege and Male Privilege: A Personal Account of Coming to See Correspondences through Work in Women's Studies," in *Race, Class, and Gender*, ed. Margaret Andersen and Patricia Hill Collins (Belmont, CA: Wadsworth, 1992); Elizabeth Spelman, *Inessential Woman: Problems of Exclusion in Feminist Thought* (Boston: Beacon, 1988).

50. See Wendy Simmonds, *Abortion at Work: Ideology and Practice in a Feminist Clinic* (New Brunswick: Rutgers University Press, 1996); Scott, "From Race Cognizance to Racism Cognizance: Dilemmas in Antiracist Activism in California," in Twine and Blee, eds., *Feminism and Antiracism*.

51. See Scott, "Creating Partnerships for Change: Alliances and Betrayals in the Racial Politics of Two Feminist Organizations," *Gender & Society* 12, no. 4 (1998):414.

52. Scott, "From Race Cognizance to Racism Cognizance."

53. See, for instance, Bonilla-Silva, *Racism without Racists*; George Lipsitz, *The*

Possessive Investment in Whiteness: How White People Profit from Identity Politics (Philadelphia: Temple University Press, 1998).

54. Kurtz, *Workplace Justice.*
55. Starr, "Is the Anti-Globalization Movement Racist?"; Ellen Scott, "Beyond Tokenism: The Making of Racially Diverse Organizations," *Social Problems* 52, no. 2 (2005): 232–54.
56. Scott, "Beyond Tokenism."
57. Susan Ostrander, "Gender and Race in a Pro-Feminist, Progressive, Mixed-Gender, Mixed-Race Organization," *Gender & Society* 13, no. 5 (1999): 628–42.
58. Stockdill, "Forging a Multidimensional Oppositional Consciousness."
59. Stockdill, "Forging a Multidimensional Oppositional Consciousness," 235.
60. Stockdill, "Forging a Multidimensional Oppositional Consciousness," 233.
61. See, for instance, Joshua Gamson, "Must Identity Movements Self-Destruct?: A Queer Dilemma," in *Queer Theory/Sociology*, ed. Steven Seidman (New York: Blackwell, 1996); Stephen Valocchi, "Not Yet Queer Enough: The Lessons of Queer Theory for the Sociology of Gender and Sexuality," *Gender & Society* 19, no. 6 (2005): 750–70; Steven Seidman, ed., *Queer Theory/Sociology* (New York: Blackwell, 1996).
62. Mary McIntosh, "The Homosexual Role," *Social Problems* 16 (1968): 182–92.
63. Michael Omi and Howard Winant, *Racial Formation in the United States: From the 1960s to the 1990s* (New York: Routledge, 1994).
64. Judith Lorber, *Paradoxes of Gender* (New Haven: Yale University Press, 1995).
65. Julie Bettie, *Women without Class: Girls, Race, and Identity* (Berkeley: University of California Press, 2002).
66. Corber and Valocchi, "Introduction."
67. Judith Butler, *Gender Trouble: Feminism and the Subversion of Identity* (New York: Routledge, 1990).
68. Norma Alarcon, "Conjugating Subjects in the Age of Multiculturalism," in *Mapping Multiculturalism*, ed. Avery F. Gordon and Christopher Newfield (Minneapolis: University of Minnesota Press, 1996).
69. Corber and Valocchi, "Introduction," 10.
70. Lipsitz, *The Possessive Investment in Whiteness.*
71. Michel Foucault, *History of Sexuality Part I* (New York: Vintage Books, 1978).
72. Gordon and Newfield, "Introduction," 5–6.
73. Frank Dobbin and John Sutton, "The Strength of a Weak State: The Rights Revolution and the Rise of Human Resources Management Divisions," *American Journal of Sociology* 99 (1998): 396–429.
74. Gordon, "The Work of Corporate Culture."
75. "Diversity at Verizon," *Verizon*, http://multimedia.verizon.com/diversity/.
76. "Diversity at Verizon."
77. Raeburn, *Changing Corporate America.*

78. See, for instance, Duggan, *The Twilight of Equality*; Gordon, "The Work of Corporate Culture."

79. See Artz and Murphy, *Cultural Hegemony in the United States.*

80. See Carlos Cortes, *The Children Are Watching: How the Media Teach about Diversity* (New York: Teachers College Press, 2000).

81. See, for instance, Dobbin, "The Business of Social Movements," in *Passionate Politics: Emotions and Social Movements*, ed. Jeff Goodwin, James Jasper, and Francesca Polletta (Chicago: University of Chicago Press, 2001); Raeburn, *Changing Corporate America.*

82. José Esteban Muñoz, *Disidentifications: Queers of Color and the Performance of Politics* (Minneapolis: University of Minnesota Press, 1999).

83. Judith Halberstam, "Notes on Failure," keynote address at the University of California, Irvine, "Failure: Ethics and Aesthetics" conference, 2006.

Chapter 3

1. See Helen Hemphill and Ray Haines, *Discrimination, Harassment, and the Failure of Diversity Training* (New York: Quorum Books, 1997).

2. For a discussion of the growth of this industry, see Margaret Stockdale and Fay Crosby, *The Psychology and Management of Workplace Diversity* (New York: Blackwell, 2003); Hemphill and Haines, *Discrimination, Harassment, and the Failure of Diversity Training*; Dobbin and Sutton, "The Strength of a Weak State."

3. Aronowitz, *The Politics of Identity*, quoted in Kurtz, *Workplace Justice*, 47.

4. See, for instance, Pierre Bourdieu, *Distinction: A Social Critique of the Judgment of Taste* (Cambridge: Harvard University Press, 1984); Bettie, *Women without Class*; Julia Penelope, ed., *Out of the Class Closet: Lesbians Speak* (Freedom, CA: Crossing Press, 1994).

5. See Bill Keller, *Class Matters* (New York: Times Books, 2005); Bettie, *Women without Class.*

6. Bourdieu, *Distinction.*

7. See Donatella della Porta and Mario Diani, *Social Movements: An Introduction* (Oxford: Blackwell, 1999), especially 41.

8. All individuals' names have been changed for purposes of confidentiality.

9. See Dudley Clendinen and Adam Nagourney, *Out for Good: The Struggle to Build a Gay Rights Movement in America* (New York: Simon & Schuster, 1999).

10. Clendinen and Nagourney, *Out for Good*, 352–53.

11. Clendinen and Nagourney, *Out for Good*, 352–53.

12. For more discussion of this trend, see Vaid, *Virtual Equality.*

13. Duggan, *The Twilight of Equality.*

14. Halberstam, *In a Queer Time and Place*, 10.

15. Rupp and Taylor, *Drag Queens at the 801 Cabaret*. Thank you also to Susana Pena for clarifying this point.

16. CSW sponsors other LGBT charitable events, supports a low-income housing project for people with HIV/AIDS, and makes small grants to other nonprofit organizations in exchange for their volunteers' labor at the pride festival.

17. A second woman, Donna, was added to the board approximately one month after I began research.

18. The decision to remove Tom from the board was made unanimously in response to information provided by CSW staff suggesting that he had violated several of CSW's bylaws and procedures (e.g. lost petty cash receipts, unjustified expenses, etc.).

19. The board consisted of five members after the addition of Chad, an elder gay white male leather activist, whom the board voted to appoint in August.

20. I was a graduate student at the time of this study, a mark of my own class mobility and certainly a measure of my cultural capital within the academy and elsewhere. However, as a young student new to Los Angeles, it was also clear that I had few of the skills and connections important to the reporters, the West Hollywood City Council, and others interested professionalizing CSW.

21. None of the board members with whom I have since spoken about this meeting could recall the specific use of the word "elitist"; however, I had pointedly described the new group as members of a gay and lesbian "elite." It is likely that prospective board members conflated these terms; however, they have very different meanings for me (i.e., the former implies an ideology of superiority; the latter references cultural capital or status).

22. Neither of the women of color spoke about being accused of elitism.

23. West Hollywood has a large Russian community with a growing business and political power base.

24. Bourdieu, *Distinction*, 372, 7.

25. Bourdieu, *Distinction*, 7.

Chapter 4

1. Boykin, "Where Rhetoric Meets Reality."

2. Armstrong, *Forging Gay Identities*.

3. See Stockdill, "Forging a Multidimensional Oppositional Consciousness."

4. Raeburn, *Changing Corporate America*.

5. Ruth Frankenberg, "Cracks in the Façade: Whiteness and the Construction of 9/11," *Social Identities* 11, no. 6 (2005): 553–71; Steven Gold, "From Jim Crow to Racial Hegemony : Evolving Explanations of Racial Hierarchy," *Ethnic and Racial Studies* 27, no. 6 (2004): 951–68; Lipsitz, *The Possessive Investment in Whiteness*; Peter McLaren, *Revolutionary Multiculturalism: Pedagogies of Dissent for the New Millennium* (Boulder: Westview, 1997).

6. McLaren, *Revolutionary Multiculturalism,* 8.

7. See, for instance, Roderick A. Ferguson, *Aberrations in Black: Toward a Queer of Color Critique* (Minneapolis: University of Minnesota Press, 2004); Ruth Frankenberg, "The Mirage of Unmarked Whiteness," in *The Making and Unmaking of Whiteness,* ed. Birgit Rasmussen, Eric Klinenberg, Irene Nexica, and Matt Wray (Durham: Duke University Press, 2001); Muñoz, *Disidentifications.*

8. See Joan Acker, "Hierarchies, Jobs, and Bodies: A Theory of Gendered Organizations," *Gender & Society* 4 (1990): 139–58; Dana Britton, "The Epistemology of the Gendered Organization," *Gender & Society* 14, no. 3 (2000): 418–34.

9. See Armstrong, *Forging Gay Identities*"; Dana Y. Takagi, "Maiden Voyage: Excursion into Sexuality and Identity Politics in Asian America," *Amerasia Journal* 20, no. 1 (1993): 1–17.

10. See Vaid, *Virtual Equality.*

11. For more discussion of the Center's early history, see Clendinen and Nagourney, *Out for Good.*

12. See Moira Kenney, *Mapping Gay L.A.: The Intersection of Place and Politics* (Philadelphia: Temple University Press, 2001).

13. Mimi Avins, "Room for Change," *Los Angeles Times,* 3 August 1999.

14. Avins, "Room for Change."

15. In 2002, Claire resigned from the Center, moved to Oregon, and returned to management consulting.

16. These employees were considered "donors" and received tickets to attend one of the Center's gala events.

17. See Raeburn, *Changing Corporate America.*

18. Vaid, *Virtual Equality,* 288.

19. Vaid, *Virtual Equality,* 298–99.

20. See Kenney, *Mapping Gay L.A.*

21. Gordon, "The Work of Corporate Culture."

22. Collins, *Black Feminist Thought.*

Chapter 5

1. Arturo Madrid, "Diversity and Its Discontents," in *The Meaning of Difference: American Constructions of Race, Sex and Gender, Social Class, and Sexual Orientation,* ed. Karen Rosenblum and Toni-Michell Travis (New York: McGraw Hill, 2000), 229.

2. Essex Hemphil, ed., *Brother to Brother: New Writings by Black Gay Men* (Toronto: Hushion House, 1991), xix.

3. See, for instance, Brett Stockdill, *Activism against AIDS: At the Intersections of Sexuality, Race, Gender, and Class* (Boulder: Lynne Rienner, 2003).

4. See, for instance, Faderman, *Odd Girls and Twilight Lovers*; Beth E. Schneider and Nancy Stoller, eds., *Women Resisting AIDS: Feminist Strategies of Empowerment* (Philadelphia: Temple University Press, 1994).

5. See Ruth Schwartz, "New Alliances, Strange Bedfellows: Lesbians, Gay Men, AIDS," in *Sisters, Sexperts, Queers: Beyond the Lesbian Nation*, ed. Arlene Stein (New York: Penguin, 1993); Nancy Stoller, "From Feminism to Polymorphous Activism: Lesbians in AIDS Organizations," in *In Changing Times: Gay Men and Lesbians Encounter HIV/AIDS*, ed. Martin Levine, Peter Nardi, and John Gagnon (Chicago: University of Chicago Press, 1997).

6. Dennis Altman, *Power and Community: Organizational and Cultural Responses to AIDS* (London: Taylor & Francis, 1994).

7. Rist, "The Deadly Costs of an Obsession"; Rofes, "Gay Lib vs. AIDS."

8. Rofes, "Gay Lib vs. AIDS"; Vaid, *Virtual Equality*.

9. See Vaid, *Virtual Equality*.

10. See the Gay and Lesbian Medical Association's *Healthy People 2010: A Companion Document for Lesbian, Gay, Bisexual, and Transgender Health* (San Francisco: Gay and Lesbian Medical Association, 2000).

11. Clendinen and Nagourney, *Out for Good*; Vaid, *Virtual Equality*.

12. Gay and Lesbian Medical Association, *Healthy People 2010*.

13. See Stockdill, *Activism against AIDS*.

14. See Schwartz, "New Alliances, Strange Bedfellows."

15. See Stoller, "From Feminism to Polymorphous Activism."

16. Rafael Jorge Diaz, "Latino Gay Men and Psycho-Cultural Barriers to AIDS Prevention," in *In Changing Times: Gay Men and Lesbians Encounter HIV and AIDS*, ed. Martin Levine, Peter Nardi, and John Gagnon (Chicago: University of Chicago Press, 1997).

17. My goal here is to not to deny the possibility of this kind of sexual fluidity, but to highlight that lesbian inclusion was dependent upon their sexual involvement with gay men in a way that was not true in reverse (i.e., gay men faced sufficient risk without having sex with women).

18. Centers for Disease Control and Prevention, "HIV/AIDS among Women Who Have Sex with Women," www.cdc.gov/hiv/topics/women/resources/factsheets/wsw.htm.

19. Kathleen Dolan, *Lesbian Women and Sexual Health: The Social Construction of Risk and Susceptibility* (Binghampton: Haworth, 2005); Stockdill, *Activism against AIDS*.

20. Halberstam, *In a Queer Time and Place*, 10.

Chapter 6

1. Halberstam, *In a Queer Time and Place*, 4.

2. Daniel Cortese, *Are We Thinking Straight? The Politics of Straightness in a Lesbian and Gay Social Movement Organization* (New York: Routledge, 2006).

3. Duggan, *The Twilight of Equality*, 50.

4. Eng, Halberstam, and Muñoz, "Introduction," 1

5. Eng, Halberstam, and Muñoz, "Introduction," 4

6. Rodriguez, *Queer Latinidad*, 6–7.

7. Alarcon, "Conjugating Subjects in the Age of Multiculturalism," 127–48.

8. Sandoval, "Feminist Forms of Agency and Oppositional Consciousness: U.S. Third World Feminist Criticism," in *Provoking Agents: Gender and Agency in Theory and Practice*, ed. Judith Kegan Gardiner (Urbana: University of Illinois Press, 1995), 208–26.

9. Muñoz, *Disidentifications*, 11–12.

10. Muñoz, *Disidentifications*, 19.

11. Muñoz, *Disidentifications*, 9.

12. Raeburn, *Changing Corporate America*, 217–18.

13. D'Emilio, "Capitalism and Gay Identity."

14. Janet Jakobsen, "Sex + Freedom = Regulation: Why?" *Social Text* 84–85, vol. 23, nos. 3–4 (2005): 285–308.

Bibliography

Acker, Joan. "Hierarchies, Jobs, and Bodies: A Theory of Gendered Organizations."
   Gender & Society 4 (1990): 139–58.
Adams, John A. "The Mainstream Environmental Movement: Predominantly White
   Memberships Are Not Defensible." *EPA Journal* 18, no. 1 (1992): 25–27.
Alarcon, Norma. "Conjugating Subjects in the Age of Multiculturalism." In
   Mapping Multiculturalism, edited by Avery F. Gordon and Christopher
   Newfield, 127–48. Minneapolis: University of Minnesota Press, 1996.
Alston, Dana, ed. *We Speak for Ourselves: Social Justice, Race, and Environment.*
   Washington: Panos Institute, 1990.
Altman, Dennis. *Power and Community: Organizational and Cultural Responses to
   AIDS.* London: Taylor & Francis, 1994.
Anzaldúa, Gloria. "Bridge, Drawbridge, Sandbar, or Island: Lesbians-of-Color
   Hacienda Alianzas." In *Bridges of Power: Women's Multicultural Alliances*, edited
   by Lisa Albrecht and Rose M. Brewer, 216–31. Philadelphia: New Society, 1990.
———. *Borderlands La Frontera: The New Mestiza.* San Francisco: Aunt Lute
   Books, 1987.
Armstrong, Elizabeth. *Forging Gay Identities: Organizing Sexuality in San Francisco,
   1950–1994.* Chicago: University of Chicago Press, 2002.
Aronowitz, Stanley. *The Politics of Identity: Class, Culture, and Social Movements.*
   New York: Routledge, 1992.
Artz, Len, and Bren Ortega Murphy. *Cultural Hegemony in the United States.*
   Thousand Oaks, CA: Sage, 2000.
Avins, Mimi. "Room for Change." *Los Angeles Times*, 3 August 1999, E1.
Baca Zinn, Maxine, and Bonnie Thorton Dill. "Theorizing Difference from
   Multiracial Feminism." *Feminist Studies* 22, no. 2 (1996): 321–31.
Baker, Patricia. "Doing Fieldwork in a Canadian Bank: Issues of Gender and
   Power." *Resources for Feminist Research* 16, no. 4 (1987): 45–47.
Berube, Allan. "How Gay Stays White and What Kind of White It Stays." In

The Making and Unmaking of Whiteness, edited by Birgit Rasmussen, Eric Klinenberg, Irene Nexica, and Matt Wray, 234–65. Durham: Duke University Press, 2001.

Bettie, Julie. *Women without Class: Girls, Race, and Identity.* Berkeley: University of California Press, 2002.

Blackwood, Evelyn, and Saskia Weiringa. *Female Desires: Same-sex Relations and Transgender Practices across Cultures.* New York: Columbia University Press, 1999.

Bonilla-Silva, Eduardo. *Racism without Racists: Color-Blind Racism and the Persistence of Racial Inequality in the United States.* New York: Rowman and Littlefield, 2003.

Bourdieu, Pierre. *Distinction: A Social Critique of the Judgment of Taste.* Cambridge: Harvard University Press, 1984.

Boykin, Keith. "Where Rhetoric Meets Reality: The Role of Black Lesbians and Gays in 'Queer' Politics." In *The Politics of Gay Rights*, edited by Craig Rimmerman, Kenneth Wald, and Clyde Wilcox, 79–96. Chicago: University of Chicago Press, 2000.

Britton, Dana. "The Epistemology of the Gendered Organization." *Gender & Society* 14, no. 3 (2000): 418–34.

Butler, Judith. *Gender Trouble: Feminism and the Subversion of Identity.* New York: Routledge, 1999.

Caraway, Nancie. *Segregated Sisterhood: Racism and the Politics of American Feminism.* Knoxville: University of Tennessee Press, 1991.

Centers for Disease Control and Prevention. "HIV/AIDS among Women Who Have Sex with Women." http://www.cdc.gov/hiv/topics/women/resources/factsheets/wsw.htm.

Chasin, Alexandra. *Selling Out: The Gay and Lesbian Movement Goes to Market.* New York: Palgrave, 2000.

Clendinen, Dudley, and Adam Nagourney. *Out for Good: The Struggle to Build a Gay Rights Movement in America.* New York: Simon & Schuster, 1999.

Collins, Patricia Hill. *Black Feminist Thought: Knowledge, Consciousness, and the Politics of Empowerment.* Boston: Unwin Hyman, 1990.

———. "Toward a New Vision: Race, Class, and Gender as Categories of Analysis and Connection." *Race, Gender & Class* 1, no. 1 (1993): 25–45.

Combahee River Collective. "A Black Feminist Statement." In *Social Perspectives in Lesbian and Gay Studies: A Reader*, edited by Peter M. Nardi and Beth E. Schneider, 521–26. New York: Routledge, 1998.

Coppock, Viki. *The Illusions of Post-Feminism.* London: Taylor & Francis, 1995.

Corber, Robert, and Stephen Valocchi. "Introduction." In *Queer Studies: An Interdisciplinary Reader*, edited by Robert J. Corber and Stephen Valocchi, 1–20. New York: Blackwell, 2003.

Cortes, Carlos. *The Children Are Watching: How the Media Teach about Diversity.* New York: Teachers College Press, 2000.

Cortese, Daniel. *Are We Thinking Straight?: The Politics of Straightness in a Lesbian and Gay Social Movement Organization.* New York: Routledge, 2006.

Cotter, Jennifer. "Martha Stewart: Global Capitalist Behinds the Domestic Label." *Red Critique: Marxist Theory and Critique of the Contemporary* 5 (July/August 2002). Available at http://redcritique.org/JulyAugust02/marthastewartglobalcapitalist.htm.

Cousino, Niki, Julie Wymann, Sarah Lewison, et al., producers. *Sisterhood™: Hyping the Female Market.* Video. Paper Tiger Television, New York. 1993.

Crenshaw, Kimberlé. "Mapping the Margins: Intersectionality, Identity Politics, and Violence against Women of Color." *Stanford Law Review*, 43, no. 6 (1991): 1241–99.

Davila, Arlene. *Latinos Inc.: The Marketing and Making of a People.* Berkeley: University of California Press, 2001.

Davis, Angela. *Women, Race, and Class.* New York: Vintage Books, 1983.

della Porta, Donatella, and Mario Diani. *Social Movements: An Introduction.* Oxford: Blackwell, 1999.

D'Emilio, John. "Capitalism and Gay Identity." In *Powers of Desire: The Politics of Sexuality*, edited by Ann Snitow, 100–13. New York: Monthly Review Press, 1983.

Diaz, Rafael Jorge. "Latino Gay Men and Psycho-Cultural Barriers to AIDS Prevention." In *In Changing Times: Gay Men and Lesbians Encounter HIV and AIDS*, edited by Martin Levine, Peter Nardi, and John Gagnon, 221–44. Chicago: University of Chicago Press, 1997.

Dobbin, Frank. "The Business of Social Movements." In *Passionate Politics: Emotions and Social Movements*, edited by Jeff Goodwin, James Jasper, and Francesca Polletta, 74–82. Chicago: University of Chicago Press, 2001.

Dobbin, Frank and John Sutton. "The Strength of a Weak State: The Rights Revolution and the Rise of Human Resources Management Divisions." *American Journal of Sociology* 99 (1998): 396–429.

Dolan, Kathleen. *Lesbian Women and Sexual Health: The Social Construction of Risk and Susceptibility.* Binghampton: Haworth, 2005.

Duggan, Lisa. *The Twilight of Equality?: Neoliberalism, Cultural Politics, and the Attack on Democracy.* Boston: Beacon, 2004.

Duneier, Mitchell. *Sidewalk.* New York: Farrar, Straus, and Giroux, 1999.

Eng, David, Judith Halberstam, and Jose Esteban Munoz, eds. "Introduction: What's Queer about Queer Studies Now?" Special Issue. *Social Text* 84–85, vol. 23, nos. 3–4 (2005): 1–18.

Faderman, Lillian. *Odd Girls and Twilight Lovers: A History of Lesbian Life in Twentieth-Century America.* New York: Penguin, 1991.

Ferguson, Roderick. *Aberrations in Black: Toward a Queer of Color Critique.* Minneapolis: University of Minnesota Press, 2004.

Ferraro, Kathleen J. "Negotiating Trouble in a Battered Women's Shelter." *Journal of Contemporary Ethnography* 12, no. 3 (1983): 287–306.

Ferree, Myra Marx, and Frederick Miller. "Mobilization and Meaning: Toward an Integration of Social Psychological and Resource Perspectives on Social Movements." *Sociological Inquiry* 55 (1985): 38–61.

Foucault, Michel. *History of Sexuality Part I.* New York: Vintage Books, 1978.

Frankenberg, Ruth. "Cracks in the Façade: Whiteness and the Construction of 9/11." *Social Identities* 11, no. 6 (2005): 553–71.

———. "The Mirage of an Unmarked Whiteness." In *The Making and Unmaking of Whiteness,* edited by Birgit Rasmussen, Eric Klinenberg, Irene Nexica, and Matt Wray, 72–96. Durham: Duke University Press, 2001.

———. *White Women, Race Matters: The Social Construction of Whiteness.* Minneapolis: University of Minnesota Press, 1993.

Gamson, Joshua. *Freaks Talk Back: Tabloid Talk Shows and Sexual Nonconformity.* Chicago: University of Chicago Press, 1998.

———. "Must Identity Movements Self-Destruct?: A Queer Dilemma." In *Queer Theory/Sociology,* edited by Steven Seidman, 395–420. New York: Blackwell, 1996.

Gay and Lesbian Medical Association. *Healthy People 2010: A Companion Document for Lesbian, Gay, Bisexual, and Transgender Health.* San Francisco: Gay and Lesbian Medical Association, 2000.

Glaser, Barney, and Anselm Strauss. *The Discovery of Grounded Theory.* Edison, NJ: Aldine Transaction, 1967.

Giroux, Henry. *The Terror of Neoliberalism: Authoritatianism and the Eclipse of Democracy.* Boulder: Paradigm, 2004.

Gold, Steven. "From Jim Crow to Racial Hegemony: Evolving Explanations of Racial Hierarchy." *Ethnic and Racial Studies* 27, no. 6 (2004): 951–68.

Gordon, Avery. "The Work of Corporate Culture: Diversity Management." *Social Text* 44, vol. 13, no. 3 (1995): 3–30.

Gordon, Avery, and Christopher Newfield. "Introduction." In *Mapping Multiculturalism,* edited by Avery F. Gordon and Christopher Newfield, 1–18. Minneapolis: University of Minnesota Press, 1996.

Gray, Herman. *Cultural Moves: African Americans and the Politics of Representation.* Berkeley: University of California Press, 2005.

Grindstaff, Laura. *The Money Shot: Trash, Class, and the Making of TV Talk Shows.* Chicago: University of Chicago, 2002.

Halberstam, Judith. *In a Queer Time and Place: Transgender Bodies, Subcultural Lives.* New York: New York University Press, 2005.

———. "Notes on Failure." Keynote address at the University of California, Irvine, "Failure: Ethics and Aesthetics" Conference. Irvine, 2006.

Hammersley, Martyn, and Paul Atkinson. *Ethnography: Principles in Practice*. New York: Routledge, 1995.

Harvey, David. *A Brief History of Neoliberalism*. Oxford: Oxford University Press, 2005.

Hemphil, Essex, ed. *Brother to Brother: New Writings by Black Gay Men*. Toronto: Hushion House, 1991.

Hemphill, Helen, and Ray Haines. *Discrimination, Harassment, and the Failure of Diversity Training*. New York: Quorum Books, 1997.

Herek, Gregory. "Gender Gaps in Public Opinion about Lesbians and Gay Men." *Public Opinion Quarterly* 66 (2002): 40–66.

hooks, bell. *Ain't I a Woman?: Black Women and Feminism*. Boston: South End, 1981.

Howe, Carolyn. "Gender, Race, and Community Activism: Competing Strategies in the Struggle for Public Education." In *Community Activism and Feminist Politics: Organizing across Race, Class, and Gender*, edited by Nancy Naples, 237–56. New York: Routledge, 1998.

Hull, Gloria, Patricia Bell Scott, and Barbara Smith, eds. *All the Women Are White, All the Blacks Are Men, Some of Us Are Brave*. Old Westbury, NY: Feminist Press, 1982.

Jakobsen, Janet. "Sex + Freedom = Regulation: Why?" *Social Text* 84–85, vol. 23, nos. 3–4 (2005): 285–308.

Johnston, Hank, and Bert Klandermans, eds. *Social Movements and Culture*. Minneapolis: University of Minnesota Press, 1995.

Johnston, Jill. *Admission Accomplished: The Lesbian Nation Years (1970–1975)*. London: Serpent's Tail, 1998.

Jordan, June. "Report from the Bahamas." In *Moving towards Home: Political Essays*, 137ñ46. London: Virago, 1989.

Keller, Bill. *Class Matters*. New York: Times Books, 2005.

Kenney, Moira. *Mapping Gay L.A.: The Intersection of Place and Politics*. Philadelphia: Temple University Press, 2001.

King, Deborah. "Multiple Jeopardy." *Signs* 14, no. 11 (1988): 88–111.

Kitwana, Bakari. *Why White Kids Love Hip Hop: Wangstas, Wiggers, Wannabes, and the New Reality of Race in America*. New York: Basic Civitas Books, 2005.

Kurtz, Sharon. *Workplace Justice: Organizing Multi-Identity Movements*. Minneapolis: University of Minnesota Press, 2002.

Levy, Ariel. *Female Chauvinist Pigs: Women and the Rise of Raunch Culture*. New York: Free Press, 2005.

Lewin, Ellen and William Leap. "Introduction." In *Out in the Field: Reflections of Lesbian and Gay Anthropologists*, edited by Ellen Lewin and William Leep, 1–30. Chicago: University of Illinois Press, 1996.

Lipsitz, George. *The Possessive Investment in Whiteness: How White People Profit from Identity Politics*. Philadelphia: Temple University Press, 1998.

Lorber, Judith. *Paradoxes of Gender*. New Haven: Yale University Press, 1995.

Lucal, Betsy. "What It Means to Be Gendered Me: Life on the Boundaries of a Dichotomous Gender System." *Gender & Society* 13, no. 6 (1999): 781–97.

Lugones, Maria. "Playfulness, 'World'-Traveling, and Loving Perception." In *Making Face, Making Soul/Haciendo Caras: Creative and Critical Perspectives by Feminists of Color*, edited by Gloria Anzaldua, 390. San Francisco: Aunt Lute Books, 1990.

Madrid, Arturo. "Diversity and Its Discontents." In *The Meaning of Difference: American Constructions of Race, Sex and Gender, Social Class, and Sexual Orientation*, edited by Karen Rosenblum and Toni-Michell Travis, 224–30. New York: McGraw Hill, 2000.

Manalanson, Martin F. *Global Divas: Filipino Gay Men in the Diaspora.* Durham: Duke University Press, 2003.

Mansbridge, Jane, and Aldon Morris. *Oppositional Consciousness: The Subjective Roots of Social Protest.* Chicago: University of Chicago Press, 2001.

McLaren, Peter. *Revolutionary Multiculturalism: Pedagogies of Dissent for the New Millennium.* Boulder: Westview, 1997.

McIntosh, Mary. "The Homosexual Role." *Social Problems* 16 (1968): 182–92.

McIntosh, Peggy. "White Privilege and Male Privilege: A Personal Account of Coming to See Correspondences through Work in Women's Studies." In *Race, Class, and Gender*, edited by Margaret Andersen and Patricia Hill Collins, 70–81. Belmont, CA: Wadsworth, 1992.

Meyer, David S., and Suzanne Staggenborg. "Movements, Countermovements, and the Structure of Political Opportunity." *American Journal of Sociology* 101 (1996): 1628–60.

Michaels, Walter Benn. *The Trouble with Diversity: How We Learned to Love Identity and Ignore Inequality.* New York: Metropolitan Books, 2006.

Mohanty, Chandra. "Cartographies of Struggle: Introduction to Third World Women and the Politics of Feminism." In *Third World Women and the Politics of Feminism*, edited by Chandra Talpade Mohanty, Ann Russo, and Lourdes Torres, 1–47. Bloomington: Indiana University Press, 1991.

Moraga, Cherrie and Gloria Anzaldua, eds. *This Bridge Called My Back: Writings by Radical Women of Color.* New York: Kitchen Table Women of Color Press, 1981.

Muñoz, José Esteban. *Disidentifications: Queers of Color and the Performance of Politics.* Minneapolis: University of Minnesota Press, 1999.

Naples, Nancy, ed. *Community Activism and Feminist Politics: Organizing across Race, Class, and Gender.* New York: Routledge, 1998.

Newton, Esther. "My Best Informant's Dress: The Erotic Equation in Fieldwork." In *Margaret Mead Made Me Gay: Personal Essays, Public Ideas*, edited by E. Newton, 243–58. Durham: Duke University Press, 2000.

Omi, Michael, and Howard Winant. *Racial Formation in the United States: From the 1960s to the 1990s.* New York: Routledge, 1994.

Ostrander, Susan. "Gender and Race in a Pro-Feminist, Progressive, Mixed-Gender, Mixed-Race Organization." *Gender & Society* 13, no. 5 (1999): 628–42.

Penelope, Julia, ed. *Out of the Class Closet: Lesbians Speak*. Freedom, CA: Crossing Press, 1994.

Raeburn, Nicole. *Changing Corporate America from the Inside Out: Lesbian and Gay Workplace Rights*. Minneapolis: University of Minnesota Press, 2004.

Reagon Johnson, Bernice. "Coalition Politics: Turning the Century." In *Home Girls: A Black Feminist Anthology*, edited by Barbara Smith, 356–68. New York: Kitchen Table Women of Color Press, 1983.

Rist, Darrel Yates. "The Deadly Costs of an Obsession." *Nation*, 13 February 1989.

Robnett, Belinda. *How Long? How Long? African American Women in the Struggle for Civil Rights*. New York: Oxford University Press, 1997.

Rodriguez, Dylan. "The Political Logic of the Non-Profit Industrial Complex." In *The Revolution Will Not Be Funded: Beyond the Non-Profit Industrial Complex*, edited by Incite! Women of Color Against Violence, 21–40. Cambridge, MA: South End, 2007.

Rodriguez, Juana Maria. *Queer Latinidad: Identity Practices, Discursive Spaces*. New York: New York University Press, 2003.

Rofes, Eric. "Gay Lib vs. AIDS: Averting Civil War in the 1990s" *OUT/LOOK* 2, no. 4 (1990).

Roth, Silke. "Developing Working Class Feminism: A Biographical Approach to Social Movement Participation." In *Self, Identity, and Social Movements*, edited by Timothy Owens, Sheldon Stryker, and Robert White, 300–23. Minneapolis: University of Minnesota Press, 2000.

Rupp, Leila, and Verta Taylor. *The Drag Queens at the 801 Cabaret*. Chicago: University of Chicago Press, 2003.

Sandoval, Chela. "Feminist Forms of Agency and Oppositional Consciousness: U.S. Third World Feminist Criticism." In *Provoking Agents: Gender and Agency in Theory and Practice*, edited by Judith Kegan Gardiner, 208–26. Urbana: University of Illinois Press, 1995.

———. "U.S. Third World Feminism: The Theory and Method of Oppositional Consciousness in the Postmodern World." *Genders* 10 (1991): 1–24.

Schneider, Beth E., and Nancy Stoller, eds. *Women Resisting AIDS: Feminist Strategies of Empowerment*. Philadelphia: Temple University Press, 1994.

Schwartz, Ruth. "New Alliances, Strange Bedfellows: Lesbians, Gay Men, AIDS." In *Sisters, Sexperts, Queers: Beyond the Lesbian Nation*, edited by Arlene Stein, 230–44. New York: Penguin, 1993.

Scott, Ellen. "Beyond Tokenism: The Making of Racially Diverse Organizations." *Social Problems* 52, no. 2 (2005): 232–54.

———. "Creating Partnerships for Change: Alliances and Betrayals in the Racial Politics of Two Feminist Organizations." *Gender & Society* 12, no. 4 (1998): 400–23.

———. "From Race Cognizance to Racism Cognizance: Dilemmas in Antiracist Activism in California." In *Feminism and Antiracism: International Struggles for Justice*, edited by France Winndance Twine and Kathleen Blee, 125–49. New York: New York University Press, 2001.

Seidman, Steven, ed. *Queer Theory/Sociology*. New York: Blackwell, 1996.

Sender, Katherine. *Business, Not Politics: The Making of the Gay Market*. New York: Columbia University Press, 2004.

Simmonds, Wendy. *Abortion at Work: Ideology and Practice in a Feminist Clinic*. New Brunswick: Rutgers University Press, 1996.

Smith, Andrea. "Introduction: The Revolution Will Not Be Funded" In *The Revolution Will Not Be Funded: Beyond the Non-Profit Industrial Complex*, edited by Incite! Women of Color Against Violence, 1–20. Cambridge: South End, 2007.

Smith, Barbara, ed. *Home Girls: A Black Feminist Anthology*. New York: Kitchen Table Women of Color Press, 1983.

Spelman, Elizabeth. *Inessential Woman: Problems of Exclusion in Feminist Thought*. Boston: Beacon, 1988.

Spivak, Gayatri Chakravorty, "Subaltern Studies: Deconstructing Historiography." In *The Spivak Reader: Selected Works of Gayatri Chakravorty Spivak*, edited by Donna Landry and Gerald Maclean, 203–36. New York: Routledge, 1996.

Starr, Amory. "Is the North American Anti-Globalization Movement Racist? Critical Reflections." In *Fighting Identities: Race, Religion, and Nationalism—Socialist Register*, edited by Leo Panitch and Colin Leys, 265–80. New York: Monthly Review Press, 2003.

———. *Naming the Enemy: Anti-Corporate Movements Confront Globalization*. New York: Zed Books, 2000.

Stockdale, Margaret, and Faye Crosby. *The Psychology and Management of Workplace Diversity*. New York: Blackwell, 2003.

Stockdill, Brett. *Activism against AIDS: At the Intersections of Sexuality, Race, Gender, and Class*. Boulder: Lynne Rienner, 2003.

———. "Forging a Multidimensional Oppositional Consciousness: Lessons from Community-Based AIDS Activism." In *Oppositional Consciousness: The Subjective Roots of Social Protest*, edited by Jane Mansbridge and Aldon Morris, 204–37. Chicago: University of Chicago Press, 2001.

Stoller, Nancy. "From Feminism to Polymorphous Activism: Lesbians in AIDS Organizations." In *In Changing Times: Gay Men and Lesbians Encounter HIV/AIDS*, edited by Martin Levine, Peter Nardi, and John Gagnon, 171–90. Chicago: University of Chicago Press, 1997.

Syeda, Sohera, and Becky Thompson. "Coalition Politics in Organizing for Mumia Abu Jamal." In *Feminism and Antiracism: International Struggles for Justice*, edited by France Winndance Twine and Kathleen Blee, 193–219. New York: New York University Press, 2001.

Takagi, Dana Y. "Maiden Voyage: Excursion into Sexuality and Identity Politics in
    Asian America." *Amerasia Journal* 20, no. 1 (1993): 1–17.
Taylor, Verta. "Emotions and Identity in Women's Self-Help Movements." In *Self,
    Identity, and Social Movements*, edited by Timothy Owens, Sheldon Stryker,
    and Robert White, 271–99. Minneapolis: University of Minnesota Press, 2000.
Twine, France Winddance. "Racial Ideologies and Racial Methodologies." In *Racing
    Research, Researching Race: Methodological Dilemmas in Critical Race Studies*,
    edited by France Winddance Twine and Jonathan W. Warren, 1–34. New York:
    New York University Press, 2000.
Wajcman, Judy. *Women in Control: Dilemmas of a Workers Co-operative.* New York:
    St. Martin's Press, 1983.
Walters, Suzanna Danuta. *All the Rage: The Story of Gay Visibility in America.*
    Chicago: University of Chicago Press, 2003.
Watney, Simon. "The Spectacle of AIDS." In *The Gay and Lesbian Studies Reader*,
    edited by Henry Abelove, Michele Barale, and David Halperin, 202–11. New
    York: Routledge, 1993.
Vaid, Urvashi. *Virtual Equality: The Mainstreaming of Gay and Lesbian Liberation.*
    New York: Anchor Books, 1995.
Valocchi, Stephen. "Not Yet Queer Enough: The Lessons of Queer Theory for the
    Sociology of Gender and Sexuality." *Gender & Society* 19, no. 6 (2005): 750–70.

Index

PROTESTANTS AND CATHOLICS ON THE SPIRITUAL LIFE

PROTESTANTS AND CATHOLICS

ON THE SPIRITUAL LIFE

Edited by
MICHAEL MARX, O.S.B.

THE LITURGICAL PRESS,   Collegeville, Minnesota

Foreword

This paperback edition contains the papers presented at the Ecumenical Institute on the Spiritual Life held at St. John's Abbey, Collegeville, Minnesota, from August 31 to September 6, 1965. They were first published in *Worship* magazine (December 1965). The participants in the conference were from the Protestant, Orthodox and Roman Catholic traditions. This book is entitled *Protestants and Catholics on the Spiritual Life* because it contains no paper by an Orthodox representative. However at the meeting Rev. Thomas Hopko voiced the Orthodox view in the discussions and in his report on the Jesus-prayer.

The chief initiator of the project was Dr. Douglas V. Steere, Quaker observer at the Second Vatican Council. It was during the second session, in the fall of 1963, that he first broached the subject to the Rev. Godfrey Diekmann, O.S.B. The idea of such a conference in which Christians of different traditions share their insights about the devotional side of religion is based on the conviction that the deepest forces conducive to Christian unity lie in a renewed prayer and spirituality of all Christians, and in the mutual help they give to each other by sharing their spiritual traditions. The spiritual heritage of Christians, based on a common faith and life in Christ, appears in a variety of forms and emphases. The chief aim of the conference was the understanding of these many facets of Christian spirituality as reflected in the churches. There have been a growing number of ecumenical dialogues in such areas as the Bible, liturgy, and theology, but in America none dealing with what must be of basic concern to all Christians: spiritual growth in Christ. Since spirituality is in essence the spirit of prayer and worship, each day began with Mass concelebrated by attending priests and ended with a prayer service led by Orthodox and Protestants.

Eight papers were presented and discussed at length. One does not appear in this paperback. Rev. D. H. Salman, O.P., of the *Centre de Recherches en Relations Humaines* in Montreal, will publish his article "Depth Psychology and Spiritual Direction" in *La Vie Spirituelle*. "Problems and Perspectives: an Epilogue" by Rev. Kilian McDonnell, O.S.B., was not delivered at the conference. Its purpose is not to summarize but to be an evaluation of the papers by a non-participant in terms of problems that might be discussed in the future by Protestants, Orthodox, and Catholics.

Michael Marx, O.S.B.

When this historic gathering had reached the concluding evening of its eight days together, the proposal was made that it might well terminate honorably with this wonderful occasion. The gathering however would not listen, but insisted that this kind of crossing of traditions and finding of congenial spirits must go on.

The result of all of this is that our working party in contemporary spirituality is to continue and perhaps even to form a small institute. The next meeting of the group has been set for September 7–11, 1966, at Pendle Hill, Wallingford, Pennsylvania — a Quaker center for religious and social studies. Papers have been planned which will be worked over by the group and then re-written and eventually published as a small book on a contemporary approach to the life of prayer. Several new members are being added to the group but its intimate character is being preserved. Many letters have already been exchanged between members of the group who have found each other across the traditions. It is clear that the lonely work that many have been engaged in has been less lonely. What more witness can we have to the ecumenical fruits that such ventures can confer upon us.

Douglas V. Steere

PROTESTANTS AND CATHOLICS ON THE SPIRITUAL LIFE

Opening Address

Douglas V. Steere

Our task at this gathering is I think a unique one. I know of no ecumenical group of Roman Catholics and non-Catholics in the last four hundred and forty odd years which has been bold enough to meet to share the insights which each possessed for this highly intimate area of spiritual practice. What we are about will require a maximum of charity from each one of us, and by charity I mean that attempt to enter into the mentality of each other in such a way as to uncover the deepest truths that are hidden in each tradition. As Dietrich Hildebrand suggests, however, we are likely to fail in this true charity if we remain fixed in the frames of each other. What we seek is a real engagement that will leave none of us as we were. If from our gathering nothing more comes than the opportunity to deepen and widen our own spiritual approach as a result of this encounter, none of us will be disappointed. We have, nevertheless, a common responsibility to take a penetrating look at the nature and role of ascetic theology in our time and to try to determine where fresh work needs to be undertaken. We may even be drawn to go as far as to assign some of that work between us. Yet in order to do this intelligently, we must know what each of us is already doing and we must freshly evaluate our respective assets and liabilities. We should also know what each of us finds creative in our own traditions and in the traditions of the others, as well as what we may find lacking or even destructive in the tradition of the other.

We have also the duty to assess the inner and outer situation of our time into which our concern for a vital spiritual tradition must come. We must look carefully at new tools such as depth psychology that have been independently developed. We may at some future time even examine the chemical devices that have been alleged to assist the initial take-off into the expanded religious consciousness. Professor Zaehner has done this from the Roman Catholic angle in his *Mysticism: Sacred and Profane*. There might also be some point in examining at some future time the spiritual practices of the non-Christian religions to see what those traditions might have to teach us.

If, in such a gathering as this, a desire should grow up for the creation of a small spiritual institute in contemporary spirituality that could assist in this process, none of us should be greatly surprised. We might however

I

conclude that these matters can be most creatively pursued by the kind of hermit-like attention to them that has always been given by concerned individuals in their separate cells of tradition, and when the time seemed auspicious to them for this sort of undertaking. It has always been interesting to me to note the way the three important books in the English-speaking world on the subject of religious mysticism by the Quaker, Rufus Jones, the Roman Catholic layman, Baron Friedrich von Hügel, and by the Anglican, Evelyn Underhill, all appeared within three years of each other between 1908 and 1911, and that no one of the three had any notion of the work that the others had been doing in preparing them. They had been like three widely separated volcanoes erupting at almost the same time, all lit by the same subterranean fiery substance which seemed bent on venting itself. Perhaps we wish to continue in this fashion.

On the other hand, it is interesting to compare our situation with that of the Desert Fathers of the third and fourth centuries who each established his own dwelling and garden and worked often for years at his task of self-purification, only to find that occasional visits to worship or confer with a neighbor were so helpful that perhaps some pooling of the common search was in order — and the situation was created for a Pachomius to make his cenobitic proposals. We must try to read the signs of our times and see what we are called upon to undertake as the result of our present gathering.

The Biblical Way of Life /
The Spirituality of the Bible

Barnabas M. Ahern, C.P.

Originally this article was presented as part of the symposium "The Word Endures Forever" sponsored by the Thomas More Association and the Department of Library Science of Rosary College, River Forest, Illinois, and printed in The Critic, *August-September, 1965:* © Copyright 1965 *by the Thomas More Association, Chicago, Illinois. After being given in the above symposium as "The Biblical Way of Life," the paper was re-worked by the author for the Ecumenical Institute on the Spiritual Life and presented under the title "The Spirituality of the Bible." But unable to prepare this second text for publication, he authorized a reprinting of the earlier paper, which had meanwhile appeared in* The Critic. *It may assist the reader in relating the present essay to the theme, "The Spirituality of the Bible," if we here include a transcript of the author's opening remarks at Collegeville:*

"Let me begin by indicating why I felt a double concern when I saw this title. I think you can well understand that here we are coming to what is normative. Previously we have been speaking of techniques, practices, and traditions, the human means that man has devised to help in spiritual living. This morning in our discussion we come to what is God's divinely revealed plan for spiritual living. And no single man can encompass that. . . . And secondly the title caused concern in this regard also, that when one speaks of spirituality in the Bible, this might lead to the impression that there are other things in the scriptures. Actually scripture is all spirituality. There is nothing in it except the tracing of God's relation to man and man's relation to God. So St. Paul meant, I think, when he said to Timothy that all scripture is inspired by God and profitable for teaching, for correcting, and for rebuking, and for instructing in justice, that the man of God may be perfect (see 2 Tim 3:16).

"This does not mean that the Bible dissolves the natural order. No. It is filled with natural things. . . . But the Bible does make it clear that from the very beginning, in creating the natural order, God created it with a definite finality; that by his free will and by his utterly gratuitous mercy God intended from the first moment that all these natural things should one day be caught up in a total supernatural relation to him; that they

3

should all be bound up in the covenantal family life of the father with the child. This teleology is present throughout the Bible.

"As we know, the actual covenant begins only with Moses at Sinai, in the Book of Exodus. And yet in the development of the scripture, all that has preceded, all the natural events in the life of Abraham, Isaac, and Jacob, are presented under the form of a covenant. In other words, the shadow of God's manifestation is thrown back over all the preparatory natural steps. And in fact the opening chapters, one to nine, of Genesis are all cast in the covenantal pattern, bringing out the truth that the sacred writer, inspired by God, saw this remarkable teleology in all things. But the manifestation did not come until Sinai. There for the first time God formally burst in on human consciousness and made very clear what his plans were for this natural thing which he had created."

Just a month ago I sat on the beach of the Indian Ocean at Mombasa, watching a file of fishermen drawing in a huge net. I was fascinated by their rhythmic lock-step and listened curiously to the song they were chanting in Swahili. During a lull two of the men approached me to ask if I would give the blessing of Christ on their haul. When I had done so, I asked the meaning of the words they were singing. They told me it was a prayer for the blessings of heaven on their catch. In further conversation one of the men referred to the other as his "brother." Because there was so little resemblance between them, I asked, "Is he really your brother?" "Oh yes," he answered. "He is from my village." For every African, a fellow tribesman is always a "brother."

The whole scene was a picture — as the Bible itself is a picture — of a way of life: God seen as present and acting; men bound together with family ties; and Christ, Saviour of the people of God.

This way of life is set forth in the Bible as in a living photo album where alternating colors, somber and vivid, fascinate the eye and where the sound of voices, clarion and dulcet, captivate the ear and ring in the memory. Unfortunately, men of the West have lost the power to see truth in a picture. We smile when we hear the spouse in the Canticle praise his beloved with the words, "Thou art like a horse in Pharao's chariots." Imagine a young man of today saying to his best girl, "Honey, you are just like a horse." We think instantly of a huge animal; we see only a heap of flesh and nothing more. The Eastern mind, on the other hand, would think immediately of the grace and litheness of the horse's movement, the beauty of its rich, thick mane, and the limpidity of its eyes. We find it so hard to see through an image to the meaning it conveys. In a culture which has canonized historicism and scientific positivism we have lost the child's intuitive power to pierce through myth and picture to the reality which alone has meaning. We miss the word because we hear only sounds: we miss the real and living pictures because we see only dark or garish colors.

For once, then, let us become children again in order to study the pictures of the Bible and to discover with the wisdom of a child's mind the way of life which the Bible unfolds. We find the scene on the shores of Mombasa renewed in a thousand ways. For to put it very simply, the biblical way of life is really a way of thinking, a constant motivating awareness that God is always present to bless, that we, the children of God, are bound together as brothers, and that we have a Saviour through whom every blessing must come.

The biblical way begins with the picture of a burning bush at Horeb and with the voice of God commanding Moses to set out on a long, weary trek. But the people who were to make the journey with Moses would ask for the name of the God who had espoused their cause. In response to Moses' query God replied, "I am who am" (Ex 3:14). He then continued, "This is what you shall tell the Israelites: 'I AM sent me to you. . . . Yahweh [He Who Is] has sent me to you. This is my name forever'" (Ex 3:14–15).

It would require centuries for Israel to understand this Yahweh who had chosen them for himself. Through the prophets whom he sent, God taught his people the mystery of his transcendence. Unlike Dagon the god of the Philistines and Baal the god of Ugarit, Yahweh was not fashioned by human hands and was alien to the whims and passions of human things. The prophet Isaiah would bring Israel to see how unique he was and how holy; he was the God "seated on a high and lofty throne" far above the rising and falling waves of the sea of humanness (cf. Is 6:1). His people were to be holy because Yahweh, their God, was holy. They were to share his transcendence and, like the eagle who was their God, they were to soar above an earth riven by vice and honey-combed with corruption.

Yahweh, however, was a God afar off only in his unchanging holiness. In everything else, he was always the God near at hand. At the very moment when he first identified himself as "He Who Is" this God was planning to save his people and to carve them away from the burning rock of Egyptian tyranny. He would always be the same, "yesterday, today, yes, and forever." At Sinai he bound himself by solemn covenant to father this people whom he had chosen. The pact was sealed with blood; for, when the victims were slain, one bowl of blood was smeared on the altar of God and the other bowl was sprinkled on the people to bind Yahweh to Israel forever. The cloud which led the people through the desert by day and the pillar of fire which protected them at night were but the faint symbol of his abiding presence. His immanence was the very source of the nation's life. In God they lived and moved and had their being.

AWARENESS OF GOD AS ALWAYS PRESENT TO SAVE

This divine presence was something more than the ubiquity of our theologians. It was a dynamically active presence, a saving presence. The God of Israel is the God who acts; his presence is instinct with love and mercy. Much later the psalmist would write of him:

> Where can I go from your spirit?
> From your presence where can I flee?
> If I go up to the heavens, you are there;
>   If I sink to the nether world, you are present there.
> If I take the wings of the dawn, if I settle at the farthest
>   limits of the sea,
>   Even there your hand shall guide me, and your right hand
>   hold me fast (Ps 138[139]:7-10).

Yahweh was always at hand, if only his people would stretch out their hand. Though his holiness was a constant rebuke to the nation's waywardness, his immanence was always present to comfort them. The spokesmen of Israel drained every color of the rainbow to paint in imagery all that Yahweh meant to them. He was the father who created them, and made them, and established them (Deut 32:6). He was the mother who could not forget her little ones (cf. Is 49:15). He was the shepherd who leads his flock into verdant pastures and guides them in right paths (Ps 22[23]). He was the faithful spouse, another Hosea, who loved ever yet again faithless Israel, so like to Gomer, wayward daughter of Diblaim. He was an eagle always teaching his young to fly (Deut 32:11).

I shall never forget the day that I stood on the barren plain at Petra with its walls of blood-red rock. Glancing up, I saw a large bird soar out from a mountain crag. Something dropped from its back like a pellet of lead. In a moment the pellet unfolded, and I saw a little bird stretching its wings to fly. Before long, however, the uprush of wind proved too strong and the little bird, once more a stone in the sky, began to drop. In an instant the mother bird swooped down and caught it on her back to bear it aloft for a second trial. This time the young bird sustained itself longer in flight;

but once more it crumpled before the wind and began to drop. But the ever-present mother saved it again for a third testing. As before, the pellet dropped, the wings opened, but this time the young bird flew off into the distance in the security of its mother's shadow. As I watched fascinated, I recalled the Deuteronomist's description of Yahweh: "As an eagle incites its nestlings forth by hovering over its brood, so he spread his wings to receive them and bore them up on his pinions" (Deut 32:11).

This is what God was to Israel — the God always at hand to save. What he began at Sinai he would consummate, leading Israel to himself. The way might be long and devious, but Yahweh was always there to ease each step of the journey. This is the theme which dominates Israel's history. It is a *Heilsgeschichte,* a theologized history. In it, God's saving action is the primal point of view.

The historians of Israel see God at work everywhere. When fire broke out in the camp, the sacred writer ascribes the fire to God (cf. Num 11:1). When Uzzah reached up his hand to steady the tottering ark, the scripture says that God struck him dead (2 Sam 6:6-7). If we were present we would say simply that the old man acted too precipitately and suffered a cardiac collapse. But the authors of scripture see things with the perspicacious wisdom of the child's mind, a wisdom which most of us lost at the age of eight. Watch the reaction of a little child who stumbles on the street. It turns to its mother with an aggrieved expression as though she were responsible for the tumble. Or again, give a piece of candy to a very little child. You will notice that it does not look at you but turns immediately to its mother. The four walls enclosing its life are the walls of parental love. In everything, the child with true wisdom sees through an incident and through an agent to the person who really counts. In the same way, scripture attributes everything to God. The biblical way of life involves an alert God-consciousness. For the people of Israel, God is a father whose wondrous providence reaches from end to end mightily and orders all things sweetly.

One might say that this God-consciousness is common to all primitive people. The Moabite stone which describes the victory of Mesha, king of Moab, over Israel, reads like a page from the Bible. This stela commemorates the battle which Mesha waged in honor of his god and recounts the signal victory which he achieved with the help of his god. But there is also a tremendous difference. Israel's Yahweh was the true God; and so the nation's God-consciousness centered in a deity who really acted in the midst of his people.

This consciousness of God was so strong that Israel delighted to see him at work everywhere. The stories of the nation's heroes are embroidered with this awareness. The book of Judges is typical. As you move through its pages you feel as though you are walking through a picture gallery. The story of each judge is fitted neatly into a stylized frame: Israel sins and is punished; the people then clamor for God's help; in response he sends a deliverer; and the deliverer, through the power of God, saves the nation. Some of the portraits show only the frame: all that was remembered were the name of the judge and the name of the foreign nation from whom he delivered his people. But in other portraits the details overflow the frame. These portraits picture heroes like Gideon and Samson, men whose characters, like that of Pope John, tended to attract stories. They were like satellites in orbit drawing other satellites to themselves. Their histories, therefore, show many legendary elements. Samson, for instance, was a perfect target for every kind of wild tale. But the tale shows its real meaning in the recurring cliché, "The spirit of the Lord stirred him" (Judg 13:25). With the wisdom of a child, Israel saw God everywhere at work to save.

Even in stories of real deeds, the thought of God was the Bible's only measuring rod. Writers of secular history would probably devote chapters to the reign of Jeroboam II, the Omride king who lifted the nation to a peak of material prosperity. He was second only to David as the nation's greatest king. Yet the Bible dismisses him with a bare seven verses, for he worked only to accomplish his own human plans. On the other hand, kings like Josiah and Hezekiah who would rate only a paragraph in secular history are given whole chapters in the Bible. These godly kings cooperated as best they could with God's saving plan; and so they walk in the limelight. Perspective counts a great deal in gauging the stature of a man. And perspectives in biblical and profane history are very different. The biblical perspective views all from God's point of view; the vantage point from which all is measured in profane history is the merely human accomplishment.

To walk the biblical way of life, therefore, means an abiding awareness of God, the consciousness that he is ever at hand to save. It was the Prophet Hosea who crystallized the conviction that God would never change in his loving fidelity to the covenant with which he bound himself to Israel. Israel could always count on his tireless mercy and his rock-like loyalty. However the nation might fail, Yahweh would love it "yet again," even as Hosea himself loved Gomer his faithless spouse. The saving mercy of Yahweh was alive with perennial dynamism. Even after the nation's sin, the heart of God still beat to the rhythm of his impassioned words through the Prophet, "How could I give you up, O Ephraim, or deliver you up, O Israel? My heart is overwhelmed, my pity is stirred. I will not destroy Ephraim again; for I am god and not man, the Holy One present among you" (Hos 11:8-9).

This faith in the unchanging love of God was but the unfolding of all that Israel had come to find in the very name of God, Yahweh. As the centuries passed, memories of the Horeb revelation became a clarion call to constant confidence. For at the very moment when God spoke of his plan to save Israel he also identified himself as the God who is. Alien to the changes of past and future, he would always be the same — "yesterday, to-day, yes, and forever." History had proven the certainty of his revelation. Rock-like in his love, he had always been at hand to save his people. And so, the Psalmist sings of him:

> Thou in the beginning, O Yahweh, didst found the earth,
>> and the heavens are works of thy hands.
> They shall perish, but thou shalt continue:
> And they shall all grow old as does a garment,
>> and as a vesture shalt thou change them,
>> and they shall be changed.
> But thou art the same,
>> and thy years shall not fail (Ps 101[102]:25-28).

God could never change in his mercy and loyal fidelity to the covenant with which he pledged himself to bring his people to himself. He was Yahweh, the God who is always the same. For everyone who walks the biblical way of life, therefore, the first need is an abiding sense of God always living, always at hand, always dynamically active to save.

COMMUNITY AWARENESS

This very mention of God's will to save instantly conjures up a second need for all who would walk the way to God traced in the scriptures. The man who lived by the scriptures must realize that God wills to save not merely the individual but the whole family of God's people. The first time God spoke of his saving plan he spoke of a people. "I have witnessed the affliction of my people in Egypt. . . . I will send you [Moses] to Pharao to lead my people out of Egypt" (Ex 3:7, 10). At Sinai, too, it was with the people that God entered into covenant. To be a true Israelite, therefore, meant not only an abiding sense of God; it meant also an abiding sense of belonging to the family of God.

Every page of scripture sounds a rebuke to ourselves who are shackled by the subjective philosophies of our own age and who are locked up in the atomistic individualism of "me, myself and I." To us the words "to save" refer only to something we call the soul. With most of us it hardly even extends to our bodies, for in our thinking we are still bound by the almost Manichean conclusions we have drawn from the Greek philosophical dichotomy of soul-body. To think of God's salvation as needfully embracing the whole people of God, to see his glory achieved only when his glorious saving power has dynamized the whole human family, to acknowledge that the earth and the sky and the mountains and the sea, as part of us, are constantly echoing our own groanings for final redemption — this mentality is almost unknown in our own day. At the very time when the world is being almost forcibly bound into unity, most men are conscious only of a centripetal force ruthlessly driving them to an even greater self-centeredness. "Am I my brother's keeper?" is today the raucous cry uttered even by men who, as members of the new Israel, should certainly realize that the whole family of God is but one person in Christ Jesus.

Such individualism is utterly foreign to the biblical way of life. In his beautiful providence God chose to intervene in the history of the human race at a time when primitive cultures were naturally God-conscious and social-minded. In Africa I saw what this meant. Though it is true, tribal life is breaking down under the impact of Western civilization, there are still vestigial remains of a strong tribal consciousness which binds men together as brothers. The individual lives in the tribe and for the tribe. Its destiny and its glory mark the measure of the individual's dignity. His name is a tribal name, and his work is a tribal collaboration. He matures as an individual through his contribution to tribal achievement. He cannot think of his personal life as something apart from the life of his people.

If, then, God created Israel to be his people, he did so because he envisaged a family life for those whom he would save. The tribal consciousness of an ancient people would provide the good earth in which the seed of his plan to save the human family would find its congenial soil.

It was needful, of course, to purify this natural social consciousness, to emphasize through Jeremiah and Ezechiel the personal responsibility of the individual, and to change a merely human family into the family of God. But a family it would always remain. The very glory of God, like that of any father, could be achieved only when the whole family became radiant with the power of his saving action. All Israel was his son. The life and the saving of the individual were inseparably bound up with the life and the saving of all God's people.

Unless we understand this we have missed the meaning of the scriptures.

The great characters of the Bible, their prayer, their work, are seen in true perspective only in the light of a dominant social consciousness. Cut a character profile of any of the saints of the Old Testament — Moses, Josuah, Samuel, David, Jeremiah. Whatever joy thrills their hearts, whatever sorrow depresses them, whatever emotion pulses in their souls — their whole life is caught up in the lives of their people. Moses pleads to be written out of the book of life if God's people were to fail. Jeremiah's prophecy flows like a flood of tears because his brothers are faithless to their father. David's very service of God knew no other end than service of God's people. As living branches of an olive tree, each true Israelite found the fullness of life only in the healthy growth of the tree which God had planted for his glory. For this they labored and for this they prayed.

This is why the scripture is a recountal of one action following another. Men became true sons of God only insofar as they worked for the family of God. Sometimes their deeds shock us. But we must remember that the moral conscience of the family of God, like the conscience of all children, had to mature. In the beginning they thought only of serving God by serving his people in whatever way came to mind. Men did not scruple over means: they were concerned only with the end. Men, yes — and women too.

Judith is typical. The book which recounts her exploits is only a "tall story," a piece of delightful midrash pointing the way for every true Israelite to walk. The heroine is called Judith because she represents the perfect Jewess, fully God-minded and wholly devoted to his people. She it is who saves Bethulia, a city with symbolic name representing that "virgin-daughter Israel" for whom Judith risks all. When the story opens the city is under siege, and the priests, craven with fear, have agreed to surrender to Holofernes unless the Lord God comes to assist them within five days. When Judith learns of their cowardice she flays them with her tongue. "Who are you," she asked angrily, "to set a time limit to the Lord?" A woman of action, she immediately took things into her own hands. Gaily bedecked, she ventured into the territory of the enemy and found herself a prisoner in the camp of the Assyrian. According to plan she gained the favor of Holofernes, only to make ready the springing of the trap which would destroy him.

After wining and dining together they went off to his tent where the captain fell upon his bed in a deep slumber. It was the moment for which Judith was waiting. At this point in the operatic version of Friedrich Hebbel's tragedy *Judith*, the heroine lapses into a soliloquy. With piercing song she soars into the stratosphere with a long aria that resembles Gilda's *Caro Nome* in *Rigoletto*. How utterly unlike the biblical Judith. The heroine of the scriptures strides to the bedside, takes Holofernes by the hair of the head, lifts her eyes to heaven and cries out. "God help me!" Then, with one swift blow, she cut off the head. We tremble with revulsion before the deed and miss the single, striking fact which the sacred writer wishes to teach: the true Israelite must be ready to brave every danger for his people. It is significant that Elizabeth in Luke's infancy narrative praises Mary, the perfect daughter of God, with the very words with which the priest of Bethulia greeted Judith on her return, "Blessed art thou among women" (Judith 13:23; Lk 1:42).

The true Israelite remembered always that he belonged to a people, the very family of God. For them he worked, and for them he prayed. Even a casual reading of the Psalms shows that many of them are really community prayers. They are alive with social consciousness; it is Israel, the family of God, who speaks to the Father. Other Psalms, however, seem remarkably personal. To the uninitiated, they voice the sentiments of an individual man speaking from the depths of a solitary heart — alone with the Alone. But this impression is faulty; it is blind to the mind of Israel. The "I" of the psalmist is the "I" of all his people. He can never forget that in him and through him his brothers speak. Every Israelite belongs to the family of God. This is his constant thought: this is the ground of his confidence. If the psalmist seems to flail the heavens with Promethean daring, it is because he is sure of the God to whom he speaks. Yahweh is father to a family whom he loves and whom he has created for his glory. Every Israelite who prays to him, as a member and spokesman of God's family, is certain of being heard.

The mind of Israel was the mind of the great Teresa. As she lay dying, the mother of Carmel whispered a word which, at first, those around her bedside could not catch. They asked her to repeat it, knowing that the last word of a saint is always his best word. How disappointed they must have been when, at last, they caught an utterance which seemed so banal and pedestrian. All Teresa was saying was the commonplace word, "O, I am so happy to die a daughter of the Church." Yet for one who knows God's saving plan, what word could be more meaningful: we are dear to God only and because we belong, as children, to the beloved family which he begot in Christ Jesus for his glory.

AWARENESS OF THE MESSIAH'S FAMILY BOND

Family consciousness dominates the biblical way of life. Because God planned to save a family, each member must be his brother's keeper — especially that one through whom God would consummate his saving plan. For too long a time we have looked upon the Old Testament expectancy of a Saviour as the hope for a unique and solitary individual. We have taken catch phrases from the prophets, cut them away from all context and, like men playing with a jigsaw puzzle, have fitted them neatly with occurrences in the life of Jesus. Faithless to the very meaning of prophecy, we have used words merely as identification tags for an individual who was to come.

This is totally foreign to the plan which God had traced for the saving of his people. When he first promised salvation he spoke only of the good things which would come to his people when, at long last, it had walked the way to find him. All Israel was his son: a whole family had been created for his glory. It was only when Israel borrowed kingship from the Aramean nations across the Jordan, that the people began to look to an individual, their king, to save them. He belonged to them: as leader and elder brother to the family of God, great things were expected of him. Through him and in him as a corporate personality, the people of God would achieve its destiny.

But kings came and kings went: and each one, more or less, failed to achieve the nation's dream. God's word, however, could not fail; he was the unchanging Yahweh, tirelessly faithful to the covenant he had pledged. So it was that Israel began to look forward to an ideal king of the future, a member of the family who would achieve definitively what no king before him had accomplished. Faith in God's unfailing promise forced men to dream of one of their own who would perfectly accomplish God's saving work because he would incarnate everything best in the family which God loved. This hope introduced a remarkable fluidity into Israel's dream of the future. The people and the Messiah are inseparably bound together.

In Isaiah's canticles (42, 49, 51, 53) it is often difficult to distinguish between the perfect "Servant of Yahweh" who is the purified nation of the messianic era and the perfect "servant" who, as an individual, will achieve victory. Zechariah represents the Messiah as "poor and needy" because the prophet knows he will embody the whole spirit of the *anawim*, the perfect Israel of the future (cf. Zech 9:9). Daniel speaks of "one like unto a son of man" who draws near to the Ancient of Days to receive all honor and glory. But for Daniel, this "Son of Man" bears locked up in himself all the "holy people of God" (cf. Dan 7).

Every page of scripture holds out the hope of salvation for the whole family of God. But its best illumined chapters make clear that the family will consummate its course only in and through a brother who, as the perfect son of God, will bring the whole people to the Father who created the family for the glory of his final saving action.

The Old Testament way of life, therefore, was really a way of thinking. The saints of the Old Law were God-minded men, ever aware of God's presence and ever conscious of his unfailing will to save them. This very fact made them also family-conscious men, for they realized that God had made himself the Father of a whole people and that his glory would be achieved only in the salvation of all their brothers. They longed for the fulfillment of his promise and, therefore, they cherished the dream that one day one of their very own would rise up to bear the whole family in and through himself to the Father who loved them. Often this vision became blurred and distorted. Often the way followed by Israel deviated into by-paths because the nation was blinded by the garish light of merely human ambitions.

But Yahweh was always there to make sure that not all the family lost its way. The nation might be reduced to a remnant; but the remnant would be faithful and, through Israel's perfect son, would draw not only the chosen people but all nations into a new Israel, the glorious family of God.

FULFILLMENT

Certainly when at last salvation came, it followed the blueprints which God had traced in the Old Testament. God, who before seemed hidden, now acted manifestly. His kingship broke through the evil of human appearances to heal the whole of man with miracles and to illumine minds with words never uttered before. Once more it was a people and a family that God worked to save. The very words of Christ's kerygmatic proclamation, stylized later in the Beatitudes, invited into the household of God all the *anawim*, all the "poor and needy" members of the new Israel. True to the Prophet's expectation, Christ himself was a member of the family. The very one through whom God worked was himself the family's elder brother. As the author of the Epistle to the Hebrews has put it, "He has not been ashamed to call them his brothers" (Heb 2:11). When Christ rose from the waters of the Jordan after his baptism his whole being thrilled with the awareness that he was truly the "servant" in whom the Father is well pleased, the perfect Israel embodying in himself the whole family he had come to save.

Matthew and Luke therefore describe his experiences in the desert with the language and imagery used in Deuteronomy to describe ancient Israel's testing. In this way the Evangelists focus light on the fundamental truth that the new Israel lives in and through him. With a personality as distinct as our own, he entered upon his work with the consciousness that he belonged to us and we to him.

The biblical way of thinking is the same in the New Testament as in the Old: God is at hand to save his people through one who himself is a member of God's family. But how pale are the lines of the preparatory blueprint in comparison with its actual fulfillment. God works truly, but this time through a man who is God. God covenants with a people, but this time with the blood of his own Son. God saves his family through one who is their brother, but this brother is God's own Son. The redeemed will always live as the family of God, but the new Israel has been predestined, and blessed, and adopted as sons "through Jesus Christ," the unique and beloved Son of the Father (Eph 1:5-6).

Summing it all up, St. Paul writes, "He who has not spared even his own Son, but has delivered him for us all, how can he fail to grant us also *all* things with him?" (Rom 8:32). In and through Christ, God has fulfilled his saving plan. Yet enigmatically the new Israel still has its course to run. The biblical way of life must still go on — now with impetuous urgency under light that cannot fail and with strength which cannot wane. We live in the period of a partially realized eschatology — with the *jetztschon* of gifts already bestowed and the *jetztnoch* of gifts already certain yet still to come. God cannot do more than he has already done: in Christ he has given us "all things." All that remains is that each man follow the biblical way of life and make his own the mind of every true Israelite in the Old and New Testaments.

BIBLICAL WAY OF LIFE IN THE PRESENT

As we have seen, this involves a multi-faceted mentality. First of all, the Christian, like the Israelite of old, must cherish a constant awareness of God at work to save not only souls, but the whole man and the whole world. God has created everything for his glory — sky and mountains, Mars and men. He is immanently present in everything; and his saving action radiates through the world "like shining from shook foil." Describing a fearsome storm, the Psalmist cries out, "The voice of Yahweh twists the oaks and strips the forest; and in his temple all say 'Glory'" (28[29]:9). The whole world utters a paean of praise to the Creator who made it and is always perfecting it. Every progress in technology, every thrust into outer space, every career developed, every talent brought to fruition, every primitive people lifted to a new level of human being, every neighborhood rehabilitated and every life made more livable, disease conquered and longevity prolonged — this is God's glory, the radiance of his saving power in the world that he loves. Today new bonds are being forged between nations. Distances between minds and men have vanished: differences in place are being dissolved through flights which circle the globe, the whole world is being forged into unity. This is God at work, the God who is always present to save and to perfect the whole world for its final glorification.

Years ago a group approached Cardinal Stritch to enlist his aid in their crusade to ban the bomb. The old Cardinal listened to them thoughtfully as they described the horrors of nuclear war. When they finished he smiled his curious little smile and said, "As you were speaking, all I could think of was the fact that in this our day we have learned at long last how, by balancing atoms, we can achieve so much good." This was the word of a man who saw all things rightly. Certainly, there are dangers in advance and progress. Man can still twist and destroy everything that God does. But the abuse does not take away the use; and man's subjection of things of vanity cannot impede the work of God who is always at hand to save and to perfect the thing he loves.

We need this consciousness of God at work in the world and need the conviction that God counts on men as instruments of his saving work. Divine Providence works through human prudence. God as a true Father gives to every son a hand in the glorious work he would accomplish. Having made the world, God commanded man to dominate it. He was to be God's instrument in perfecting himself, and the whole world, that one day Christ might raise up this glorious creation, wholly perfected, and present it to the Father as his work — and ours.

For too long a time some Christian people have feared material progress, because, in myopic short-sightedness, they have looked upon it with the eyes of Manicheans. They have failed to glimpse the tremendous truth that the whole world is God's, that Christ's blood is upon the rose, and that God's glory will not be perfect until the whole world has been made ready, with every secret mastered and every latent power developed, to be our halcyon abode with God through all the ages of eternity.

But if God is so much at work in the world which is our home, how much more vitally he must be at work in the hearts of men. "Because you are sons," St. Paul writes, "God has sent the Spirit of his Son into our hearts"

(Gal 4:6). That Spirit prompts us constantly to cry out "Abba, Father." But he is also at work, to empower every man for the building up of the body of Christ. We are living in the days of reassessment and of new ideas. Some see in this only a danger sign to be feared. They forget that these things may be of the Spirit, who divides to everyone according as he will (2 Cor 12:11). Certainly every new thing must be tested; God is not always at work in the whirlwind. But men, above all those in authority, must learn to listen and to adapt to the authentic voice of the Spirit. St. Paul's rule knows no exception, "Do not extinguish the Spirit. Do not despise prophecies. But test all things; hold fast that which is good" (1 Thess 5:20-21).

It is for us to watch for God at work and to assist with every power of our being whatever he is doing to save the world and men.

THE FAMILY OF GOD

Secondly, men of the new Israel must realize that God has created a *people* for his glory. Life with God means necessarily a family life; for we are his sons only because, through baptism, we have been united to Christ who is the first-born of many brethren. To live for God and with Christ is an anomaly and even an impossibility if men would attempt to live independently of their brothers. Obviously, many considerations must rule our day-to-day dealings with others. It would be illusory to think that membership in a family dissolves instantly radical human differences in culture and background, in social and educational levels. But these human differences cannot dissolve the fundamental truth that we are all "one body in Christ." The problems of the moment cannot obscure the need to work out the eventual conclusions of St. Paul's reminder: "All you who have been baptized into Christ, have put on Christ. There is neither Jew nor Greek; there is neither slave nor freeman; there is neither male nor female. For you are all one person in Christ" (Gal 3:27-28).

Differences between Catholic and Non-Catholic are often very real. Yet there are many areas of agreement which bind us together; as there are many fields of work in which we can collaborate for the betterment of all. As for areas of disagreement, how often these melt away under the flame of charity which should burn in every ecumenical dialogue. If only we could learn to emphasize what we share in common, how much closer we would come to that unity for which our Lord prayed.

Our destiny to live as the family of God must give new meaning to a fully Christian attitude towards the family of nations and of races. Striving for mutual understanding and readiness to help, a truly efficacious desire for peace and harmony are truly essential if one day the family of God is to embrace all those whom God has called his own and with whom he has entered into a family covenant through the blood of his Son.

To build up in us this family consciousness, the fathers of the Vatican Council have made possible a new corporate form of worship. Active participation in the liturgy is difficult for some, because they have been schooled for years in that form of personal and subjective piety which thinks only of the Lord and oneself. Perhaps the hearts of these people are full of charity for their brother. But now they are asked to make that charity real by giving vocal expression to it — even in their prayer life. Let them but remember that liturgy is a family feast where father and children are united at the same table. What is more natural than that all be united in the spoken words of love. For St. Paul and for the whole early Church, the Christian service was life's great opportunity for a brother to help his brother in the loving presence of their father: "In all wisdom," he writes, "teach and admonish one another by psalms, hymns and spiritual songs, singing in your hearts to God by his grace" (Col 3:16).

God made us a family; and his glory, like the glory of every father, will be fully radiant only when his love and saving action permeate every heart.

CHRIST OUR BROTHER

Thirdly, the biblical way of life means the awareness that Christ is truly one of us. Though he is God's own Son, he has not been ashamed to call us his brothers. Only too often we see the Christ of earth, the Christ who saved us, as hieraticized by the glory of his divinity. If there is any tract in our theology which needs revision it is the tract on the incarnation; for at times its theses do little justice to the truth of faith that Christ "emptied himself" to become a man like ourselves (cf. Phil 2:7).

It will take us all eternity to understand fully the limitations which Christ accepted in order not merely to live among us but in very truth to be one of us. We find it easy to accept the fact that Christ hungered and thirsted, that he slept and suffered. But we often overlook how truly he was "at home" here in this world of ours, how much he loved his work as a carpenter, how strongly he desired to be a success among the people whom he loved. We fail to appreciate his tears over Jerusalem because we forget that he was truly a Jew and patriotism burned in his heart as in ours. We wonder at his tears over the dead Lazarus, because we find it awkward to think of him as one of ourselves with warm and real emotions. We cannot understand his fearful agony in the garden, because we have never ad-mitted how strongly he clung to life and how heartbroken he was over the obvious failure and frustration of all that he had tried to do.

Yet it is only when we realize Christ's humanness that we come to understand how perfectly he has saved us. He has not only acted as God; but, as our brother, he has walked the very way of striving and uncertainty, of joy and of sorrow which we must walk in our way to God. He is our Saviour precisely because, in death and resurrection, he bore us all, locked up in his heart, to the warm welcome of a Father's home. This Saviour has walked the very way which we must follow if we are to be saved. United to him we renew each day, through the power of his spirit, our death to selfishness and our life unto God. He is at once the way of our going, the truth of our groping, and the life of our ephemeral passing. In him and through him, we learn to walk the biblical way of life, ever conscious of God at hand, ever devoted to God's family, and ever clinging to that best of all brothers who is truly one of us and truly God's Son.

The Role of Monastic Spirituality
Critically Discussed

Jean Leclercq, O.S.B.

To treat of the role of monastic spirituality from a critical point of view does not merely imply bringing out its content, but likewise marking its influence; it does not mean solely acknowledging both its content and influence, but appraising them. Monasticism has more than once in the past been a subject of discussion; today, however, the question takes on a new significance: monasticism is discussed outside and inside the Catholic Church, even by monks, and rightly so. We have here an aspect of the activity and a manifestation of the vitality of the Church in our time which seeks — *ecclesia quaerens* — better to grasp the meaning and to justify the values it has received from tradition, so as the better to transmit them, and ever more faithfully respond to their demands.

Some general notion of monasticism must be the point of departure in such an inquiry. Monasticism must therefore be considered in all its breadth. To restrict it to ancient or recent forms of the Benedictine institution would be unduly to limit its scope. The Trappists, the Carthusians, the Camaldolese, the Hieronymites, the Poor Clares, the Dominican nuns, and others offer so many manifestations of the "monastic phenomenon"; they represent sometime extreme forms of that phenomenon, but forms which, by the very fact of their being extreme, are clear and significant. The fact of monasticism must likewise be considered in all its traditional depth by bringing to light all the elements common to it in its successive periods, from its origins in the fourth century to our time. The studies that have been made in our generation by excellent theologians and historians of monasticism will greatly facilitate the present study.

Finally, beyond all those varied historical manifestations, the essential element of monastic life must be discerned. We will find it expressed in the well balanced and impartial considerations of an Italian Benedictine:

"If we consider tradition in the past, there is no doubt that Benedictine monasticism belongs to the *contemplative* type of religious life even if, as history shows, it has never excluded a certain amount of varied activity. But in our time, activism threatens to upset everything and to do away precisely with that contemplative character which seems essential to mo-

20

nasticism in every age. In some instances, we may wonder if the monastery and the monk still preserve the essential of a life which in itself is, at least in a certain measure, a contemplative life, and which, at all events, must favor the contemplative life. Who can deny that precisely in our world of today, monasticism is called upon to incarnate values that are above all contemplative, and to bear witness to their importance and their pre-eminence?"[1]

Let us now try to make this rather general notion definite, and to view it in the light of the data of history, or better, tradition. It will then be possible to form a worthy judgment and to indicate the role which monasticism can play in the Church of today. Let us consider its chief elements and show what were and what are their advantages, but also their dangers, nay even their ill-effects.

ESSENTIAL ELEMENTS OF MONASTICISM

If we wish to consider these elements as a whole, before giving attention to each one in particular, we can say that monasticism has simply given an institutional form to practices and aspirations that were inherent to every life in Christ. In addition to the laws of the Church imposed on all, the monks made obligatory for themselves those institutions they had created within the Church. In so far, and in so far only, did they go beyond the Christians in general. They pledged themselves to practice the Christian life according to those particular norms which they had freely established or chosen, not without an inspiration from the Holy Spirit, under the control and with the approval of Church authorities. There was no question of a Christian ideal different from that of all, nor of a Christian life more perfect than that of the generality of Christians, but of a complex of means destined to favor the seeking for perfection imposed on all Christians, and to make clear and concrete certain demands of that imitation of Christ which the Gospel proposed to all men, and which, from their origin, monks have always made their essential aim.[2]

What were the principal means they chose? In the first place, that fundamental attitude of the Christian which consists in not being *of this world* made them leave the world. They no longer wished to be *with the world*. Spiritual death to the world of sin, detachment with regard to this passing world, became for them separation from the world. They went into

[1] F. Visentin, in C. Vagaggini, *La preghiera* (Rome 1964), pp. 946 f.

[2] Texts are cited by U. Ranke-Heinemann, *Das frühe Mönchtum, Seine Motive nach den Selbstzeugnissen* (Essen 1964), pp. 83–100: "Das Motiv der Nachfolge."

the desert, into solitude; and this flight from the world, this search for solitude, gave rise to the terms "monks, monasteries, cloisters," used to designate their persons and their homes. The ascetics who did not leave the world, even if they practiced celibacy, voluntary poverty, and a life of prayer, were not regarded as monks.[3] Dom Guéranger's concept remains true: "Separation from the world, in itself, makes the monk."[4] The life of a monk is a life of solitude: whether he is alone, as in the case of the hermit, or whether he lives in community, he has set himself apart from ordinary, and even Christian society.

If he leaves the world, it is in order to be with God. He goes into solitude to "seek God," according to a biblical principle unceasingly repeated in monastic tradition. This seeking God and his kingdom manifests itself in an effort toward keeping "the remembrance of God." These expressions, drawn from scripture, and the reality they inspired were illustrated by means of a vocabulary that had lost the philosophical meaning it had in the language of ancient Greece which spoke of "contemplation" and "contemplative life." This new element explains the predominant part which was always given to prayer in monasticism: the life of monks is a life of prayer and, in this sense, it is a contemplative life.[5] Theirs is a prayer of adoration and of praise, but also a prayer of intercession and supplication for all those whom God loves and wishes to save. This sense of universal solidarity appears in maxims such as those of Evagrius: "Happy is the monk who regards as his own the salvation and progress of all men,"[6] and, "The monk is one who, although separated from all, is united to his fellowmen."[7] A third essential element of monasticism consists in an intense awareness of the need of "conversion," *metanoia*, inherent to every life in Christ. It was usually expressed in self-accusation inspiring a constantly renewed effort with a view to mortifying "sinful flesh," and not only avoiding sin, but repressing inclination to sin. This accounts for the importance given to confession and penance. The life of a monk is a life of

[3] Cf. J. M. Leroux, "Monachisme et communauté Chrétienne d'après S. Jean Chrysostome," in *Théologie de la vie monastique* (Paris 1961), p. 149.

[4] Unpublished conference given at Solesmes, which has been quoted several times.

[5] The demonstration has been made for the Rule of Saint Benedict by A. de Vogüé, "La Règle de S. Benoît et la vie contemplative," in *Collectanea Cisterciensia*, XXVII (1965), pp. 89–107, and, for the remaining part of the Middle Ages, in the pages I have written on the same problem, *ibid.*, p. 108–120, under the title: "La vie monastique est-elle une vie contemplative?"

[6] *De oratione*, 122, P.G., 79, 1193.

[7] *Ibid.*, 124, 1193.

penance; the monk is a voluntary penitent; and on this point also, he is responsible for others. It will suffice to cite a dictum of Saint Jerome which became classical and entered in that manual of medieval canon law, generally called the *Decretum Gratiani*: "The role of the monk is not to teach, but to weep over his sins and those of others." [8]

Detachment with regard to the goods of this world became for monks a renunciation of all property, voluntary poverty. The life of a monk is a life of poverty; the monk is a "poor of Christ."

Submission to the will of God, in imitation of Christ who always did the will of his Father, became obedience to a superior, who represented God. That obedience tended to be total, absolute, but was always free and voluntary. It was practiced at first toward a "spiritual father," and then, in cenobitic life, toward the father of the community, the authority of the latter being well defined and limited by a rule. Obedience was regarded as necessarily bound up with renunciation, for it seemed at least as important and difficult to renounce one's own will as to renounce one's own goods. It seemed likewise required by charity. If monks voluntarily submitted to one another, if those among them who exercised authority themselves submitted entirely to the law of God, it was in order to discern and carry out all together God's design on each and every one of them. Monastic life is a life of obedience; the monk is an obedient man.

Until now no mention has been made of celibacy, since originally celibacy was not strictly a monastic concept. It had existed before monasticism was established: consecrated virginity is attested in the epistles of Saint Paul and throughout the first three centuries of Christianity. However, as soon as monks adopted the various essential elements of monasticism that have been pointed out, they likewise adopted that form of complete, definitive chastity, which is voluntary and perpetual celibacy. Chastity could be practiced in other states of life, as, for instance, in marriage; it could take on other forms. The monks adopted a specific form: to be alone in the way they understood it, to be a "monk" (to be single), necessarily means to practice continency in celibacy. Monks will often be referred to as "continent" men.

Such were from the very beginning and throughout history — notwithstanding variations in modes of application — the chief characteristics of monastic life. Having stated them, we can now attempt to pass a critical judgment on them.

[8] *Contra Vigilantium*, 15, P.L. 23, 351.

ADVANTAGES AND DANGERS OF MONASTICISM

Let us try to ascertain the advantages and dangers of monasticism, so as the better to estimate afterward the consequences they entailed.

We may say that the principal advantages were the following:

Monasticism helped the Church discover or perceive more clearly certain demands of the spiritual program proposed by the Gospel.

It showed monastic life as an example, one of the possible realizations of the life in Christ, illustrating certain aspects of the evangelical message.

It offered thereby a possibility, a help, to generous Christians who wished to adopt the same practices.

It set up examples of sanctity: apart from the martyrs, most saints that were venerated in the ancient and medieval Church were monks.

It brought forth a spiritual literature that transmitted and elaborated the experiences and the teachings of monks. Ascetic literature of all times, but especially that of the Middle Ages, strongly bore the influence of great monastic authors, such as Saint Jerome, Saint Basil, Cassian, Julian Pomerius, the compilers of the Merovingian age (e.g., Defensor of Ligugé), the writers of the Carolingian epoch (e.g., Smaragdus of Saint-Mihiel), and later those of the twelfth century, particularly Saint Bernard.

But it is fitting to lay stress on two chief services monasticism rendered the Church. In the first place, it introduced into the life of many Christians, both clerics and lay persons, spiritual practices that had been proper to the monastic life at the beginning. Retreat (that is, as the term itself indicates, a certain anchoretism for a period of more intense solitude and recollection), spiritual direction, manifestation of conscience to a spiritual father, meditation, spiritual reading, were of monastic origin.

Self-accusation in particular contributed much to revivifying penance. From the very first generations of monks, as the most ancient of the *Apophthegmata* of the Fathers bear witness, a deepening of the Christian conscience had been observed among them. Little by little, everyone acquired a more and more intimate and intense conviction of his condition of sinner and experienced the need to acknowledge it and to mortify himself in order to do penance.

"It was in the same period — late fourth and early fifth century — that a new concept and practice of penance began to prevail. Public penance was not given up officially; but because of the length and severity of the penitential practices imposed and above all because of the non-repeatable character of the sacrament and its humiliating aspect and disabling consequences, there was a strong tendency to postpone it until proximity of death seemed to urge it and at the same time to preclude occasions for further sin. These considerations were similar to those which often caused the delay of baptism. It is not necessary to enter into the controversial question as to how early so-called private penance was introduced into the Church. It is probable at any rate that St. Basil, St. Augustine, and other Fathers of that time had the inadequacies of public penance in mind, when they insisted so strongly on the biblical and earlier ascetic conception that a true spirit of penance should extend far beyond gross sin to everything which is not pleasing to God. And this was one of the great functions of monasticism: to demonstrate in practice that spiritual perfection and complete detachment from sin are ultimately one and the same thing, that the safest way and perhaps the only way to cease being a sinner is to become a saint. It is in the ascetic-monastic milieu, therefore, that the beginnings of what today is called private penance, and even repeatable confession and absolution, are to be found." [9]

Another important role of monasticism was to react against the spiritual emptiness engendered gradually in some milieus with the development of institutions and even with the appearance of a certain "legalism," as well as with the material growth of the Church. Monks exercised a sort of "prophetic" protest against every form of mediocrity. [10] It has been remarked, with regard to Cassian, that in some of its representatives monasticism was not unlike Protestantism. [1] There were striking voices, like those of St. Jerome, St. Peter Damian, St. Bernard, Blessed Paul Giustiniani, and today, Thomas Merton. But there was also—and there is still—the silent protest of so many unknown monks and nuns proclaiming in their own way, by their life, the message to which writers give expression. By the very fact that they exist and are known to exist, such contemplatives set all Christians on their guard against the temptations of an easy or superficial activism. That prophetic function is a form of witnessing on the part of monks to the eschatological character of the Church. More consciously than others, they already live for the other world; and they remind all that beyond this world, there is another; that beyond the present, there is the kingdom to come. They remind the Christians they should not be satisfied with this world, although they may desire to make it better. They remind them that human

[9] Gerhart B. Ladner, *The Idea of Reform* (Cambridge, Mass., 1959), pp. 309f.

[10] Cf. J. Fontaine, art. *France*, in *Dictionnaire de spiritualité*, col. 792.

[11] A. de Vogüé, *Monachisme et Eglise dans la pensée de Cassien*, in *Théologie de la vie monastique*, pp. 220 and 223.

progress and "development" under all its forms and in all domains remain ordained and subordinated to an encounter of persons with God in Christ.

Finally, one of the secondary roles of monasticism was to put at the disposal of the Church a generous personnel, ready to be employed in the difficult works of evangelization or reform of manners at times and in countries in which others were not assuming those functions. So it happened — less than it is said at times, but in a way that cannot be passed over in silence — that bishops or popes, in particular circumstances, asked monks to enter the clergy, or to become members of the hierarchy of the Church, or again to devote themselves to agricultural, cultural, pastoral, or missionary activity.

Now, what were the dangers to which monasticism was exposed and to which it yielded?

The first was to go too far in the realization of a legitimate ideal, and in the first place to exaggerate the practice of asceticism. Hence the excesses, the abuses and extravagances of certain forms of mortification in ancient monasticism, or at the time of St. Peter Damian, de Rancé, or Dom de Lestrange. On the whole, these excesses were not so serious as a free literature likes to put it at times today. Those who read the sources and know how much to attribute to their literary genre and to their humor admire the moderation and the good sense with which the *Apophthegmata* of the Fathers of the desert or the writings of subsequent great authors are filled. But the danger of exaggeration was real and was not always avoided.

In the realm of ideas, there was the temptation to give too much value to human effort, at the expense of the efficacy of grace: Pelagius was a monk, and Pelagianism is a typically monastic error.

Another danger was to regard as an absolute, as an end, what was only a means, and consequently to present monastic life as the model for all Christian life, and as the point of reference in relation to which Christian life should be judged. That accounts for a certain fashion, nay, a certain snobbishness in the fourth and fifth centuries, for example, for what has been called the "Egyptian way of life."[12] It is clear that this engendered pride and vain self-complacency in many a monk.

History also witnessed instances in which monks tended to separate themselves from "la grande Eglise," either by having no hierarchy, or by opposing an authority of a charismatic nature to that of ecclesiastic institution; or again, by rejecting the doctrine of the Church on certain points, or by living without the sacraments, even, strangely enough, the Eucharist.

[12] J. Fontaine, *loc. cit.*, col. 792.

Others gave in to an individualism, or, what is worse, an egoism, which impelled them not to care for their neighbor and his salvation, nor for the good to be done the neighbor here and now. The prophetic protest at times resembled an Adventism or a Millenarianism ignorant of the concerns of the Church. At times, monasticism gave the impression of being, with regard to the Church, what sects are with regard to Churches.

Moreover, when spiritual fervor disappeared or diminished among certain monks, there was a tendency to think that the institutions which that interior fervor produced were sufficient in themselves, without the continuance of that enthusiasm which had brought them into existence. This could lead to a community life without charity, to a life of celibacy without chastity, to one of poverty without privation or detachment.

CONSEQUENCES OF THE BENEFITS AND DISADVANTAGES

Having observed the advantages and dangers monasticism presents, we can note a few of the facts that can be explained by these data.

The advantages enable us to understand why the authority of the Church always encouraged the monastic institution as a whole, insured its protection, and took its defence when it was necessary. It was a bishop, St. Athanasius, who wrote the *Life* of St. Anthony, the father of all monks; a pope, St. Gregory the Great, did the same for him whom we call "the patriarch of the western monks," St. Benedict. Both wished to illustrate and to commend that mode of life; and we might cite many instances in which leaders of the Church, from St. Augustine to Paul VI, affirmed the legitimacy and the high value of monasticism.

The benefits of monasticism explain also how Christians always discerned its significance and saw in it an example of Christian generosity and an incitement to fervor. This accounts for the vast diffusion of monastic literature, to mention only one of the signs of the importance attributed to monasticism. Lives of monks, texts written for or by monks, nearly always enjoyed a certain prestige and have exercised an influence on spiritual writings up to our own day.

On the other hand, the drawbacks and the dangers of monasticism account for the criticisms directed against it. We have seen that one of its functions was to criticize, in the measure in which it protested; but it also needed to be criticized, and it was indeed, on the part of monks themselves, as well as on the part of other Christians. At all times there were churchmen who reproved certain monks for the abuses, the excesses, and the deviations that have already been pointed out. It will suffice here to cite a few examples taken from different periods.

In antiquity, already in the fourth and fifth centuries, a certain reaction against monks can be observed, a certain mistrust in their regard on the part of Christians, both lay and cleric, living in the world and satisfied with "l'Eglise établie." They were opposed to the diffusion of the ideal of continence, which threatened to permeate the lives of even married people. Who then would give the Church new sons? They worried about the ideal of voluntary poverty. Who then would come to the help of the needy? Who would administer the properties of the clergy? They feared that the ideal of separation from the world would deprive it of men experienced in the work to be done. Who would preach and convert the world?

And so, we notice a certain opposition to St. Martin on the part of bishops and members of the clergy of Gaul, and an opposition to both St. Martin and St. Jerome on the part of members of the Roman clergy.[13] But we also see monks finding fault with other monks: St. Jerome found St. Martin and his disciples too moderate.[14] St. Basil criticized Eustathius of Sebaste and his groups of ascetics.[15] St. John Chrysostom rebuked certain monks for their sadness, the relaxing of their discipline, and for their tendency to believe their observances were infallible means of sanctification;[16] he reproved them for their indifference with regard to the salvation of their neighbor,[17] and for their want of charity.[18] St. Augustine upbraided slothful monks who did not want to work and for whom he wrote his treatise *De opere monachorum*. The praises Cassian reserved for the Egyptian monks were nothing else than indirect criticisms addressed to the monks of Gaul; he put the latter on their guard against the gyrovagues, the sarabaites, and the false hermits.[19] Rules were written to preserve monks from the exaggerations and the deviations to which they were exposed; thus the Rule of St. Benedict begins with a censure of bad monks. The function which doctrinal definitions filled in the domain of faith — the exclusion of errors, was performed by monastic legislation in what concerned discipline — the condemnation and elimination of abuses. So a continuous criticism of monasticism was carried out in antiquity both by monks and by churchmen.

[13] Cf. A. de Vogüé, *loc. cit.*, p. 231.

[14] Cf. J. Fontaine, *loc. cit.*, col. 795, and "Vérité et fiction dans la chronologie de la Vita Martini" in *S. Martin et son temps* (Rome [Studia Anselmiana, 46] 1961), p. 232.

[15] J. Gribomont, "S. Basile," in *Théologie de la vie monastique*, p. 113.

[16] J. M. Leroux, *op. cit.*, pp. 167f.

[17] *Ibid.*, p. 169.

[18] *Ibid.*, p. 171.

[19] A de Vogüé, *loc. cit.*, p. 221.

In the Middle Ages, criticism of monasticism was at the bottom of all those efforts at renewal that we call reform, whether the initiative had been taken by a prince, as in the case of the Carolingian reform, or by bishops or councils, by monks like St. Odo and the abbots of Cluny, St. Peter Damian, the Cistercians and St. Bernard, or again by popes like Gregory VII in the eleventh century, Alexander III in the twelfth, and Benedict XII in the fourteenth. Monasticism was in a state of continual reform, which supposes a constant self-criticism. And one of the roles of monasticism in the Middle Ages was to keep up in the Church the idea and ideal of reform.[20] A historical phenomenon such as the Gregorian reform in the eleventh century was not accomplished only by a new legislation; it was helped by a renewal and a deepening of religious mentality to which monasteries contributed a large part.[21] Again in the thirteenth century, we see monasticism criticized and called back to the demands of its vocation by an Odon de Cheriton [22] and by the theologians of the Mendicant Orders.[23]

The epoch of the Reformation was one of those during which monasticism was subjected to the most violent criticism. In the life of Luther himself we observe an evolution on this point; at first he tended to reinforce laws, to re-establish observances in the Augustinian Order to which he belonged; later, he came to make a complete break with vows and observances, and to elaborate a theology that would justify such a rupture. This radical criticism was maintained in Protestantism, and reinforced, in our times, by new arguments borrowed from history. An attempt was made to explain the appearance of monasticism by the influence of religions or philosophies foreign to Christianity, or again, by economic circumstances or an opposition to the hierarchical Church.[24] But the problem has just recently been taken up again on its true ground, that of theology.[25]

In our time, monastic life is the object of criticism, some of which comes from historians, philosophers, and theologians who attribute to certain tra-

[20] G. Ladner, *op. cit.*, pp. 319–426: "Monasticism as a vehicle of the Christian idea of reform in the age of the Fathers."

[21] I gave some indications on this point in *Témoins de la vie spirituelle en Occident*, (Paris, 1965), pp. 166-174.

[22] I have furnished evidence under the titles *Pétulance et spiritualité dans le commentaire sur le Cantique*, in *Archives d'histoire doctrinale et littéraire du moyen âge*, XXXIX (1964), Paris 1965, pp. 43–47, and *Odon de Cheriton ou Hélinand de Froidmont*, to be published in Paris in 1966.

[23] Let us think for example of the sermons of Humbert de Romans, O.P.

[24] An "aperçu" of these various attempts is given by U. Ranke-Heinemann, *op. cit.*, pp. 9–12.

[25] R. H. Esnault, *Luther et le monachisme aujourd'hui* (Geneva, 1964).

ditional attitudes of monasticism — such as separation from the world, "contempt of the world," contemplative life — a Platonic, pessimistic, dualistic, "anti-incarnational" origin or savor. Others react against a monasticism too "installé," too little conspicuous for solitude, austerity, poverty, and simplicity of life. A book like Louis Bouyer's *The Meaning of Monastic Life* represented a protest of this kind. Recently, the *American Benedictine Review* published articles raising questions regarding concepts and practices of monasticism as a whole [26] and of that of the United States in particular.[27] Thomas Merton did not fail to bring up the problems which the Cistercians of the strict observance have to face.[28] In a recent letter he affirmed, "I have consistently held that a monk can speak from the Desert, since there is no other place from which he has a better claim to be heard." And one of his latest essays ends with the following sentence which vibrates with the tone of the great prophetic and protesting voices: "But one thing is certain, if the contemplative, the monk, the priest, the poet merely forsake their vestiges of wisdom and join in the triumphant empty-headed crowing of advertising men and engineers of opinion, then there is nothing left in store for us but total madness." [29]

Regarding the "nabis," those prophets who were at times "charismatic leaders" of the people of Israel, a comparison has been made between "the efficaciousness of their protest against an excessive attachment to terrestrial goods and that which monasticism and other ascetic movements of the same kind have exercised in the Middle Ages." The historian who made the comparison also offers the following observation, which we ought to be able to apply to monasticism of any period:

"By walking out of the circle in which they had lived hitherto, by making palpable, both in their dress and in their living a secluded life in special colonies, their opposition to any kind of comfortable worldliness or cultivation of self-interest, so that they might dedicate themselves utterly to the religious idea, they brought home once more with unmistakable severity to a nation that had become too flabby and soft, that 'life is not the highest

---

[26] "Problems Facing Monachism Today," in *American Benedictine Review*, XVI:1, 1965, pp. 47–56 (German translation in *Geist und Leben*, 1965).

[27] A. Tkacik, "The Twentieth Century Monk," *ibid.*, XVI:2, pp. 242–246.

[28] "The Monk in the Diaspora," in *Commonweal*, 1964, pp. 741–745, and in *Blackfriars*, 1964, pp. 290–302. H. Urs von Balthasar and others have remarked that in our last generations, some of the Christian voices that were most listened to were monastic voices, such as those of St. Theresa of the Child Jesus, Sister Elizabeth of the Trinity, Charles de Foucauld, Dom Marmion, and Thomas Merton.

[29] *Symbolism*, published in the Indies in 1965, p. 29.

good,' and that there is something greater than earthly progress and the enjoyment and multiplication of worldly goods."[30]

ACTUALITY OF MONASTIC SPIRITUALITY

If we wish to form a comprehensive judgment on the role and value of monastic spirituality, we must distinguish what is proper to the life of monks, such as practices, observances, and modes of existence, and what is ancient, traditional, sound and applicable to everyone. The latter comes from Christian sources common to all members of the Church, namely the scriptures, the liturgy, and patristic literature. The way in which monasticism has utilized and lived by these has remained simple, a stranger to the methods, techniques, and at times, the complications which more recent "schools" have introduced to answer different needs. The monastic way of serving God and praying to him lies at equal distance from the individualism that appears in the writings of many spiritual authors from the end of the Middle Ages to the nineteenth and even the twentieth century, and, on the other hand, from the tendency to a collectivism, signs of which are discernible today.

But the monastic life has its limitations. If sometimes in the past it has been presented as *the* model of Christian life, that was a deviation or an abuse of terms, which might well be explained in part by circumstances. We see better today that it is only *a* model, one of the possible realizations of the life in Christ, one of the means of carrying out and illustrating some of its demands. The movement of ideas provoked by the Council will contribute to this equitable re-evaluation, this re-equilibration, if we may so speak. Monasticism is not made to answer all the needs of the Church. In itself it is neither oriented toward the priesthood, nor turned toward evangelization or any other ministry. Many of its authentic representatives, beginning with the cloistered contemplative nuns, are strangers to clerical life and to any exercise of direct apostolate. "Non omnia possumus omnes": we cannot all do everything.

What is essential and, in this sense, specific to monasticism is the primary place it gives to prayer, under both its forms: private and communal. In the nineteenth century, the second has been regarded at times as a sort of specialty of monks, and especially Benedictines, by the fact that the celebration of the liturgy was hardly performed by any others. The role which Dom Guéranger and others in Europe played in the liturgical renewal from the middle of the nineteenth century to the middle of the twentieth,

[30] Walther Eichrodt, *Theology of the Old Testament* (Philadelphia, 1961), pp. 326f.

and which the Benedictines continue to play in the United States in our times, should not make us forget that traditionally the divine office is only one of the forms of prayer for monks, one of the observances by which they seek union with God. Today, in proportion as the liturgy is again becoming pastoral, the leadership of the liturgical movement is gradually passing into the hands of those in charge of pastoral work, and these are not monks. At the same time monasticism is laying more and more emphasis on the *lectio divina,* and many incline to think that an institution of religious life which grants less time to reading than to the office cannot claim to be Benedictine, since it does not conform with one of the fundamental prescriptions of the Rule of St. Benedict. Moreover, that element of solemnity which had developed in the Benedictine liturgy at the time of the baroque and in the nineteenth century tends everywhere to be reduced. That evolution cannot but bring monasticism back to its true function in the Church.

Its role is to permit certain forms of piety, what we might call "pietist movements," to be realized within the Church itself. In them, the monks sustain their fervor; they are in the Church, without entirely breaking away from the world. They detach themselves from the world, but their culture has always exercised an influence on the world.

Their role is to affirm, at the same time and in their own way, the lordship of Christ over all that exists, the primacy of eschatological anticipation, docility to the charisms of the Spirit, and obedience to the Church and its institutions. When one of these elements tends to weaken, monasticism loses something of its vigor; it runs the risk of becoming a well established institution, but one devoid of fervor, or of being a group of fervent persons whose enthusiasm is uncontrolled and lacks continuity. If the values of monasticism are no longer or not sufficiently found in some institutions which ought to preserve them, they appear in new foundations and institutions. The whole history of monasticism, and certain of its manifestations of vitality in the Church today, illustrate this fact. But it would be as fallacious to wish to depend on a purely spiritual tradition, without any connection with history, as it would be illusive to think that fidelity to the past suffices to justify an institution.

Finally, the principal role of monasticism is to remind everyone that the first condition to fulfill in order to transform society is to transform ourselves by leading the life in Christ as fully as possible, and to do this for the glory of God. This is particularly true during a period marked at the same time by a return to the sources and by the emergence of new forms of Christian fervor and action, more and more "secular" in appearance in that they are practiced in the world. If monasticism remains different, it does not for that reason judge them. It admires them, learns some lessons from them, and helps them as much as possible. Nevertheless, monks and nuns know that, for them, the best way of preaching the law of the Lord is to reform themselves with total generosity.

The Puritan and Pietist Traditions
Of Protestant Spirituality

Horton Davies

Our understanding of both the Puritan and Pietist elements in the spiritual tradition of seventeenth and eighteenth-century Protestantism will require us to shatter the common stereotypes suggested by each term. "Puritan" is wrongly equated with a blue-nosed, kill-joy attitude to life. This stereotype was popularized by Shakespeare's Malvolio in *Twelfth Night* of whom it was said, "Thinkest thou because thou art righteous there shall be no more cakes and ale." Lord Macaulay, the historian, perpetuated the stereotype in affirming that the Puritans banned bearbaiting not because this gave pain to the bear, but because it gave pleasure to the spectators. Yet the Puritans introduced opera into England and re-introduced seriousness in religion. Edmund Spenser, the superb allegorist, and stateman-poet John Milton prove that in Puritanism, Christianity and culture were closely allied. As for Pietism, it is a great mistake to think of its leaders such as Spener, Zinzendorf, or the Wesleys, as lyrical spiders, forever spinning a saccharine subjectivity from their insides. Theirs was a deeply disciplined love of God which they communicated in hymnody that expressed the renewal of life in Christ on a firm biblical foundation.

One might as well begin by some brief definitions. By Puritanism I intend that highly egalitarian and radical spiritual theocratic movement which arose within Anglicanism, included the Presbyterians, the Independents or Congregationalists, and the Baptists of England, and possibly also the Society of Friends, which replaced a monarchy with a commonwealth, the Book of Common Prayer with a Directory or Manual of Worship, prescribing the topics of prayers but not the very words, and which claimed that instead of tradition it used the Bible as its authority for doctrine, church government, and devotion. The Puritans are, I would suggest, to be distinguished from the Society of Friends by the fact that for the former the Bible was primary and the Holy Spirit secondary, whereas the authorities were reversed for the Quakers. This worship was marked by: biblical loyalty — all worship was a response to the word of God; the edification of the elect of God; intelligibility, and a strong ethical direction (sanctification, if you will). It rejected liturgy as a lame man might a crutch when he believed himself healed. It was iconoclastic in its rejection of symbolism and ornaments. It is believed that it is the inner testimony of the Holy Spirit which alone makes worship, whether public or private, acceptable to God. Austere it was, but also invigorating. Theologically it was Calvinistic, with its high evaluation of preaching and its relative depreciation of the sacraments of baptism and the holy supper.

Pietism, like Puritanism, was a movement originating in opposition to the formality and complacency of the state religion of the day. Puritanism reacted against Episcopalianism in England; Pietism reacted against the desiccated orthodoxy of the Lutheranism of the day in Germany and in the Methodism of John Wesley, against the moralistic smugness of the eighteenth-century Church of England. Puritanism was a movement of the will and the mind — we are not likely to be allowed to forget that. It has been pointed out that "in contrast to other pioneers, they made no concessions to the forest, but in the midst of frontier conditions, in the very throes of clearing the land and erecting shelters, they maintained schools and a college, a standard of scholarship and competent writing, a class of men devoted entirely to the life of the mind and the soul." [1] Pietism did not lack leaders of independent mind like Spener, Franeke, Gottfried Arnold, and John Wesley, but it glowed with men of good heart who worked for the revival of religion, of missionary enthusiasm, and of such charitable foundations as orphanages — all on the basis of a biblical piety. Their influence has been seen in the parent church of Lutheranism and most decidedly in Methodism. Unlike Puritanism, Pietism had no particular quarrel with the liturgy, except possibly a feeling that it encouraged too cold and formal a spirit in church attendance. At least we can say that the liturgy was to be supplemented by free prayer and Bible readings in the gathering of the little *ecclesiolae* with the *ecclesia*. In the case of Wesley we know that he prepared an abbreviated version of the Book of Common Prayer for the use of his preachers in America when he was divided from them by the American Revolution. The Puritans, you will recall, proposed the Directory of Public Worship in 1644, which was an abolition of the liturgy.

FREE PRAYER OVER LITURGY

In view of the great liturgical movement of the nineteenth and twentieth centuries, it would seem that we are exhuming a tradition in worship and spirituality that is dead because it is when not anti-liturgical, at least a-liturgical.

I will forbear to count noses as an index of truth, but I must remind you

[1] Perry Miller and Thomas Johndon, *The Puritans* (New York, 1938), pp. 11f.

that this is an exceedingly vigorous tradition in Protestantism, and even in such communions as the Lutheran and the Episcopalian which proudly use a liturgy, there will be many ministers and laity for whom free prayer in the home will be thought to be the apex of conversation with God, an intimate and necessary supplement to the liturgy. For the Presbyterians, Methodists, Congregationalists, Baptists, Disciples of Christ, and for thousands of those Christians whom we so disparagingly and unfairly refer to as sectarians, from the Pentecostalists downwards, public worship is synonymous with free or extempore prayer, at least as used in a supplementary way. They share with the Society of Friends the uneasy feeling that to pray through a liturgy is to approach God *second-hand*.

In order to understand a viewpoint so apparently opposed to the liturgical movement and to the traditions of Roman Catholicism, Orthodoxy, Lutheranism, and Episcopalianism, we must go back to the origins and hear the proponents of the view. It may give patience as a consequence of insight. Those who argued that prayer is the fruit of deep meditation upon the Bible and a knowledge of God's people advanced five arguments for the superiority of free prayer over a liturgy:

First, there was the conviction that a constant use of set forms of prayer deprived ministers and people of the gift of prayer. John Owen, Puritan divine, former Dean of Christ Church, Oxford, and Vice-Chancellor of Oxford University, wrote in 1662, that as a result of the reintroduction of the Book of Prayer with the Restoration of the House of Stuart in 1660: "we daily see man napkining their talents until they are taken from them." [2] The point was put more vehemently by the anonymous author of the 1641 book *The Anatomy of the Service Book* who asks: "What, we pray you, is the procreant and conservant cause of dumb dogges that cannot barke; idle Shepheards, saying Sir Johns; mere Surplice and Service-Book men, such as cannot doe so much as a Porter in his frocke; for he doth Service, and the Priest onely sayes service: is it not the Service-Book?" [3]

Secondly, it was urged that set forms of prayer could not meet the varied needs of differing congregations and occasions. While a liturgy is comprehensive in its appeal, it lacks the particularity and intimacy of free prayer. Isaac Watts says: ". . . it is not possible that forms of prayer should be composed that are perfectly suited to all our occasions in the things of this life and the life to come. Our circumstances are always altering in this frail and mutable state. We have new sins to be confessed, new temptations and

[2] John Owen, *A Discourse Concerning Liturgies and their Imposition, Works*, ed. Goold (Edinburgh, 1862) xv, 52.

[3] *The Anatomy of a Service Book*, Second edition (1652), p. 47.

sorrows to be represented, and new wants to be supplied. Every change of providence in the affairs of the nation, a family, or a person, requires suitable petitions and acknowledgments. And these can never be well provided for in any prescribed composition." [4] Here we gain a clue into how two different conceptions of prayer reflect differing ecclesiologies. Liturgical prayer stresses the historic and corporate nature of the Church in "Common Prayer"; free prayer suggests the intimacy, even spontaneity, of the little family church of the elect where each individual counts exceedingly. If liturgical prayer adequately reflects what is held in common by all Christians, in its creed, its collects, its confessions, however abstract the phrasing, free prayer meets particular requirements. Moreover, liturgical prayer does not demand that a pastor should know the members of his congregation well; free prayer presupposes the smaller compact Christian community. Liturgical prayer requires a parish as a background, with the wider horizon of the nation or the international community; free prayer suggests not Israel so much as the remnant, i.e., the compact unit of the congregation as a worshiping family. To sum up, Watts helps us with the reminder that "generals [generalization] are cold and do not affect us. . . ." [5]

Thirdly, it was argued that to require the worship of God through set forms was to insist that they were as important as the scriptures. The use of set forms could not be said in the same breath to be an indifferent matter (*adiaphoron*) and yet required. Vavasor Powell, a leader of the Baptists, condemns the imposition of the Prayer Book by King Charles II in these words: "Either such Liturgies or Common Prayers are indifferent or not indifferent; if indifferent, then they are not to be imposed upon Christians but they are to be left to their liberty, as Christians were left by the Apostles; but if it be not indifferent, then unless a *Prescript* can be shewed from God (it being in his Worship) it is no less than Will-Worship, forbidden *Col.* 2.23." [6] For the Puritans the requirement of the Book of Common Prayer was trespassing on the Divine Rights and on human liberty.

Fourthly, it was urged that familiarity bred contempt.

The final charge against set forms of prayer was that they had brought persecution in their train. Vice-Chancellor John Owen accuses imposers of liturgies of bringing "fire and faggot into the Christian religion." [7]

This seems a formidable indictment, but, of course, the defenders of

---

[4] Isaac Watts, *Guide to Prayer, Works,* ed. Russell, iv, 127.

[5] *Ibid.*

[6] Vavasor Powell, *Common Prayer-Book No Divine Service* (1661), p. 7.

[7] John Owen, *A Discourse of the Work of the Holy Spirit in Prayer, Works,* ed. Russell, iv, 23.

liturgies had an equally formidable weaponry to employ. Bishop Jeremy Taylor, the Anglican divine, argued that extempore prayer was the product of mental laziness, urging that the real issue was: is it better to pray with consideration than without? Also in his *Two Discourses* Taylor declares that extempore prayer leads to ostentation rather than to edification. The same author's third argument against free prayers is that the people cannot give their voluntary assent to such prayers until they have carefully considered them, which, of course, time does not permit. Another Anglican, Dr. Henry Hammond, insisted that it was a great weakness of the Puritan plea that it presupposed that all ministers could express themselves felicitously, fluently, and publicly.

Perhaps my readers have been perplexed as to how, with the many examples of set prayers in the Old Testament (for example, at the consecration of the Temple) and in the New, especially the Lord's Prayer, the Puritans could claim that their innovation had biblical sanction? They believed that the Lord's Prayer was a pattern of true prayer rather than a prescribed prayer, especially as the versions of it in the two Gospels varied. But over above this, their profound sense both of original sin and of the initiative and support of the Holy Spirit forced them in the direction of free prayers. Their authority was the clear assertion of St. Paul in Chapter 8 of the Epistle to the Romans that "the Spirit helpeth our infirmities for we know not what to pray for as we ought." To use set forms was to quench the Spirit and to forget that 1 Corinthians 14:16 had insisted that only the pastor's voice is to be heard in prayer, to which the people are to add their "Amen" as proof of concurrence.

There were, of course, trivial subordinate arguments dependent on very subtle eisegesis. The one which amuses me most is the supposedly irrefutable argument from God's word for the abolition of responsive prayers. The authority for this assertion is the Levitical prohibition of the meat of that most repetitious of birds, the cuckoo! Within both Puritanism and Quakerism the really valid protest was against the idolization of the institution, the absolutization of the finite, and the reminder that God alone comes to his people with sovereign freedom, when they would prefer him to be so predictable, even channelable! The freedom of free prayer was not libertinism; it was the freedom of obedience learned in listening to God after reading his word.

PREACHING AND HYMNODY

Another feature of Puritan worship was the raising of preaching to a sacramental level — the exhibition of Christ incarnate, crucified, risen and exalted for the criticism and comfort of the elect. Let me merely remind you of Richard Baxter's definitions of preaching to give you a glimpse of the august, objective, and authoritative conception of preaching held by the great Puritans. "It is no small matter," said Baxter, "to stand up in the face of a congregation, and deliver a message of salvation or damnation, as from the living God in the name of our Redeemer. It is no easy matter to speak so plain that the ignorant may understand us; and so seriously that the deadest hearts may feel us; and so convincingly that contradicting cavillers may be silenced." [8] The same author provided the classical description of the urgency of preaching: "I preached as never like to preach again, and as a dying man to dying men."

I need hardly remind you that Pietism's preaching tradition is hardly less distinguished, for John Wesley the ex-Oxford don, became the greatest extension lecturer on committed Christianity in the English-speaking world and was superbly aided by his henchman, George Whitefield, in England and America.

It might also be recollected that it is the Free Church tradition of worship which has contributed so superb a fund of hymnody to the modern church, beginning with Puritan Watts and Pietist Charles Wesley. It is perhaps too often forgotten that those in the Puritan-Pietist tradition sing their creeds in their hymns. The greatest of them are, as was John Wesley's first Collection of *Hymns for the Use of the People called Methodist*, primers of theology, lyrical expressions of the radiance of the Christian experience. It was Isaac Watts who first in the modern world had the daring to make his author David speak like a Christian, and to make the great leap from a paraphrase of the Psalms to a Christian hymn.

FAMILY AND PRIVATE PRAYER

It is not now as vigorous as it used to be, but one of the glories of the Puritan-Pietist traditions was the high level of the practice of family and private prayer; indeed, the gathering of praying households is what made the experience of Sunday worship such a Pentecost of expectation. The Reformed tradition of spirituality, said Dr. C. S. Lewis, lowered the honors standard but greatly improved the quality of the pass degree. This high quality of intra-mundane and familial spirituality is the strength of the Puritan and Pietist commitment to God. God's covenant which is "to you and your children" was invariably read at baptismal services and welded each family into a solidarity in Christ. The head of the family, who had

[8] Richard Baxter, *The Reformed Pastor* (1860), p. 128.

promised at the baptism of his children to supervise their Christian nurture, was in duty bound to teach them the scriptures, to have them recite the main headings of Sunday's two sermons, and to instruct them in prayer and praise. If conscientious in his duty, he would conduct family prayers twice a day. Baxter's *Christian Directory* presupposes that each adult will pray privately each morning and each night as well as engage twice a day in family worship.

Samuel Clarke gives us a moving illustration of the ardor of Puritan private devotions when describing the practice of John Cotton, the treasure and terror of Boston: "He began the Sabbath on the Saturday evening: and therefore then performed Family duties after Supper, being larger than ordinary in Exposition, after which he catechized his children and Servants, and then retired into his Study. The morning following, Family Worship being ended, he retired into his Study untill the Bell called him away. Upon his return from the Congregation, he returned again into his Study (the place of his Labour and Prayer) into his private Devotion; where (having a small repast carried him up for his dinner) he continued till the toling of the Bell. The publick service being ended, he withdrew for a space into his afore-mentioned Oratory, for his sacred addresses unto God, as in the forenoon: Then came down, repeated the Sermon in his Family, prayed, and after Supper sang a Psalm, and, towards bed time betaking himself again to his Study, he closed the day with Prayer. Thus he spent the Sabbath continuously." [9]

It is of enormous significance that each Puritan and many a Pietist who was in earnest kept a daily spiritual ledger or diary. On this was marked not only the sins but the resolutions to do good and each night the tally of resolutions and acts was kept. Misguided, intense, over-introspective, the Puritans and Pietists may have been, I agree; but I doubt if any people have more espoused honest religion. Bare, austere, functionally designed, their worship and their meeting-houses were — the Methodist churches happily more comfortable — but Pietists and Puritans were never at ease in Zion and never comfortable in their sins. If their worship lacked the comprehensiveness of a liturgy, and in jettisoning tradition lost some of the balance of the historic Christian life, if it was insufficiently aware of the teaching power and suggestiveness of symbolism and over-aware of direct didacticism, these are not irremediable defects. What is irreplaceable in their worship is its biblical basis, its undeviating loyalty to God as King of kings and Lord of lords, its deep simplicity, its spirit-prompted spontaneity (how-

[9] Samuel Clarke, *A Collection of the Lives of Ten Eminent Divines &c.* (1662), p. 69.

ever rapidly that might degenerate into cliches), its sense of the privileges and responsibilities of the elect of God, and its recognition that a Christian is *contra mundum*, not to escape it but to learn from it. Puritanism's weakness was asperity, the thin patience of the elect; Pietism's weakness was a syrupy sentimentality; together they make for that telling of the truth in love which is the heart of the Gospel and of Christian worship and ethics.

It is not within the scope of this paper to bring the story of the Puritan-Pietist tradition to the present. But I must not fail to point out that the denominations in this tradition — Congregationalists (United Church of Christ), Baptists, Disciples, Methodists, and Presbyterians — have in the twentieth century recovered, with the rest of Christendom, a liturgical and corporate piety for which I have provided evidence in *Worship and Theology in England: The Ecumenical Century: 1900 to 1965* (Princeton, N.J., 1965). It is now recognized that liturgical and charismatic are not competitive or disjunctive terms but complementary ones, for the people of God follow the shape of the liturgy as they are joined with our Lord's offering of himself as the word in preaching and the sacrifice in the Eucharist in the power of the Holy Spirit.

Common Frontiers in Catholic and Non-Catholic Spirituality

Douglas V. Steere

Our whole enterprise of ascetic or spiritual theology must always wrestle with a certain inner contradiction. No one has expressed it better than Augustine when he declared that "We come to God by love and not by navigation."

It is possible to become so concerned with trying to chart the navigational routes most suited for quickening the inward life of the people of God, that we will be tempted to forget Augustine's warning. Yet Catholic or Protestant or Orthodox, we all face this common paradox. To forget that "we come to God by love" is to forget both prevenient grace, whose pull and lure have initiated our coming, and to forget, too, that in responding to this grace, our own surge of love is not readily predictable or chartable and may vary vastly between persons and traditions and epochs — making the task of the spiritual theologians in the map room almost impossible of accomplishment. For many religious thinkers not only is the task unmanageable because of this complexity, it is also undesirable because it implies that the priority seems to be given to navigational techniques and courses, and not to grace and the spontaneous answers of love. This hints at a succumbing to Pelagianism, to the accent upon justification by works, perhaps even to the personal accumulation of merit by devotional practices, instead of resting all on God's supreme act in the atoning grace of Christ and on a man's spontaneous response as the recipient of redemption.

Thirty years ago I had a long visit with Karl Barth in his home in Bonn. I was staying at Maria Laach at the time, and I journied in from Andernach for the visit. I spoke of the role of private prayer as a means of putting us into the stream of grace and even spoke of how impressed I had been by the rhythm of the daily Benedictine liturgical cycle as a means of exposing a community to this baptism of grace. Barth repudiated both roles and denied that either had the slightest significance as far as my own, or the monks' redemption was concerned. He insisted that for himself, he knew that he hung suspended between heaven and hell, that the weight of his sins would most certainly sink him to hell, and that only the intervention of the supreme act of grace wrought in Christ would ever be sufficient to lift him and to overcome this terrible gravitational force of his sin. He implied that this act of Jesus Christ was enough, that anything else was utterly irrelevant, and that anyone who wasted his time or trust on these practices was to be pitied.

There are few in classical Protestantism who would be quite as brazen as to put his emphasis as bluntly as Barth did to me. But actually, there is a very strong undercurrent in classical Protestantism that would find in these remarks what they deeply believe; and in the United States, at least, neo-orthodoxy has had little time for the devotional side of religion and has often regarded it as specious humbug and self-deception.

What I have been describing is not exclusively a Protestant problem. For extreme Augustinian "Grace-is-all-ism" in either confession would rule out the place for human decision and effort in either the initial experience of redemption, or in the subsequent progressive movement toward the basic re-orientation required. The Roman Catholic Church has on at least two conspicuous occasions repudiated such a position in favor of a more moderate attitude. Barth's central affirmation about the need of grace stands, but at the same time, we cannot rest easy with the conclusions he draws from it about the channels that may be the agencies through which that grace may most readily flow.

I have accented this paradox because it is always implicitly present in the Protestant discipline and is a common factor to Protestant and Catholic both. If we were to define ascetic theology as the nurture and deepening of the human responses to the grace that is lavished upon men, we should not come far afield. For ascetic or spiritual theology in its final sweep seeks always to make that response more adequate and more complete, and it implicitly assumes Leon Bloy's famous line at the close of *The Woman Who Was Poor* that "man has only one sorrow — not to be a saint" — if we were to define a saint as "one in whom God has more and more his undivided sway."

Implicit, too, in our discipline is a view of the nature of man, and it is a view that, in spite of all of our various differences of accent, we might, I believe, agree upon: namely, that as a creature, man's loving back to God is spasmodic, inconstant, and anything but continuous, that he requires infinite encouragement, and that there must be countless occasions of restoration to an awareness of the constant action of grace. I believe we could also agree in assuming that conversion is continuous and that, in spite of a man's intentions, there is no such thing as the total commitment of a man to grace. Instead there are ever new areas in a man's life, and in the life of his time in which he is immersed, that call out for further yielding. For us both, "How do I become a Christian when I already am one?" is more than a rhetorical question. All of this means that man is an unfinished creature and a node of unfinished creation even when he has been drenched with grace, and that he requires all the skilled assistance that can be given him in this continuous process of increasing self-surrender and inward abandonment to the grace that the Christian life calls for.

THE DIMENSION OF THE UNCONSCIOUS

To indicate in still another fashion the scope of our field, it is challenging to turn to C. G. Jung and to see how he has put the matter of the redeemed or still-to-be redeemed unconscious life of Christian men in our time:

"The divine Mediator stands outside as an image, while man remains fragmentary and untouched in the deepest parts of him. . . . It may easily happen, therefore, that a Christian who believes in all the sacred figures is still undeveloped and unchanged in his inmost soul because he has 'all God outside' and does not experience Him in the soul. His deciding motives, his ruling interest and impulses do not spring from the sphere of Christianity, but from the unconscious and undeveloped psyche, which is as pagan and archaic as ever. Not the individual alone but the sum total of individual lives in a people proves the truth of this contention. The great events of the world as planned and executed by man do not breathe the spirit of Christianity but rather of unadorned paganism. These things originate in a psychic condition that has remained archaic and has not been even remotely touched by Christianity. The Church assumes, not altogether without reason, that the fact of having once believed leaves certain traces behind it, but of these traces nothing is to be seen in the march of events. Christian civilization has proved hollow to a terrifying degree: it is all veneer, but the inner man has remained untouched and therefore unchanged. His soul is out of key with his external beliefs; in his soul the Christian has not kept pace with external developments. Yes, everything is to be found outside in image and in word, in Church and Bible, but never inside. Inside reign the archaic gods, supreme as of old: that is to say, the inner correspondence with the outer god-image is undeveloped . . . and therefore has got stuck in heathenism. Christian education has done all that is humanly possible, but it has not been enough. Too few people have experienced the divine image as the inner-most possession of their own souls. Christ only meets them from without, never from within the soul; that is why dark paganism still reigns there."[1]

---

[1] C. G. Jung, *Psychology and Alchemy*, pp. 11f.

It will do no good to hedge by ruling out such a statement on the ground that Jung, like all psychotherapists, fails to distinguish between the "psychical" and the "spiritual." Ascetical theology cannot escape the responsibility of examining the deep underwater therapy that may be required to touch these depths that Jung has described: to touch the dream life, or to touch the vital axioms — the principles from which we make our choices. For unless a man's unconscious life is involved in his redemption, how little in him will be permanently altered, how heavy will be the shadow that he casts, and how opaque he will be as a window to transmit this grace to others!

Just as Paul, after his most violent and polemical "Grace-is-all" moments in the Epistle to the Romans, moves over to the kind of conduct that can alone channel that redeemed life, so even the most avid classical Protestant, when you put him to the test, insists that a "forgiven man" who owes his redemption utterly to grace must nevertheless channel that new life and be quickened in that new life through drastic changes in his relations with his fellows and through yielding ever fresh areas in his own life to God, areas that may until then have been withheld. The Epistle of James may be called the epistle of straw, but even classical Protestants have discovered that it is hard to make the bricks of a Christian life if you leave out the straw.

INDIVIDUAL RESPONSIBILITY

Yet there should be no concealing of our differences of accent in this matter, for Protestantism in general lays more emphasis upon the school of individual responsibility in these matters than Roman Catholicism, and it is highly sensitive to any claims that would declare or even imply that the priest, or the saints, or the virgin, or the institutional church stand as an indispensable intermediary. The mediation of Jesus Christ is the only help required, and the individual Protestant believes that any other mediator is not only superfluous, but is a dangerous intrusion that is not only capable of exploiting the individual person, but that may even rob him of his direct touch with the true source of redeeming grace and of his personal responsibility before it.

There was something very beautiful in Abbot Herwegen's gentle rebuke to me when, as a young professor some 30 years ago, I came to Maria Laach to make a month's spiritual retreat. I asked him for someone to lay out a retreat for me, and he told me I had come to the wrong place, that I should have gone to the Jesuits who believed in individual spiritual pilgrimages. The Benedictines, he pointed out to me, had no hope of salvation by their own prayers or inner yieldings. If they were saved at all, it was as a member of the Benedictine family and all quite unselfconsciously as the result of the family Opus Dei. He capped it with a fine story of a Benedictine abbot's encounter with a departing visitor, and of the visitor's congratulating him on having an abbey of pious monks. To this, the abbot replied with a tone of sadness that he wished the visitor might have been able to tell him instead that he had a "pious abbey."

As an introduction to the flair and flavor of Benedictinism, these remarks of Abbot Herwegen's were magnificent. But on further thought, they are, in their full significance, less impressive. For unless each monk in that monastery is in growth, unless each monk *is* in his own special way being led to give himself more and more completely to God; in other words, unless the Benedictine house is more than a spiritual beehive: a religious collective where all of the individual responsibility has been transferred to "the family" or to those in spiritual authority who enforce the rules, it may seriously be questioned whether any such cenobitic religious institution may be justified before the standard of the deepest ascetic theology. I know that the best Benedictine thought today would heartily agree with this.

THE QUAKER TRADITION

Even though most Quakers, whose tradition I know better than most non-Catholic practice, consider themselves as a third force in the Catholic-Protestant struggle, they nevertheless share the Protestant accent on individual responsibility in this matter of growth in the response to grace, and they go so far as to insist, in George Fox's words, that "Jesus Christ is come to teach his people himself" and to refer to the Holy Spirit's available guidance to the soul of man in Isaac Penington's words: "There is that near you which will guide you. O wait for it and keep to it."

The classical type of corporate worship among the Quakers has always schooled them in looking for the minimum of outside help in finding, in being bidden by, and in following this ever-present Guide. For in its classical form, this corporate worship consists simply of the group gathering in a very plain room devoid of all ornamentation and sitting together for at least an hour in an attitude of prayer, turning inwards and waiting on God. In the course of this meeting for worship, Quakers often experience what they speak of as being "gathered" in the presence of Christ. Their own lives seem to be judged, and areas that require amendment are opened to them. Consciousness of sin and of the fact that "the One who shows us our sins is the One who heals us" is common, and Quakers also know what it is to experience in the meeting the forgiveness of sin and the inward absolution. There are often times in the meeting when there is an inward baptism of thankfulness akin to adoration; times of intercession for persons and situations; times when the gifts are accompanied with tasks to be done, which may even come as specific leadings or concerns; and times of having reservations stripped away and "disponibilité" and expendability restored. All of these inward experiences of communion and baptism and ordination for work to be done that so often take place in the Quaker meeting for worship are a further confirmation of renewal and guidance in the absence of mediation, even the mediation of the customary outward sacraments. And what Quakers here experience corporately, they often find coming to them privately through the week with a sense of direct guidance that again seeks to draw the implications of the encounter of grace for specific human obligations.

When a seventeenth-century Quaker, John Roberts, was arrested for worshiping in other than the Anglican way, he is reported to have said to Bishop Nicholsen before whom he was brought, "Miserable sinners you find us, and miserable sinners you leave us . . . you must always be doing what you ought not: and leaving undone what you ought to do, and you can never do worse. What use is religion if it does not give a man the power to change and the strength to resist temptation?"

This statement of John Roberts could be the query of a pharisee. Perhaps it was. But it could also be the question put by one who felt profoundly the individual's unmediated accountability to the indwelling Christ for following out the guidance that came to him. It could also be a window through which ascetic theology, whether in Roman Catholic or non-Catholic hands, might view its ultimate task and might in some degree measure its ultimate effectiveness. For if our ultimate task is to nurture the response which individual human beings make to the infinite donation of redemptive grace that draws at their lives, can it do this unless it finally succeeds in quickening this ultimate seed of accountability in the breast of the Christian?

In both the Protestant and Catholic traditions, there dare not be any blunting of the responsibility to listen for and to follow this "bird in the bosom," this "guest we have within us." If, in ascetic theology's guidance in the use of spiritual direction, confession, private and public prayer, fasting, devotional reading, or the service of the poor and the afflicted, it should happen that we dry up or diminish a man's inner responsibility to God in Christ or to his following the direct guidance of the Holy Spirit, and instead increase his dependence on the outward apparatus that we may provide, far from favoring him, we may have permanently crippled and deformed the very center or seed in him which God has bid us to arouse and to encourage. Here is a common element in our heritage that may be something of a norm by which to judge our methods.

It might be instructive to take three areas of ascetic theology that are, I would presume, of central concern to Protestant and Catholic alike, and to examine them both for the common ground and for the differences of accent which they may reveal: 1. spiritual direction, 2. the cultivation of the practice of private prayer, and 3. the encouragement of personal involvement in some acts of costly responsibility for our fellows.

SPIRITUAL DIRECTION

It would seem clear that Catholic and non-Catholic alike must admit the need of adequate personal counsel for those who feel a yearning to put their lives more completely into God's hands. Certainly the monastic life and later the life of the in-the-world orders have demanded this. Since the Catholic Renaissance of the sixteenth century, there would seem to have been a vast increase in the Roman Catholic effort to provide this service more and more extensively to the laity who wished it. Francis de Sales, who wrote his *Introduction to the Devout Life* (issued in 1609) specifically for lay people, calls the fourth chapter of the first book of his Christian classic "The necessity of a guide, in order to enter on the path of devotion and make progress therein" and declares, "Do you wish in good earnest to set out on the way to devotion? Seek out some good man to guide and conduct you; it is the admonition of admonitions, 'Although you may search,' says the devout [Teresa of] Avila, 'you will never find out the will of God so assuredly as by the way of this homely obedience, so much recommended and practiced by the men of old.'"[2] Francis de Sales develops this virtue of absolute obedience to a spiritual director and adds, "The guide ought always to be an angel in your eyes . . . do not look upon him as a mere man . . . trust him in God who will favor you and speak to you by means of this man putting into his heart and into his mouth whatsoever shall be requisite for your happiness . . . this friendship must be strong, sweet,

[2] Francis de Sales, *Introduction to the Devout Life*, tr. Allan Ross (London, 1930), p. 10.

holy, sacred, divine and spiritual. . . . Pray to God to give you such a one [and] remain constant and do not seek for any others." [3] For Teresa of Avila, obedience was such a condition of opening the way for grace that she once declared, "It is more meritorious to pick up a needle in obedience than to eat and drink nothing but bread and water for a whole year."

From the Protestant side, the role of spiritual direction was from the outset heavily discredited by identifying it with the confessional and with the whole apparatus that grew up around monetary penances and indulgences. In its traditional form, spiritual direction plays almost no prominent role in Protestant practice apart from the only partially-reformed Anglican Church where the Caroline divines of the seventeenth century and the Anglo-Catholic movement of the last 130 years have both strongly advised it. A contemporary Anglican authority on ascetic theology, Martin Thornton, says, "Spiritual direction is our greatest pastoral need." [4]

In spite of Protestant neglect, the basic need in this area could never be entirely ignored, and it is interesting to read the large group of personal letters of spiritual counsel which Quakers like Isaac Penington and George Fox wrote, or to read the fascinating spiritual journals that all Quakers were encouraged to set down, in order to see how these were used as guides in a fiercely democratic tradition that would have recoiled from acknowledging any such obedience to another man as Francis de Sales suggests. The Moravians and other German pietists have a similar literature, and some day we may be supplied with enough knowledge about the early Methodist class-meetings to see that they played no small role in supplying spiritual guidance. A certain amount of pastoral guidance has, of course, always been present throughout Protestant history, and more recently this has been accentuated with the coming of the tidal wave of psychological counseling that has swept through the Protestant theological seminaries in our time.

It is important to note how wisely our Catholic brothers have distinguished the confession of sins and the direction of souls. Even though both functions have often been carried on by the same priest and with the same parishioner, yet they have been so rightly seen as quite different functions. It would be well if the same distinction could be made by Protestants between a pastor's psychological counseling and the spiritual guidance of souls. For the latter is a program for encouraging increased abandonment to God, and while certainly it is not entirely separable from the counselor's

[3] *Ibid.*, p. 12.
[4] Martin Thornton, *English Spirituality* (London, 1963), p. xiii.

attempt to find "who's the matter with you" or to achieve a remission of obnoxious symptoms and an adjustment to the social situation, yet the goals are anything but identical.

Because Protestantism in general — and this would perhaps even hold for the Anglican community — would find the notion of abject obedience to a spiritual director of the kind described by Teresa of Avila or Francis de Sales so alien to their relation to their clergy, and because the clergy would be neither willing nor in many cases qualified to assume any such role, such types of spiritual direction as we have in Protestantism have often come in much more informal and completely non-authoritarian contexts: from prayer groups and confraternities; from two laymen conferring together on their common need; and from pastor to layman in highly empirical fashion as between two friends engaged in a common quest. The impression which a non-Catholic has of Roman Catholic practice in the matter of spiritual direction, as in all other phases of ascetical theology, is that it is regarded as an adjunct of the sacramental and liturgical structure and authority of the Church. If this impression is correct, then in the case of spiritual direction, the priest, whether he wishes it or not, possesses an authority which creates a certain "Distanz" between him and the parishioner, and, as an officer of the Church, the spiritual direction which he gives is likely to be in terms of the Church's liturgy and its fullest use. Roman Catholic retreats that I have attended have almost invariably centered on some aspects of the liturgy.

Closely associated with this liturgical context for Roman Catholic spiritual direction (even when one knows well that it belies Catholic theory in the matter) is another impression, namely, that there is a hidden assumption that lingers on in the minds of the Roman Catholic clergy that spirituality, if it is to be fully invoked, means a kind of commitment which fully professed men and women may be able to approach, but which life in the world will almost certainly prevent, and therefore it is best to ask little and to expect still less of lay aspirants to a spiritual life.

With a more human and less authoritarian Roman Catholic Church in prospect; with a quickened Roman Catholic concern for laity and their problems, a laity many of whom may not be restored to the supernatural life by liturgy alone; with an ever deeper sense of the unique and highly personal character of each situation of personal direction, Roman Catholic and non-Catholic alike are confronted with the necessity for a thorough examination of a non-authoritarian, empirical, and much more tentative type of spiritual guidance that will nevertheless carry sufficient weight to have it honestly and persistently worked at by the layman. Both of us require a searching to find how this direction can be undertaken with a consciousness that the Holy Spirit is the ultimate spiritual director and that the true spiritual guide will always keep this foremost and see his role as trying to work with the soul-friend to see what God is drawing him to at this stage in his life. This is certainly more than Fox's "Take them to Christ and leave them there," but it is a good deal less than the authority many a spiritual guide even in our own day has been known to assume.

While most Protestants and Catholics would, I presume, admit that spiritual direction is an art rather than a science, and while Protestants find Catholic manuals on the subject incredibly systematized and routinized, and seemingly less aware than they should be of the layman's life in our day, nevertheless the almost complete absence of any real attention to this particular function in Protestant theological seminaries is a reflection of the progressive inward impoverishment of the Protestant tradition in our time and points up how desperately we need help — and how important is our task in this field of spiritual theology.

The evangelically oriented groups who comprise a growing sector of the Protestant world seem to be so absorbed in confronting their people with the message of redemption and mobilizing their converts for witnessing to this message that the stages of further yielding and communion are largely neglected. Thomas Traherne, the seventeenth-century Anglican priest-poet, can speak to all Christians in the *Centuries of Meditation* when he says that to contemplate God's love "in the work of redemption, though that is wonderful" is not all. Still greater, he suggests, is the end for which we are redeemed: a communion with his glory. Perhaps a major focus in the spiritual direction of the future must be in guiding people to make some progress during this life of ours in the practice of communion; for surely, Martin Thornton is right when he says, "not to long for progress is to fail in prayer."

CULTIVATION OF THE PRACTICE OF PRIVATE PRAYER

Archbishop Temple spoke for Catholic and non-Catholic alike when he said "What we need more than all else [is] to teach the clergy to be teachers of prayer." [5] Here we would seem to be on common ground. For the cultivation of the practice of private prayer, while again not uninfluenced by our respective public cycles of worship, is nonetheless something that cuts

[5] F. A. Iremonger, *William Temple* (London, 1948), p. 35.

across all of our traditions. If we could express in simple terms the objective of what we were trying to accomplish in the life of prayer, I believe that this common ground might be even more evident. Would it be going too far to suggest that what we are after in the nurture of prayer is a continual condition of prayerfulness, a constant sensitivity to what is really going on? For if grace is continually laying siege to every life; if Pascal was not deceived when he wrote "Jesus shall be in agony until the end of the world," endeavoring to tell us afresh that this costly redemptive process is still going on and is forever drawing at our hearts for our healing, for our reconciliation with God and with each other, and luring us into a sense of unlimited liability for each other, then are not all acts of prayer simply precious devices for mobilizing our uncollected faculties and compelling them to wake up and pay attention, and to join the ranks of what is so costingly and tirelessly already at work?

If we turn to such an aspect as the prayer of intercession and the question is put as to whether intercession could possibly affect the life of someone who did not know that anyone was holding him up in prayer, we very swiftly reveal the condition of our spirituality in this area. Intercessory prayer among non-Catholics is used for a large spectrum of purposes including success in all phases of life not exclusive of worldly affairs; it is widely used by healing groups within the Protestant Churches who put great store by it; and it is used in a kind of simple and unthinking way of trust by our more conservative minded denominations. I do not believe that I exaggerate, however, when I suggest that none of these groups have thought out an adequate theology or metaphysics of what might be involved in the act of intercession. In the more conventional Protestant denominations, apart from a small group of the devout, it is doubtful if there is any real belief in the efficacy and significance of secret intercessory prayer. Even public prayer that includes such elements is tending to become perfunctory. Most Protestants in this large group would agree that intercessory prayer is efficacious in tendering the one who prays, and most would go further and admit that the one prayed for, if he should be one who is ill, would benefit by this proof that he was not forgotten and that he was an object of concern, provided that he knew that his prayer had been made for him. But to think that there is a realm where intercessory prayer poured out secretly by individual persons or, say, by a closed Carmelite convent of nuns could lower the threshold of the heart to the continuous siege of the Divine Redemptive love, that these prayers matter, that they matter terribly in order to reach situations, persons, and the heart of the world — this, in Protestant terms, and in an intelligently worked out, theologically grounded, and philosophically plausible way, is hard to come by in our world today.

I stress the Protestant situation because I know it best, but I learned at the Vatican Council and through many visits with members of spiritual orders of the Roman Catholic Church that even in that communion where it still remains publicly correct to applaud the contemplative orders who intercede for the sins of the world and who give themselves almost wholly to such prayer, abundant doubts are being cast upon its importance when it comes to the real matter of priorities. The pressure to push the contemplative orders out into the world and to get the monastic orders more and more to commit themselves to what the hard-pressed local bishops and society in general would regard as "useful" activist work is an ever-growing one. This would seem to indicate therefore that both confessions face a common problem of shoring up intercessory prayer against erosion and of being compelled to think it through afresh and to state its significance with the greatest skill that we can mobilize. And what has been said of this very revealing type of prayer, namely, that of intercession, holds equally for the whole spectrum of prayer and its effective cultivation amid the Himalayan dispersions of contemporary living.

PERSONAL INVOLVEMENT IN RESPONSIBILITY FOR OUR FELLOWS

When in 1920 Baron Friedrich von Hügel undertook to direct the spiritual life of Evelyn Underhill (Mrs. Stuart Moore), she was already in middle life, married, and one of Britain's most accomplished writers. The Baron began by insisting that she "visit the poor." These two afternoons a week of immersion in the life of the London poor were not suggested with any primary idea of doing *them* good, but rather of restoring her to a responsible personal relation with the brave, bold, boisterous stream of suffering humanity which makes up Christ's earthly body. It worked in her case and brought her nearer to people, and in their midst she found Christ.

Much of the spiritual re-vitalization that has come to those who have taken part in the recent freedom walks and in all kinds of civil rights demonstrations with their physical risk, their rough and tumble days bedded down in Negro churches and homes, their spells in jail in company with their Negro brothers, has come through this same restoration to a responsible relation with what, until then, was a severed limb of Christ's body. Many Catholics and Protestants have found the nearest they have ever come to sensing what is really meant by abandonment to God has come in these experiences, and they know them as authentic means of kindling the life of God in their souls. Walter Hilton, writing in fourteenth-century England in a concluding supplementary chapter to his *Scale of Perfection* says of this form of spiritual exercise, "If thou be diligent with all thy skill and ability for to deck and adorn His [Christ's] head, that is, for to honor Him with the remembrance of His passion and of His other works done in His humanity with devotion, love, and thanks to Him for the same, and forgettest or neglectest His feet . . . and lettest them [the brethren] to decay or perish for want of looking to, or to want clothing sufficient, or other necessaries . . . then dost thou not please Him nor doest Him any honor; thou seemest to kiss His mouth by devotion and spiritual prayer but thou treadest upon His feet, and defilest them, in as much as thou wilt not tend to them . . . and surely He will more thank thee and reward thee for the humble washing of His feet when they are very foul, and yield an ill savour to thee, than for all the curious pointing and fair dressing or decking what thou canst make about His head, by the devoutest remembrance of His humanity." [6]

How close the fourteenth and the twentieth centuries, as well as the Roman Catholic and the Quaker traditions, come together may be seen by laying alongside this passage, a paragraph from a French Quaker servant of God, Marius Grout, who died in 1946. "If contemplation, which introduces us to the very heart of creation, does not inflame us with such love that it gives us, together with deep joy, the understanding of the infinite misery of the world, it is a vain kind of contemplation, it is the contemplation of a false God. The sign of true contemplation is charity. By your capacity for forgiveness shall I recognize your God and also by your opening your arms to all creation." [7]

True ascetic theology in all the ages has not been blind to the spiritual direction that Jesus gave to all his future followers in the closing portion of the twenty-fifth chapter of Matthew, and that Francis of Assisi confirmed in the love that he lavished on the inmates of the leper hutch at Rivo Torto. The whole tradition of Catholic charity and of Protestant service has had freshly confirmed for it in every generation that Christ's body is truly to be found among those in need and is meant to be tended there, and that those who would serve him must open their arms to all creation. When Joseph's brethren were given the terms of their receiving further grain to save them and their families from the famine in Israel, they were told that

---

[6] Walter Hilton, *Scale of Perfection* (London, 1908), pp. 329f.

[7] Marius Grout, *On Contemplation* (Birmingham, 1945), p. 1.

they must produce their younger brother Benjamin, who had remained at home. Joseph is said to have put this into words which God may be speaking to us today. "Except you bring your brother with you, you shall not see my face."

An Irish Catholic pointed out to one of my friends that Quakers worked for the poor but rarely joined them. This may come too close for comfort to our whole Protestant tradition of charity. Roman Catholics have often taken that further step and their train of fearless saints puts us all deeply in their debt as we see what it means to become truly vulnerable, and how, when it is done in true abandonment, Christ is seen to live again and miracles break out all over the place.

While much care must be taken to distinguish this type of spiritual discipline from the compulsive but much applauded social activism that it can all too readily degenerate into, surely this third element is one that all of us face as a common element in contemporary spirituality and one that we must come to terms with. Difficult as it may be to guide and to control, it presents any ascetic theology in our time with a laboratory which could provide experiments releasing a whole new level of spiritual power to renew the Church in our time.

Contemporary Non-Catholic Spirituality
And the Guidance of Souls

John B. Coburn

The purpose of this paper is to present some of the forms of spirituality — or emphases of spirituality — which are emerging in the contemporary Protestant world with particular attention paid to the guidance of souls.

At the outset we must confess the traditional language difficulty. There is, in any ecumenical discussion, the problem of using the same words but giving them different meanings. For this paper there arise immediate problems for Protestants and some Anglicans, even in the title assigned: "Contemporary Non-Catholic Spirituality and the Guidance of Souls." The problem words are "spirituality," suggesting perhaps a separate identifiable substance such as "mentality" or "physique" or "left arm," and "souls," as though there were a "nous" that could be uncovered near the pituitary gland. "Guidance" is not an entirely happy word, if by it we mean to imply that the function of some people was to guide (as in a guided missile) other people in ways of Christian living. "Guidance," however, is to be preferred to "direction" which implies more strongly an absolute authority of one person over another in the spiritual life.

The poverty of words congenial to Protestant thought in this area is worth noting. "Piety," though once honored, has because of its affiliation with pietism become so identified with biblical fundamentalism and obscurantism that it is now highly suspect. It also tends to imply an individualism which is inconsistent with the social nature of man and the Church.

Even the word "prayer" represents a problem when it is interpreted (as it is by some) to mean disengagement from the world and therefore a retreat into a fortress — theological, devotional, or ecclesiastical — removed from life. A similar difficulty is related to the phrase "personal religion" as though it were both exclusively individualistic and directed God-ward only and so not interested in man.

On the other hand, such traditional Catholic phrases as dogmatic, mystical, and ascetical theology either have no meaning for Protestants or raise such negative — even hostile — emotions as to render them nearly useless in dialogue.

The point need not be labored: how are we to find words which are acceptable to Catholics and non-Catholics alike? The language problem,

56

of course, reflects a more basic difficulty. The words used by Catholics and Protestants carry different meanings because they come out of different ways of thinking about the life of the Spirit. In the Catholic world, spirituality is interpreted to be the growth in grace that comes in the life of an individual member of a family in response to the grace infused in baptism. It tends to be marked by "stages" of growth; sin is gradually overcome by discipline and participation in the Church's sacramental life; its aim is perfection and it is completed in the fulness of life with God and the whole company of heaven. The key word is "incorporation" in God's life through membership in the life of the Church.

For the Protestant the key words are "relationship" or "encounter": "speaking and acting" on the part of God; "hearing and acting" on the part of man. God creates us. He addresses us. We listen and respond in faith by grace. The Word dwells amongst us, is spoken by the preacher of the Word. Emphasis is not so much upon growth as it is upon the progress of a pilgrim where at each step of the way he is open to hear what God has to say and then responds by his actions toward his neighbors and God. Stress is upon the action of God right now and the response of man right now.

So behind the difficulty of words there lies this area where the spirit of Catholicism and the spirit of Protestantism approach the spirit of Christian life differently.

THE CONTEMPORARY PROTESTANT "MOOD"

Apart from the biblical fundamentalist position which (perhaps) unfortunately cannot be represented in this paper, it is best summed up in the phrase of Bonhoeffer: "To be a Christian is to be a man." To be sure, this is not always placed within its larger context: "To be a Christian does not mean to be religious in a particular way, to cultivate some particular form of asceticism (as a sinner, a penitent or a saint), but to be a man. It is not some religious act which makes a Christian what he is, but participation in the suffering of God in the life of the world." [1] This sets the mood: man and the study of the human situation provides the starting place. Rather than beginning with God, the beginning is with man.

It is, however, not man's being as substance understood philosophically which engages his interest, but man acting existentially. What concerns man are his actions, his decisions, his involvement in human affairs, how he

---

[1] Dietrich Bonhoeffer, *Prisoner for God: Letters and Papers from Prison* (New York, 1959), p. 166.

may be a man of his times, how he may come to know himself through his actions. Thus there is an understanding of Christ as "the man for others" and the consequent necessity for Christians to act decisively for others. What develops is an emphasis upon engagement in this world, upon understanding the forces immanent in this life, and an impatience with reliance upon traditional transcendent forms as helpful in understanding how God acts.

At the same time there is a breaking down of the distinction between the sacred and secular, the holy and the profane. The whole world is God's; it is his created order; the entire earth is the arena for his actions. Let us not, therefore — so runs this mood — try to place him in special sacred places like churches or tabernacles. He is in the world, and we must find and serve him there. Let us — it follows — not try to extract man's spiritual nature from his total nature; let us deal with him as a whole.

To explore the background for this mood would be interesting and rewarding but beyond the scope of this paper. It obviously rises out of our contemporary culture which in turn has been formed primarily by secular humanism and the scientific method. More than any others, Marx, Darwin, and Freud are the founding fathers. The culture has become technological, industrial, urban, de-personal, secular. The scientific method is the way to knowledge. Linguistic analysis determines the meaning of words and the validity of communication. The critical approach is the only test of truth. The material world is the real world. The world of poetry, images, myth, imagination is a fairy tale world; it is not really real.

Furthermore, since the scientific method provides the key to knowledge and since this method has revealed more knowledge in this generation than in all the generations of mankind before ours, of what real importance, then, is the study of history? The past means little. The only times are our times. Furthermore, if the findings of the scientific method are relative and changing, where is the absolute? If fact and value cannot be identified, can value in fact survive?

The culture, then, is secular, scientific, and impersonal. Its problems are immense and beyond the power of any individual to control. Since it is not evident that personal meaning can be found in those massive areas of a technological society, a man turns inward to seek meaning in personal terms. At its best it is an "I-thou" relation of trust with another human being: a wife, a friend, a family. But privatism and personalism do not always provide meaning; man is not always trustworthy. So there is the isolated man, "alone in the crowd," the separated man, not understood, alienated (even from himself), the fragmented man, set in a society hostile to him, too great to cope with.

Therefore, he becomes the man who concentrates upon himself. The more he can express himself — so runs this mood — the more of a whole human being he becomes. The significant words are these: the *whole* man is the man who is *free*, who is *authentic* or truly *himself*. He must be *unfettered*, live life as *he sees it*, and *express* himself; in most instances he will repudiate *authority*, discard any concept of a transcendent *deity*, avoid *discipline*, reject anything given, such as *tradition*. It is the self — *my self*, not your self or another's self, or my family's self, or my country's self — which determines the meaning of *my* self.

Let me give an illustration. It is a negative one: the growth in suicides, particularly among university students. At least part of the problem has to do with the difficulty a person has in an industrial, technological, impersonal society in taking the meaning of life seriously. Young people are overwhelmed by everything — examinations, the constant competitive pressures of studies from pre-kindergarten days, society, the bomb — and not a single significant part of any of this can they ever possibly control or change. Everything is too massive. They tend to feel, therefore, that if they cannot change anything else, at least they can take charge of their own life and if they want to — take it. This is one place where they have absolute control and where they are complete.

It is, however, with the translation of this mood into affirmative terms of Protestant spirituality that we are concerned. They emerge in the following ways:

THE WHOLE MAN

It is the "whole" man who is given guidance — not the "spiritual" man. The "spiritual" life is all of life, not a special segment of it. Therefore, the more the whole of life can be understood, the better. Whatever insights are given into understanding man — from whatever source (Christian or non-Christian) — are to be welcomed as instruments of the Spirit.

The Spirit moves upon the raw material of human existence in all its forms and depths, the evil as well as the good. The "spiritual" life is life "in the Spirit" and reflects the whole man in Christ. Thus spiritual guidance presupposes more and more a framework of a pastoral relationship which involves the whole man.

An early step in guidance, then, is to discover how to reinforce in a healthy way the ego strength of the counselee. Guidance now means the exploration of ways by which the authentic self may be discovered and affirmed. Here the insights of disciplines which deal with interpersonal relationships — depth psychology, for example — are invaluable. The first steps in guidance, therefore, have to do with "listening" so that the real self may begin to reveal itself, i.e., the whole self.

THE WHOLE WORLD

Since the self is always found within a social context — family, work, community — the spiritual life is fostered within this social context.

The world, in other words, provides the material which the Spirit shapes. It is not in the ecclesiastical realm that a man lives most of the time, but in the world. Hence such phrases as "holy worldliness" or "religionless Christianity" take on particular meaning today. There are no specially sacred areas where one acts "religiously." One must act fully as a whole human being in every area of the worldly life.

It is, therefore, the issues of life itself which shape the devotional life. The sources for prayer are those which arise out of the human condition. The world that Jesus knew was his world and important for him, but it is our world which is important to us, and the more we know about our life here the better.

Training in what is known as ascetical theology will, therefore, come not simply out of a monastery separated from the world, but along the road that leads from Selma to Montgomery.

To make the same point but with different language: spirituality is bound to *mission*. The life of the Spirit is the life of the Christian (his whole life) where God has placed him in the world. So, while he may very properly have a church life which is important, it is his life in the world where most of the raw material of his life is found, and it is within this raw material that the Holy Spirit dwells. That is where the spiritual life is developed. Training in mission, therefore — that is, how a man makes his Christian witness in the world — is his spiritual training, and the life that he lives in the world is his spiritual life. Not all of it, to be sure, but most of it.

This point may be put still another way. We frequently assume that as Christians we bring God or Christ to the world. The fact is, of course, that God is already in the world; the "hidden Christ" is already moving in the hearts of men and in their corporate lives. Our task is to try to discern where this Spirit is already living and moving — where reconciliation is taking place — and to cooperate with him in the world of human affairs. It is there especially that his activity counts and our spiritual life is lived.

Involvement in the issues of the day, then, is the only way by which the spiritual life can have any meaning. A man must be a man of his own times. This is not to say that involvement is an end in itself, for it is not. A Christian is involved in social issues for that is where the Spirit is, and his response is to the Spirit in and through the issues. Involvement takes place that God may be served as man is served for the transformation of society. There is, in other words, always a dimension beyond the social — a continuing relation with him who is the Lord of this world and for whom service is undertaken.

LAY SPIRITUALITY

In many areas of Christian living, therefore, spiritual guidance may properly come from laity rather than from clergy. It is lawyers, for example, who can best speak to one another and wrestle out what it means to be a Christian lawyer; and so doctors, teachers, businessmen, housewives, and bartenders. The clergy may properly become more and more "resource personnel" and less and less "spiritual" directors, more concerned with putting laity — or special kinds of laity — in touch with each other rather than keeping them in a personal relationship to themselves.

Why is it the almost universal practice, for example, that clergy conduct retreats for laity? Why don't we have it the other way around: laity conducting retreats for clergy? What special insights do clergy have into holy worldliness? They may know holiness in the ecclesiastical world (and they may not too), but that is a very small part of the world to the layman.

Indeed, is it right that the central focus of retreats, or of schools of prayer, or of spiritual conferences, be always on the relationship between the "worldly" laity who come to be instructed by the "holy" clergyman? Where is the place of the "holy community"? Indeed, is it not the "holy people of God" rather than the "holy man of God" of which the Bible most often speaks? If the spiritual life is indeed all of life, will not the laity properly instruct more and more?

This means some measure of guidance through *small groups*, where intimate sharing and listening is possible. The center of the content may be derived from both interest or vocational groups and Bible study groups. Again they will become less clergy dominated. There may develop, then, prayer groups where common concerns may be discussed in mutual trust. At its best this interest in prayer will not be developed as an end in itself but incorporated within both the vocational and Bible study groups. These groups in addition help to provide a bridge between the individual and his "personal" religion and the larger, more impersonal act of corporate worship.

"HIDDEN" CHRISTIANITY

The recognition that to be a Christian is to be a man of his times in the world means that he may live as a Christian in a "hidden" fashion and in fact may not *do* anything as a Christian in any way different from the non-Christian. He will simply do it from a different motivation and with a different purpose. "And whatever you do, in word or deed, do everything in the name of the Lord Jesus, giving thanks to God the Father through him" (Col 3:17).

The function of a Christian teacher, for example, is not to convert but to teach — to teach with all the resources at his disposal — because he wants to express his love of God and man. His teaching may be no different than another teacher's, but his purpose will be different: to expose students to Truth, i.e., to God. This is so with every occupation in God's world. In other words, day by day Christian living may not be very dramatic; indeed it may almost always be quite routine and unexciting. The point is that it be done for God in his world and in man's.

The ethical decisions that a man makes will, therefore, be those that arise out of his own situation. They will be similar to but not exactly like the situations of other men. Principles — primarily the Summary of the Law — will be important. But the counsel of intelligent and informed Christian men will be equally important. The ambiguous relativities of each situation will weigh more heavily than counsels of perfection understood in a simplistic fashion.

People will seem more important than principles. And the willingness not to have one's own way will become one of the great marks of growth in spiritual maturity. In any case, the key will be obedience to love within the context of the moment and in the light of one's total experience. Thus the rationale for "situational ethics." This is not to disregard an absolute principle such as the Summary of the Law; it is to translate this Law of Love as the law of life into personal terms, and to make relevant relative decisions in the light of the absolute principle.

In all of this there will be an increased willingness to make one's witness in a "hidden" fashion and a reluctance to identify any particular position — especially one's own — as the Christian position. This is especially true in a complex age and in a society where so often the Christian answer simply is not known. Christian modesty in the face of the massive problems of contemporary society will not be unbecoming.

CHANGING PATTERNS OF PERSONAL PRAYER

While it is true that God's relationship to man, his creature redeemed and forgiven, remains the same, man's understanding of that relationship and his response to God change from age to age. In the present age so far as Protestantism is concerned the following patterns seem to be emerging:

1. The prayer of thanksgiving is the prayer to begin with and remains the central prayer. This is to affirm the self in relationship to God by thanking him for the gift of the self, for what he has done in the unique personal situation given. In the search for the "authentic" self it is to affirm whatever "authenticity" can be found and to relate it to God as the author of "authenticity." Inasmuch as the self is found only in relation to other selves, this means thanksgiving for those selves as well; so intercession may easily follow. The main point, however, is the strengthening of the self in relation to God and to God's continuing action of love. It is affirming the self in the light of God's goodness rather than the denying of the self in the light of man's sin.

2. The prayer of adoration (which incidentally is a phrase which usually embarrasses Protestants) becomes the prayer of the will: to want God where one is. This is to affirm God in one's situation, to declare that he is present and involved even when he cannot be seen and above all to want him there. This is not to say glibly that one can see God in all situations, for he acts hiddenly as well as openly; it is simply to say one wants him where one is.

3. The prayer of confession thus becomes a more inclusive prayer than one which concentrates upon "my sin, my own sin, my own most grievous sin." It will include what I want for myself, my desires, my hopes, my confession that I do not want God in my situation, that at times I do not want to adore him, and that at times I would like not to find him. It will be the *whole* man who comes under examination, not simply acts of the past. Confession will, then, not be so easily manipulated as a means of obtaining an easy conscience, but will become a steady and continuing form of prayer for the honest presentation of the whole sinful man to the God who continually forgives.

This may not be the place to discuss sacramental or private confession, but at least reference must be made to it. Traditionally, of course, Protestantism has protested against the private confession of sin to a minister of

God (although Luther encouraged it) on the grounds that confession could be made directly to God and there was, therefore, no need for a priestly mediator. Today this seems to be changing. Part of the Lutheran world now endorses it; most of the Anglican world recognizes (if it does not practice) it; listening to troubled souls pour out their sins and giving assurance of God's absolution are part of the pastoral care of an increasing number of Protestant clergy. I can only give my own testimony that there is here a means of grace which is indispensable for some, may be of help to most, and should be offered more generously to all Protestants.

4. Petition and intercession then arise out of the context of one's own situation. They will be related in the beginning primarily to the effect of one's actions upon others. What is the Christian action that I must take? What will this mean for others? How can they be helped? How can God's will be done for them? May it be done? How through me? Beyond this, intercession may arise from no more than the hope and faith that God is concerned about all his children, and if we are bound together in his Spirit we are bound to bring them to God, for it is the Spirit who prays within us.

CHANGING PATTERNS OF MEDITATION AND CONTEMPLATION

1. Contemporary forms of meditation begin with man rather than God, with this world rather than the biblical world, with my life rather than Jesus' life. The purpose of meditation may be to help one become transformed by the Spirit of Christ and to try to "think God's thoughts after him," but the approach to those thoughts today begins humanly rather than divinely. Thus the beginning of meditation arises from our own life, our pondering, debating, thinking, wondering, reflecting, questioning, as preparation for decision making and acting. The *Exercises* of St. Ignatius, for example, hold little appeal for the modern Protestant mind, but the *Prayers* of Michael Quoist have great appeal. The sharp difference is due to the form of the latter: first human situations (The Bald Head; The Pornographic Magazine; Hunger; The Subway; Prayer Before a Twenty-Dollar Bill), then biblical treatment, and all within a free, unstructured style of address to God.

(It may be — to digress for a moment — that the classic which speaks best to this day is *The Cloud of Unknowing*. We are — so far as confidence in traditional proofs of this existence or transcendence of God are concerned — in an age overshadowed by a cloud through which we cannot penetrate. And we are not clear how the "God above God" has penetrated and continues to penetrate to us.)

2. The understanding of contemplative prayer is also changing. No longer is it to be understood as a "stage" of prayer to be attained by a select few as a result of a long interior struggle after other "stages" (vocal prayer and meditation) have been attained. It is rather a prayer which may be a very natural prayer even for beginners. Thus the prayer of simple regard may be a part of the interior response of many from the outset.

This means an emphasis on and expectation of simplicity in prayer throughout — not simply at the end of a progressive series of steps. It denies, in fact, the assumption that stages in prayer are invariably either necessary or desirable. They are, rather, woven together, with changing patterns to be sure, but never in separate, distinct steps.

THE ROLE OF THE SPIRITUAL DIRECTOR

There are certain characteristics that mark the Protestant spiritual director.

1. The first is that he himself must be not only a man of prayer, but one who is himself trying to respond as fully as he can in his own life to what he believes God's will is for him. He must have his own spiritual "growing edge," and that is where he must live. He never, in other words, "has it made" so that he may relax, write a book, and tell people the principles upon which the spiritual life may be built. The living relationship between the two individuals rests, at least in part, upon the degree to which the Spirit is actually living in the director.

2. His knowledge of depth psychology must be such as to enable him to identify the person disturbed enough psychologically as to require professional psychiatric help and to make the proper reference, and to use on an elementary level some of the tools made available by this discipline. For example, he must learn to listen so that he might hear what lies behind the first words spoken. It is a commonplace that a counselee frequently speaks first of a superficial problem in order to reveal later the underlying problem if he learns he can trust the director. What is presented as a technical religious question — "please explain the mystery of the Trinity" — may reveal a human problem — "how can I tell my father to get off my back and still let him know I want to love him?"

3. The purpose of guidance is to help a man come to discern *for himself* what God's will is and to respond to it. The director will then see that his counselee considers the variety of ways of looking at his situation, to balance one way over against another; to consider alternative ways of acting; to help him see himself and the ambiguity of his own motivations and concerns; to use his reason as intelligently as possible; to suggest various inter-

pretations of the events in his life. It means helping him see how God is involved in his situation, how God is acting (either openly or in a hidden fashion); to help him, in a word, to see with the eyes of faith.

The purpose of guidance is also to encourage him to *act* in faith — even with his own ambiguities and with the full will of God not known, but with sufficient light for the moment.

The director, then, is to set his counselee free from himself. Although he may at certain times be quite specific and directive in counsel, his underlying aim is to establish the other in his own life before God freely. I think it is von Hügel who said, "Those we love most we disengage most from ourselves." Once a man has decided what God wants him to do and wants to do it, then the director supports him in that decision.

This "setting free," this establishing of a man before God himself, is one of the great tasks of the director. A man has personal dealings with God in his interior life, and the more he can learn to trust God as his spiritual director (with whatever helps a director may give from time to time) the better.

This does not mean that a person is free simply to decide what he wants to do and then does it by stating this is God's will. The fact is that frequently what God wants us to do is precisely what we do not want to do. Perhaps most often the things God wants us to do are what we do not want to do. We squirm and try to avoid them, but finally with his help we come through and do them as well as we can.

It is equally true, however, that there are times when it is not at all clear what God's will is. So far as we can determine there is no moral issue involved which would give us direction. God seems neutral. There is no indication of what he wants. When this occurs, God is saying to us: "What do *you* want to do? If you can do it for my sake, then go do it."

In other words, the spiritual or Christian life is a joint life of man's cooperation with God's grace. God does not always give clear-cut direction. On those occasions when after prayer, reflection, and counsel there is no clear indication of what God wants and no moral dimension is apparent, then we are free — urged — to do what *we* want to do. So we do it — for God's sake and not our own — and his will is then carried out just a little further into the world. There is an area here of Christian freedom where God is depending on us, and where in Christian maturity we are meant to act independently — but always for his sake and work.

4. There are two dangers in the spiritual life that the director has an especial responsibility to watch out for. First of all, there is the failure of a

man to act when he knows what God wants him to do. This is to dull the growing edge. The fact is that God does not ask a man to do anything without giving him the power to do it. The director may, therefore, help the counselee think again about what God may be calling him to do and hold out constant encouragement that if it is indeed what God wants, then it can be done.

The other danger is that a man will give up. The sin of despair is the hardest to help a person with. The virtue of hope is a great anchor in the Christian life. Therefore the holding out of hope is part of the Christian answer in guidance, along with the affirmation that the heart of the Christian life is not in attaining perfection — that may lead to despair — but in beginning again, right now, today. And that is all that matters. The Christian life is always a series of new beginnings. Our hope is in Christ and in what he has done. Therefore we are to look up, take hope, and begin once more.

Christian hope means not simply that there is always a tomorrow which can under God be a better tomorrow for a man and his society, but it is also a present reality. When a man's hope is in Christ, then he is set free to be his authentic self right now and participate as completely as he can in his life's struggles without fear or any sense of meaninglessness. So constant encouragement, constant support, countless reminders to forget the failures that are behind and to begin once more are some of the helps the spiritual director is to provide.

5. The spiritual director need not take himself too seriously. God is going to get his work done if *he* is taken seriously. Therefore, the attention of the director is primarily on God's Spirit at work in the relationship in the life of the other, in the situation where he is trying to break through. How can he speak for the Spirit? When is judgment the right word? When forgiveness? When should he probe and cut? When to urge? When is the slow quiet word to be spoken? When the immediate word? When to let fire burn? When to rest? The Holy Spirit is at work in the counselee to bring him to his best self; how to help, then, rather than hinder? And how except to pray in the Spirit as he and his counselee meet each other in him?

PRACTICAL CONSEQUENCES

Certain implications suggest themselves as a result of the type of emphasis presented.

1. The place of a rule of life — especially for beginners in the life of prayer — must be rethought. At the present time the normal procedure is to suggest that a rule of life consisting of time set aside each day for prayer,

meditation, and Bible reading be adopted. There is at the outset the imposition of a new "law" in devotional practice. When this law is not obeyed, guilt follows and frequently despair. The danger is that the new life for the new Christian becomes a burden rather than an inspiration.

It may be that at the beginning — at least for certain people — the only rule of life should be to have no rule. If freedom and self-expression — however much they must be channeled and tempered with growth in spiritual maturity — are authentic notes of the movement of the Spirit today, then it is possible that rules imposed which restrict that freedom actually prevent the growth and maturity sought. Perhaps the first steps in guidance should be to remove all burdens which tend to increase a sense of guilt. For some people the way to begin is to affirm "being" rather than concentrate on "becoming" and not to add anything that will restrict or distort natural growth. A man is justified by faith through grace, not by his works. He is acceptable even when he knows he is unacceptable — that is a first step, not to "become" acceptable.

To be sure, growth is desired and discipline provides a means to growth, but the best discipline is that which is self-imposed and the result of one's own struggle to find the best way for one's own life. The best spiritual counsel, therefore, is that which suggests and prompts rather than commands or orders. Suggestions of various rules may properly be made, but gently, tentatively, and without pressure.

Emphasis upon a rule of life tends to give the impression that discipline is an end in itself. It is not. God is the end. And at the beginning of the way to God emphasis upon an imposed rule may be a hindrance rather than a help.

2. "Prayer for busy people" raises the problem of time. The pressure of the tempo of life in our modern industrialized society is quite simply a completely different pressure from that when most of the devotional manuals and ascetic practices were developed. Certainly the monastic ideals of the eighth century have little reality for the man of the twentieth century — clergyman as well as layman. Contemporary man — even the ecclesiastical one — simply cannot live with the leisure possible in an agricultural society.

How, then, can man "on the run" be helped to pray? How can he have interior dialogue with God while talking with men? How can he be hid with Christ while open to the world?

The issue is sometimes placed within the poles of engagement and disengagement, involvement and retreat; God "in the spaces" and God "in dialogue." How may both be affirmed as necessary and proper ways for prayer and personal response to God? The solution lies in affirming both/and rather than either/or. Yet the fact remains that most busy people do not believe they can pray. What is the best prayer for them?

The feeding of the Spirit in a regular, ordered way through prayer, meditation, and Bible reading cannot be done without some sense of being with God and paying attention directly to him. How may modern man be encouraged to "find" time when he says, "I have no time." The fact is, of course, that he does have time, though he may not have leisure. Can he not be taught to pray while driving, to intercede in a subway, and to offer thanks while walking? The "interior dialogue" of being mindful of God, thinking of him and responding to him from "time to time" throughout the day is as possible for a banker as a farmer.

If contemplative prayer may now be regarded as a possibility for the beginner as for the advanced, this leads to a new understanding of what has been termed traditionally "the sacrament of the present moment." The affirmation of one's self within the context of his immediate situation can mean also a new acceptance and affirmation of God in that situation. Are there ways by which his will may be discerned in the present moment while man is on the run? Can God be praised by the running? Is he running too?

3. Spiritual reading may take a wider form than normally accepted. While there still will be a central place for Bible study and the reading of commentaries, while there still will be a place for traditional reading of an inspirational nature, new emphasis will be placed upon reading secular literature to discover God's Spirit at work in books that speak only of man's spirit. All contemporary literature which describes man's struggle to discover himself, to affirm meaning, to wrestle with good and evil, to establish justice and mutuality, to express the love of man for another, will be proper spiritual reading. Indeed, this exercise to see how God is at work in the secular world, to praise him for it, to identify oneself with it, may be an increasingly useful way to strengthen one's own spiritual life set in the midst of that secular world. There is in reading an opportunity to "reason together" with an author *and* with God about his work in the world.

4. There is no absolute way in the devotional life; there are only different ways. Absolutes are now suspect. It is a day of relativities. What one man discovers as his way of prayer may not be another's. He may affirm his understanding, but that may not be the understanding of another. His responsibility is to help another discover his own way and to support him in that way no matter how different it may be from his own. We are in a time of

great movement with an infinite variety of ways being prepared by the Spirit.

PERSONAL PRAYER AND CORPORATE WORSHIP

To speak of a relation between personal prayer and corporate worship is not to imply that corporate worship is impersonal. It is not. All worship is, of course, personal — just as personal as private prayer. But we are referring now to the action of the gathered people of God in their corporate response to God through the liturgy.

This is expressed most fully in the contemporary liturgical movement which perhaps best illustrates the central focus of Protestant concern with involvement in this world as the means for proper expression of spirituality. Along with a new understanding of the place of baptism as the entrance into the company of God's people, there has come a new understanding of the place of the Eucharist as the central act of Christian worship.

This movement is recapturing the sense of the corporate nature of life and of the Christian Church. The centrality of the Eucharist is being rediscovered both as an offering by man of God's creative world to God and the receiving back from him within the form of bread and wine of Christ's body and blood. This again is to break down the distinction between the Church and the world, the sacred and the secular.

There is a central theme in the spirit of the liturgical movement which sets certain emphases.

Worship is an *act*. It is what people do. It has to do with the will — to acknowledge God's worth — not with the emotions.

It is an act of recollection — recalling the historical events in which God has acted. It is an act of suffering — of ourselves, our souls and bodies, since he first offered his Son as propitiation for our sins. It is an act of anticipation — of the eschaton, of his coming again.

Worship is a *corporate* act. We are members one of another each with a part to play, laity as well as clergy. We have a responsibility toward one another. Even the preaching of the word is a corporate action where the Spirit who dwells in the congregation is the instrument both for the speaking and the hearing of God's message.

Worship is, furthermore, a corporate act which is *sacramental*. It is an outward and visible sign of inward and spiritual grace. It is something that God does which enables us to respond. In the act of communion, as St. Augustine so forcibly reminded his flock, we who are part of Christ's mystical body, receive our share in the body's life. "If then you are the body of Christ and his members, then that which is on the altar is the mystery of yourselves. Receive the mystery of yourselves." Here is Christian self-affirmation in its fullest sense.

And, finally, worship is *completed* back — in the world. That is, worship is lived. It is the life of Christ in the life of Christians. Where we are is where Christ is. The fact of a person being the bearer of Christ in the world individually is thus derived from his participation in the corporate act of the Church.

So we complete the full cycle back in the world. That is the arena where we live our spiritual lives for that is where we live as human beings. When contemporary Protestantism attempts to help a man in his spiritual life it will stress the world and the necessity to be involved in that world. It will recognize the danger that arises from this stress upon involvement: that the Christian faith may become absorbed into humanism alone or identified solely with contemporary culture. Christianity is always something more than modern man and human society.

Contemporary Protestantism will also emphasize the freedom he has as a Christian to determine God's will for himself with the authority of the Christian tradition and the witnesses of Christians within the context of his own situation. It will recognize again a danger: emphasis upon freedom may be interpreted to mean self-will unfettered by discipline. The stress upon the "authentic" self may easily lead to the "self-indulged" self. It is not human freedom but freedom in Christ which is at the heart of man's free relationship with God.

Finally, contemporary Protestantism will provide for him at least one guide in the person of a fellow Christian who will relate to him on the deepest level of a personal relationship as the representative of all God's people. He may be a "friend in Christ" rather than a "spiritual director," but the purpose of the relationship will be the same: to be informed, directed, controlled, guided by the indwelling of God's Holy Spirit. Thus may he know that it is God himself who is with him to direct him, and so to strengthen him that whatever he does he does for the glory of God who in his Son is both the author and finisher of his faith — and of his spiritual life, his whole life.

A Modern Approach to the Ascetical Life

Bernard Häring, C.SS.R.

It is difficult in the age of the Second Vatican Council to present the Catholic approach to the spiritual and ascetical life in a simple manner. We have become convinced of the fact that there is a legitimate place for pluralism within the unity of the Catholic Church, indeed that it is inevitable. All of us live in the world as though in a tower. Each person has his own window from which he observes reality. But no one imagines that he sees the total reality. Therefore while everyone takes that which he sees very seriously, he must at the same time maintain a reverent dialogue with those who have a different perspective.

In spite of this variety of approach the Council has still been able in a remarkable fashion to set certain common perspectives in a clearer light.

NOT SELF-PERFECTION BUT HOLINESS

On the thirteenth Sunday after Pentecost the Church prays: "Almighty and eternal God, grant us an increase of faith, hope, and charity; make us love what you command that we may attain that which you promise." This prayer expresses the classical view of the spiritual life. Primary emphasis is laid on the truth that God takes the initiative and that we receive everything from him. Faith is therefore taken not so much as a virtue of man or a quality of the soul in the Aristotelian sense. Faith is understood essentially from the point of view of God's revealing himself. Faith is a dialogue in which God himself speaks first. He reveals himself and opens up man's heart to receive that revelation. God glorifies his truth by allowing man to share in it. We can describe faith as the grateful, joyful reception of the saving truth. In this connection, of course, the Christian is always mindful of the fact that Christ is the truth. So faith is a grateful "yes" to Christ, who utters a saving "yes" to us. He sanctifies us in the truth.

A life which is sanctified in the truth, sanctified in Christ, is a life under the law of faith. Thus Gospel and Law need not be separated. The good news of Christ is the fundamental law of faith. Faith itself denotes the great turning, the great conversion: "Be renewed in spirit and believe in the gospel" (Mk 1:15).

Life under the law of faith means praise of God, praise of his salvific truth. This faith is found first of all in the celebration of the mysteries of salvation. There Christ speaks of his bride. "There Christ continually proclaims his gospel" (CL 33). And the bride of Christ, in the assembly of the faithful, answers with praise-giving faith. But the mystery does not stand alongside of life; it must determine the basic structure of life. This means that the entire Christian life is to be considered as a joyful grateful listening to God, who speaks to us in Christ — and therefore in everything that happens. Thus, one's entire life is a response in faith, wherein everything is viewed in the purifying light of the saving mysteries.

"Grant us an increase of hope." Hope is not to be understood from the standpoint of human longing. It is God himself who desires to have someone join with him in extolling his gracious love, and who says to man: "I am the salvation of the people." Hope is a gift of the redeeming love of God. Its power consists not so much in our yearning to be happy, but rather in God's desire to make us happy. Christian hope is not only a reaching out for future blessings. It is in addition always a praise-giving, thankful "yes" to the present moment of salvation. Of course this salvation is not yet fully apparent. For that reason faith and hope are essentially ordered to growth. There is, therefore, a tension between the "already" and the "not yet," but in such a way that the salvation which is already ours urges us on to greater development and to the expectation of the full revelation of the blessed freedom of the children of God.

"Grant us growth in charity." Charity as understood by Christian faith is not a love which we might claim as our own accomplishment, but rather the love by which God has loved us first and by which he makes us capable of returning love to him in Christ. In this love, which God showers in our hearts through his Holy Spirit, God glorifies himself. He is love. His love is a colloquy between the divine persons, a colloquy which he wishes to share with men. For the Christian, love of God and fellow men is not simply a means to secure his own happiness. The love which has its source in God is the basis of the dialogue: "I — Thou — We." Our fellow man is essentially included in the love by which God loves us and by which we love him in return. For it is in one and the same love that God loves you and me, that he loves us, his family, his chosen people.

Thus to love God means basically also to love his commandments, for his commandments are an expression of his love and guideposts to a perfect love. Growth in love therefore involves a constantly more joyous "yes" to God's commandments. It means establishing an ever-widening synthesis of all ethical obligations under the unifying principle of love. It is this love which leads a man to pray through the entire course of life: "How can I repay the Lord for all that he has done for me?"

Next to the emphasis on the service-oriented character of the hierarchy and the whole Christian life, there is probably nothing more characteristic of the theology of the Second Vatican Council than this search for synthesis. This synthesis between the celebration of the mystery and one's daily life, between Gospel and Law, is crucial to the understanding of Christian morality.

By its solemn teaching on the general vocation to sanctity consisting in the love of God and neighbor, the Council has made utterly impossible any disjunction between moral theology and asceticism. Ascetical discipline is not something apart from moral theology; it rather underscores an essential characteristic of moral teaching, namely, the law of growth, the constant need for effort, purification, and self-analysis.

TWO BASIC ASPECTS OF PERSONALISM

In the light of the gospel we can see two essential aspects of a personalistic conception of life. Both these aspects emphasize the value of the human person, yet they are basically opposed to each other.

That personalism which can be termed "Adamitic" looks primarily to man himself and is concerned with all else only to the extent that it serves man's own glory or his search for happiness. Everything apart from man is taken to be simply a means. Adam wants to be wise in his own right; he yearns for an area of freedom which he has not received from God; he seeks his life in himself. This Adamitic personalism finds clear expression in the Aristotelian system, which restricts the moral ethic to the categories of end and means. The Stoic ethic is also Adamitic, based on the self-perfection of the individual. In this context God and the "other" are certainly not rejected, but they are related mainly to the perfection of the individual person.

Likewise the Buddhist, who seeks to free himself from the restless demands of life, does not find his "Thou." He remains stranded on the ego whether he conceives of this as a complete emptying of self or as an ultimate fulfillment.

Pharisaism, which makes use of the law of God as an instrument of self-justification, is the embodiment of an ego-oriented personalism, even though it pays constant lip service to God and his law.

Adamitic personalism is characterized by the fact that the emphasis on self obstructs the view of the Thou or at least relegates it to second place.

Tersteegen gives voice to a profound Christian experience when he observes that gazing on self leads to sickness whereas openness to the Thou brings health. The triune life of God consists precisely in this contemplation of the Thou. The Father is entirely himself when he imparts all his power, wisdom, and love to his Son. The Son is entirely himself by receiving himself from the Father and giving himself back to him. The Holy Spirit is the gift, the bond of love.

The personalism of the redeemed is a personalism in Christ, the incarnate Son of God. Christ's morning prayer, the basic characteristic of his entire life, is: "You have fashioned a body for me, O Lord [a human nature]. I come to do your will." His evening prayer, the fulfillment of his personalism, is "Into your hands I commend my spirit." The Christian personalist finds his true self by looking at Christ, for in this way he sees himself as loved by him who is the personification of love.

In Catholic thought of the last 20 years, biblical personalism — as developed on the Catholic side by Ferdinand Ebner and in the Jewish tradition by Martin Buber — has received great prominence. The best of Catholic and Protestant thought has come together in such personalism. It is the personalism of the "I — Thou — We." In the presence of God this personalism affirms the following: Everything that I have and am is a word of the love of God. I can therefore find my true self only by listening to God, only by a life that is totally a response of gratitude and love.

God calls each person with an inexpressible, non-transferable, unique name. Nevertheless this name can only be discovered in a dialogue of adoring, trusting love of God. God calls each one directly into being. He gives him individuality and personality through his creative word. Yet God wants to bring each one to complete self-consciousness, to fulfillment of his name through the message of a love which involves one's neighbor. A person is therefore not able to find his Thou in God — which alone can make him happy — if he does not make contact with the beloved messenger of God. No one can realize his own proper self if he uses his neighbor merely as a means for self-fulfillment. Only in openness to the Thou, to his dignity, to his uniqueness, to his needs, can a man come to a genuine, healing experience of his self.

THE TRUE MEANING OF ASCETICAL SELF-CONTROL

Adamitic and Christian personalism struggle with each other in the heart of the Christian. Thus there arises the need for control, for examination, to determine how far we understand our life as a true openness to the Thou of God and neighbor. It is in this way only that we can find our true self. Ascetical self-analysis concerns itself with the actions of the person, not in the terms of self-perfection or self-liberation, but as the answer to the great question: Is my being really open entirely to God and to the Thou of my neighbor? Christian self-control is neither destructive of self nor turned in upon self. It is rather a stage in the struggle for a fuller expression of faith as listening and response, a stage along the way of hope as man's complete gift of himself to God, and along the path of charity as man's glorification of God through selfless service of neighbor and community. Thus self-control is dedicated to the adoration of God and the service of the community. Everything is seen in the light of the great reality of love for God and love for neighbor.

Life-fulfillment and self-control must stand in proper proportion to each other. Self-control and all ascetical practices must be at the service of life. But there is always the danger that the ascetical concern for the perfection of self will be valued above the perfection of life, that is, above this openness for God and neighbor. The reflective point of view, namely, one which turns back on self, can reduce one's ability to live spontaneously; it can encroach upon openness for the Thou if the guiding principle is perfection of self.

There is an asceticism of many individual practices, mortifications, and penitential exercises which are more or less legitimate in themselves. But such an asceticism may lead to an escape from life and genuine duty. True Christian asceticism must be above all an asceticism that remains true to life. This means a self-denial related to life, a life which is understood as an adoring love for God and a serving love for one's neighbor. It must be a renunciation which is oriented to the blessed freedom of the children of God. But this means an openness for God and neighbor. Out of this freedom for God and neighbor the fullness of the individual self can develop.

The Christian life must take its proper place in life itself, that is, it must be directed toward an ever improving encounter with God and neighbor. There is of course also the need to get ready for the great opportunities of life. One must take thought beforehand and review them after they have taken place.

Self-examination before acting is essentially a matter of "discernment of spirits." This is in the great Christian tradition, one which has received an especially strong development in Benedictine spirituality. A truly traditional Christian moral theology is not based primarily on casuistry, but on the signs which enable one to analyse the spirit, signs such as inner peace of soul. When an idea or a wish, an undertaking or a plan strengthens this inner peace of soul, furthers the prayer life, or arouses joy, then one can assume that it comes from God. An additional fundamental guideline for the discernment of spirits is a faithful response to the grace of those particular God-given opportunities for good in terms of service. Christian casuistry can be integrated into such a spirit, as Paul, for example, did in the letter to the Romans and the first letter to the Corinthians when he solved the problem of the "strong ones" and the "enlightened ones" (Rom 14; 1 Cor 8). In the last analysis it is a matter of how our actions affect the salvation of others. Thus our efforts in the interest of the salvation of others is not to be subordinated to our striving for personal salvation. Rather, personal salvation, for one who is motivated by the true spirit of God, is seen as the fruit of our concern for others. Max Scheler expressed this conception of Christian asceticism when he said that self-enrichment, which is the basic value of action, is, as it were, borne on the shoulders of the action itself. Action is seen essentially as the response to a value, as the fulfillment of genuine dialogue.

Self-analysis allows one to form a particular, positive resolution. The Christian life, it is true, must be spontaneous, a response to the *kairos*, to the God-given opportunity for good here and now. But it would be naive to think that such spontaneity is possible without self-analysis and without conscious purpose. A conscious striving for the specific goals of purification and growth must be part of the spirit of watchful waiting upon God. Christian asceticism, above all in connection with the teaching on the sacrament of penance, has constantly stressed the great value of particular resolutions. Obviously, these may not be arbitrary but must be the product of a genuinely Christian self-examination. The goal must always be a greater openness toward God and a more useful service to the Thou and the community.

SCRUTINY AFTER ACTION

At certain times the Christian must re-examine his actions and analyze his motives to determine the effect of his conduct on his neighbor and the community. He must look back to see whether his actions and intentions have deepened his interior openness to God and fellow-men. Once a Christian has become accustomed to make such a periodic examination, he will more readily become instinctively aware of any disturbance to the magnetic needle of his life, that is, he will see immediately when his needs and desires are no longer directed to God and neighbor. One of the basic requirements of Christian asceticism is the ability to enter into profound, uncompromising confrontation with oneself whenever the gift of God's grace has been spurned and a particular opportunity for doing good has been ignored, or whenever something positively wrong has been done. Evil consists in the insulation of self from the appeal of value, and ultimately from the person who embodies this value. Self-examination opens the way to a new encounter in a spirit of humility and contrition. A Christian should often pray for the grace to be able to repent and renew his good resolution as soon as possible after any failure. Every sin, that is, every "no" to the invitation of love leads to a disorientation of the whole person, if this refusal is not followed immediately by an attitude of humility and renewed love. Sorrow is a personal encounter with God, who gently calls us back to himself. It is a renewed, more humble "yes," an expression of trust in the mercy of God, a song of humble praise.

CHRISTIAN ASCETICISM AND THE SACRAMENT OF PENANCE

All that has been said above receives its full significance when we consider it in relation to the sacrament of penance. A sacrament is an encounter with Christ. Christ's role is all-important here, man's part is simply response, faith. In this sacrament the Lord, who sees man's sin but also his desire for conversion, utters his forgiving word. Since confession is an encounter with Christ, a contemplation of Christ, and an awareness of self only with the eyes of Christ, it affords a genuine opportunity for liberation from the Adamitic, and development of the redeemed personalism. The saving action of Christ in the sacrament is at the same time a sanctifying action. The Christian who has been comforted and liberated by the Lord's mercy will be all the more attached to him by the sweet bonds of gratitude. His continued striving for an ever-deepening spirit of conversion is above all a hymn to God's mercy and redeeming justice.

For the sincere Christian the sacrament of penance is not a matter of law; it is not a continuous turning from death to life. It is rather the continuous working out of that which was begun in baptism, the greater purification of a soul still turned to God. We may call it the second conversion, that is, perseverance in the light through a constant struggle against the darkness that seeks to extinguish it.

The sacrament of penance, precisely when it is not a matter of obligation due to the presence of mortal sin, is an expression of the prayer: "Grant us an increase of faith, hope, and charity." Such growth is a struggle against evil. It is a glorification of God made pure by a more humble life.

We are enabled through God's grace to experience this continuing conversion over and over again as a new beginning. This does not mean that a person should live in constant disabling fear of having lost God's grace. Rather he expresses gratitude for God's repeated words to us: "Behold I make all things new." It is a new beginning by virtue of God's new gift to the soul making it more intensely new. This progress is accompanied, however, not by a satisfied glance at the self-perfecting ego, but by looking at Jesus and neighbor, by praise and humble thanks.

This does not mean that the self is entirely to be excluded. On the contrary it is included in the experience of the love of Jesus, who is truly concerned for us, who really helps us to find our true self when we turn to him and turn with his love to our neighbor.

As this continual conversion develops there occurs a change of emphasis. Human freedom is seen more and more as a sharing in the freedom of God. A synthesis between freedom on the one hand, and docility and obedience on the other is gradually developed. Obedience is understood more and more in relation to grace, and the law is recognized ever more clearly as an expression of life in Christ Jesus. The consciousness of a constant need for conversion brings with it also a true understanding of the law. The new law is the Holy Spirit, who fills our hearts with love, which is the fulfillment of the law. But we have not yet given our full allegiance to this law; we have not yet given ourself over completely to the direction of the Holy Spirit. Therefore we still need external laws to guide us. But this is not law for law's sake. Its task is to remind us of our sinfulness and to lead us at the same time to Christ, from whom we expect cleansing and holiness. The fruit of this developing conversion is a broadening synthesis, whereby the law is interpreted in a truly theological way as a call to humility and even more as a call to heed the graces of the Holy Spirit. Continuous conversion is expressed by a growing willingness to accept personal responsibility and co-responsibility. It is also evidenced by the greater personal character of our prayer, which now expresses a deeper longing for the coming of the Lord.

ASCETICISM AS WATCHFULNESS

As a result of biblical study and liturgical renewal the eschatalogical virtues are receiving greater attention in ascetical teaching. The Christian life is an expression of hope. But hope is nourished by the daily coming of the Lord in grace and by the expectation of his final coming at the parousia. Watching and waiting for the Lord's coming becomes the spontaneous expression of the virtue of hope. Nor is this to be understood only in reference to the sacraments. The Lord does come to his people and to each communicant in the Eucharist. He is present with his grace in every sacrament. But this understanding of the coming of the Lord in the sacraments is not to be taken in isolation from the rest of life. Rather it gives the entire Christian life its meaning and direction. For the Lord comes whenever we encounter the "other." The Lord comes in all the signs of his providence. The biblical ethic is an ethic of *kairos*. It is not we who make plans for ourselves; our lives are directed by God. Christian wisdom consists in the acceptance of this divine plan as it is manifested in revelation, in the signs of the times, and in the large and small events around us.

Watchfulness and genuine understanding of the divine plan of salvation are possible only through the spirit of prayer. We will be able to be watchful and wise in a truly Christian manner only if we put ourselves in the presence of God by humble prayer in every hour of decision. The genuineness of sacramental piety and of one's prayer life discloses itself in this watchfulness. Watchfulness is related to the law of grace. But grace does not stand in contradiction to life; rather it gives it direction by making us attentive to the challenge of the hour, to the needs of one's neighbor. Watchfulness expresses itself first of all in gratitude, but gratitude leads us to humble obedience to God's grace and to the summons of the hour.

UNITY OF PRAYER AND LIFE

A conception of prayer based largely on the fulfillment of certain prescribed prayers destroys the unity of the Christian life. It is extremely important that our very way of speaking about prayer express the oneness of prayer and life. Once again the attitudes of Christian personalism become crucial. Such an outlook views faith, hope, and charity very much as a dialogue or a response. Prayer as an expression of faith, hope, and charity involves attentiveness to the word of God in all its ramifications. God speaks to us as the creator. But creation is not simply something that happened a long time ago. It denotes rather the continued creative activity of God who preserves us in life and directs the fate of the world. In prayer a man listens to Christ and to every word which proceeds from his mouth. He is attentive to the message of the Church, especially as it is revealed in the lives of the saints and in the celebration of the liturgy. He pays heed to the directives of just laws. He beholds the glory of the heavens which sing the praises of God. He contemplates history which is God's masterpiece, the story of God's dealings with his people. Prayer is response and praise. It is a yearning humble effort to understand God better and to follow him more perfectly. Understood in this sense, prayer embraces all of reality.

There are certain high points in prayer. For the Catholic Christian these are the celebration of the sacraments. Here we are absolutely certain that God is speaking to us in Christ Jesus through his Church. In the sacraments we participate in a most intimate way in the response which the Church, the bride of Christ, extends to her bridegroom. And our own personal prayer is closely joined to this personal and community prayer of the liturgy. It involves direct contemplation of God and demands a readiness to follow him, but always in relation to the tasks and duties of life. These actions in their turn must manifest an openness to God, a willingness to engage in his service.

If we regard prayer as a listening and a response to God, we will understand morality in terms of responsibility in the fullest sense of that word, namely, listening to God speaking to us in those circumstances of life in which we encounter our neighbor, his love, and his needs. Responsibility takes the stuff of life, our own self with its talents and weaknesses, and above all the Thou of neighbor and community, and includes it all in its response to God. Thus life itself becomes a prayer. Prayer is watchfulness, docility, openness, and a valiant effort to bring all things back to their source in God. This is the full meaning of the Christian ethic of responsibility. All values are taken seriously in such an approach. The religious and secular spheres are carefully distinguished, and the multiplicity of duties, values, and attitudes is taken into account. But there is also a synthesis, a re-establishment of Christ in the very center of life.

There are those, also within the Catholic Church, who would tend to undervalue praying as such, arguing that one's whole life is after all a prayer. Obviously such a conception is naively optimistic. Only the person who considers himself completely purified and in possession of a full Christian personality would maintain that his life has become a perfect prayer. The actual times of prayer retain their value, for they give explicit expression to our adoring faith, hope, and charity. Indeed, they are absolutely necessary, for they work as an integrating factor in life. Only the person who takes time for such a direct dialogue with God will be enabled to structure his life in an attitude of responsiveness to God. Prayerful dialogue with God is the pre-condition for a genuine encounter with the Thou. On the other hand, the daily reverent contact with the Thou of neighbor and the We of community will give to our encounter with God a certain closeness and relevance to life.

ASCETICISM IN TOUCH WITH LIFE

The danger of asceticism is that a man will concentrate too much on himself and flee the true demands of life. Therefore special care must be taken to keep asceticism in contact with one's true obligations in life.

The fundamental norm of Christian asceticism is the paschal mystery of the suffering, death, and resurrection of the Lord. The risen Christ sends us the Holy Spirit, and in his power we must seek to "put to death" the disordered desires of the ego-oriented personality. Christ gives himself back to his Father; he commits himself into his hands, and in the same act he gives himself for the salvation of his brothers. Thus an asceticism genuinely relevant to life is always directed simultaneously to God as an act of loving adoration and to neighbor as a deed of serving love. This is the way to overcome the artifices and intrigues of a nature turned in on itself and thus to attain to the true freedom of the children of God.

Mortification is therefore not so much a battle against self as such; it is a struggle against a distorted and selfish mode of life. Self-denial does not demand hatred of body; it involves rather a struggle against pride of spirit, against self-glorification and self-justification. But beyond this it seeks to bring the body and all the passions under the rule of a spirit turned toward Christ.

Asceticism is a life-and-death struggle. If we do not destroy the desires of the Adamitic, self-sufficient personality, they will destroy the Christ life within us. Clearly, however, we will be able to overcome the desires of the old man only through the power of Christ, only by looking to him and trusting in him.

Christian mortification receives its life-giving power from the joy of Easter. Yet this joy cannot be fully realized unless we are willing to pay the price of constant combat against self-centeredness. Conscious of our own sinfulness, we must be ready to struggle continually against all selfish and unruly desires.

The new law in all of its elements and aspects is a law of grace and joy. In St. John's Gospel our Lord prefaces the solemn announcement of his new law ("Love one another as I have loved you") with the words: "I have told this to you that my joy may be in you and your joy may be complete" (15:11). Christian asceticism and Christian life will be true to life in the fullest sense if they proceed from the gospel, which is the source of all truth. But the core and summit of the gospel message is the good news of the resurrection of the Lord, who has been crucified for us. All asceticism must give clear expression to this truth.

The paschal mystery is the full expression of conquering love. For that reason asceticism may not remain something which is simply set along-side of Christian love or which perhaps even detracts from the vitality of Christian love. Asceticism will be true to life if it becomes a yes to the duty of constant purification which is inherent in love, if it shows itself ready to bring those sacrifices which are demanded by true love for God and neighbor.

Asceticism deals with a love for God and neighbor which is still in the process of development. Because of this it must at times seek that particular form of expression which is best able to foster fraternal love in various cultures and eras and among differing individuals. It must at times confront those dangers which could disturb a person's inner freedom and his readiness for service to neighbor and community.

OPENNESS TO THE WORLD AND THE SPIRIT OF POVERTY

Schema 13 of the Second Vatican Council (The Church in the Modern World) certainly presents the basis for the further development of the theology of material things. Whoever seeks first the kingdom of God gains at the same time an awareness of the nature of all of creation as the manifestation of God's fatherly love and the means to express fraternal charity.

The theology of material things and of the world has a very fundamental bearing on the direction of Christian asceticism. It is only when the world is fully understood in its true significance that the complete meaning of asceticism is manifest. The world is before all else the good creation of God, inviting us to praise him and to be united in the bonds of brotherhood. Of course the world has become tainted — against its will, so to speak — by the sins of Adam and his descendants. The world is under man's dominion, and he is a sinner. But as God's good creation, and even more as the creation redeemed by Christ, it cries out to redeemed man. For it is through him that it can share in the freedom of the children of God. In addition, "world" in the Johannine sense denotes, at times, those men who by faith have received the revelation in Jesus Christ, but who have deliberately resolved to reject him.

In Christian asceticism we have a harmonious response to the world in all its aspects. Asceticism is the readiness to suffer in the struggle against a world that is God's enemy. It is readiness to give witness to Christ, so that those who are seeking the truth may be led to faith. It is above all warfare against one's own sinfulness and against the insidious forces in the environment in order that the true meaning of created reality may once more be revealed.

A truly relevant asceticism is sensitive to the yearning cry of all reality for a full participation in the freedom of the children of God. Asceticism will be relevant if it is not tied to any one program or involved in legalism, but is open to the realities of any given situation — if it is willing to go out and meet God's world.

A requisite for an asceticism open to the world is the spirit of poverty. By poverty we do not mean lack of possessions, but rather that attitude which is expressed in the first beatitude: "Blessed are the poor in spirit, for theirs is the kingdom of heaven" (Mt 5:3). Whoever is poor in spirit — this is always a gift of the Holy Spirit — renounces the inordinate desire for possessions. He is able to acquire, not without struggle against selfishness, a purified love of all values and all earthly realities. Only in this way can he become involved in worldly affairs, eager for genuine cultural activity, concerned about economic possibilities, open to the need of institutional reform, and in all of this remain sensitive to the claims that his neighbor has upon him. The man who is poor in spirit rejects the use of things simply as a means. He recognizes in them the gift of God. He perceives in them the call of God. He is able to appreciate their true worth, for he sees them as a sign of the love of his heavenly father. But because of this he understands as well that he is challenged to give them up or modify his use of them whenever the needs of his fellow man demand it.

PIETY AND ASCETICISM FOR THE LAITY

Chapters 4 and 5 of the Constitution on the Church make it abundantly clear that a truly Christian asceticism is in no sense the private domain of religious. The layman is a full-fledged Christian. Therefore all the arguments for the necessity of asceticism are as valid for the laity as they are for priests and religious. The Christian who lives in the world, no less than one living in a religious community, must bear full witness to the Christian faith and life, even though the emphasis may be different for one group or the other. The witness given by the religious may tend to stress the truth that "this world as we see it is passing away" (1 Cor 7:31). The layman, on the other hand, will seek to fulfill his apostolic mission by more direct involvement in worldly affairs and by his effort to build up the secular order. Nevertheless, the full truth about God and the world must remain for both of them the fundamental guiding principle. Their witness must be integrated in such a way that they can help each other.

We may take as an example the relationship of the religious life to marriage. The virginal state gives testimony to the eschatalogical aspect of Christian life. In this way of life the establishment of a home and family cannot be the ultimate value. The specific task of the religious is to manifest heartfelt love for Christ, and, in Christ, for fellow man. But the full meaning of the celibate life is grounded in the truth that marriage and family have a profound dignity and value. The celibate Christian must realize that the vitality of virginal love would soon be stifled if married love were not genuine and redeemed. He must know that our Lord could hardly be pleased with a renunciation of marriage if marriage itself is not highly esteemed. A married person, on the other hand, discovers in marriage and family an authentic path to salvation and holiness. But at the same time he is grateful to the celibate for the benefits his witness confers on marriage. He is in a way indebted to those who have given up marriage for the sake of the kingdom of heaven, for they help him understand more fully the inner freedom within marriage and the family. In this way his conjugal and parental love will be in accordance with the law of purification and growth.

A profound appreciation of material values and of the mission of the lay person in the world, the esteem given to a life lived according to the evangelical counsels of voluntary poverty, obedience to a superior guided by the Spirit, and celibacy for the sake of the kingdom, manifest the full scope of the Christian life. There is both openness to the world and renunciation of the world; there is the full positive paschal acceptance of the world as well as the willingness to practice restraint and self-denial in the interest of the salvation of all.

Today's Ecology of Devotion

John Oliver Nelson

From age to age, "contemplation" differs as its *templum*, the locus of its pursuit, changes. More, the whole life of devotion is affected as its common *oikos* shifts from century to century. So it is that in relation to prayer and worship, considerations of *ecology* (study of an organism's reaction to its environment) have great meaning as we seek understanding and renewal in this field.

Clergy and scholars of religion, hedged about with books and in a sense living within the classic structure of faith and "the known universe," sometimes downgrade such ecological concerns even when these are grippingly impressive among lay and secular people. Indeed it is frequently the dated antiquarian appearances of saintliness in the modern world — like a quaint Gothic chapel amid cyclotrons — which make piety unacceptable and irrelevant to many men and women and youth. They simply shrug that they live now "in a different world." At the moment when we agree with them, the faith is compromised or lost: it is *not* a different world, but the same universe in which God has dwelt through all human history. Some clergymen do find that they can set up a little enclave within which the classic life of the spirit can be maintained despite the new environment. (Although the actual place is not important: sometimes the most cloistered and withdrawn analyst of the contemporary scene is the most relevant or even *avant garde*.) Thus piety often seems to be linked with ancient, unexamined theology and cosmology — whereas impiety rejoices at being thoroughly up to date, relevant, cheek-by-jowl with the freshest achievements of technology and social change.

In this brief ecological discussion, all that can be attempted is an attention-calling gesture toward some main areas in which worship, liturgy, and the practice of prayer must surely be re-translated. We do face (as the several synopsizing sections below seek to indicate, *seriatim*) a new universe, a new individual, a new statement of the Gospel, new corporateness, and new liberty of opinion and action. It is under such rubrics as these that Christian faith must look to its age-old task of becoming imminently, contemporarily relevant, aware of all reality and experience as the gift of God and the arena of God's working by the incarnation in Christ. If modern thinkers, and the common folk who follow them, are not to settle for purely secular mysticisms

86

and Promethean or nationalist cult practices, our approach to the ecology of devotion is a study and program of profound urgency in the Church.

A NEW UNIVERSE

To many churchmen and social critics, it was a shocking revelation to see the reaction of some hundreds of thousands of laymen — Protestant, Catholic, Jewish — to Bishop John A. T. Robinson's little book, *Honest to God.* Their enthusiasm in getting hold of the first several chapters of this book (even though a great many readers bogged down later in the text) was a startling indication of where "ordinary people" are actually living today in terms of cosmology. As the Bishop rather casually pointed out that today the Deity cannot be "up there" or "out there" nor "in there," but rather is himself the very ground of being, multitudes of college-trained readers in a dozen countries exclaimed that "at last some theologian has begun to make sense." Theologians themselves brushed the book off by saying that Robinson was just popularizing Paul Tillich. The Church of England tended to say merely, "Look what doctrinal leeway we give our bishops!" Editors said (and the Bishop partly agreed) that he should have waited and written a more careful book. Pastors threw up their hands, often, and objected: "All question and no answer!" But laymen in significant and surprising numbers exulted that here was a view of the universe and God which made more sense than what the Church has been saying.

Further evidence of where many modern Americans stand was found in widespread interest in Bishop Robinson's Ascension Day sermon in Boston. There he asked if the main difference between our Lord and the astronauts was that they maneuvered their way back to earth whereas our Lord went shooting off into space? The query was of course absurd, and reminiscent of the earliest Soviet cosmonaut's laughing report that he had found "no evidence of God" in outer space. But the gusto and seriousness with which contemporary, educated Americans regarded these considerations is of deep importance. Not just the Sunday supplement stories of science fiction or exploration of the Milky Way, but the solid assumptions of campus and suburb and laboratory, seem very frequently at odds seriously with the main lines of Hebrew-Christian interpretation of the universe. The comment of an illustrious Scottish theologian, Thomas Torrance of Edinburgh, that "de-mythologizing would not be needed if mythologizing of an unscriptural sort had not first taken place," is doubtless accurate. But the fact is that both Christians and secularists have wrought their own myths about reality, sometimes in such picturesque and naive terms that the wholeness of cosmic truth is utterly obscured.

A noted Christian leader of great erudition remarked recently in personal conversation, "I still pray, *up.* . . ." But can we enable modern devout people to kneel and relate to the vast, brooding, seeking, omnipresent God who our Lord said "sees in secret"? Freud has made laymen suspicious of "the father image" projected into the skies. Ernest Hocking has reiterated in our century the claim that "in Christ we see the human face of God." C. S. Lewis declared, "If the choice of mental image is between a benign old Kingly man on his throne, and an oblong blur, give me the former every time!" But the traditional teenage "leap" from lesser deities — parents, Scouters, clergy — to the infinite God must be informed and given definiteness.

When the Psalmist found the heavens declaring the glory of God, his mental realization of that glory was *toto coelo* other than that of the Cape Kennedy scientist or even the contemporary grade schooler who knows the stars. Are "the four corners of the earth," "the Lord looked down upon the children of men," "he has founded it on the seas and established it on the floods" translatable in current dimensions? How anthropomorphic should our teaching and apprehending of the grace and strength of God be in a time when we begin to suspect that the energy within a neutrino may be the same as that in a personality?

Some of the task, obviously, is just terminology. Alongside the realities of the Shepherd Psalm, can there be such prayer as, "O Lord, whom we know in the countless light-years and numberless galaxies of your creation, and also in the positron and neutron and every intricate pattern of matter . . ."? Together with, "O God of heaven and earth," could there be such formulae as "O Ruler of sphere and stratosphere"? Some of the crude and sensational liturgies used by the jazz-mass generation have elements which do strike the imagination and responsiveness of the day, and these should possibly be sorted out from among cheaper or more trivial statements of prayerful intention. Fresh forms of prayer, like those of John Baillie or Father Quoist, have often been like water to the thirsty soul among students and critics of the faith.

Not just the language but the place of worship may need reorienting. Prayer offered in a gigantic nuclear laboratory or on a launching-pad, or under the shadow of a gargantuan cyclotron or linear-acceleration colossus, may speak in the new language. In offices and clubs, on ski slopes or in basketball courts, not the clerical figure performing his liturgical role, but the whole group of laymen lifting their allegiance in vernacular phrases right where they work or play, can be a worthy relating to the modern milieu.

It has been said that the characteristic experience of God among modern men is of the *remoteness* of Deity, the mystery, vastness, unknowableness — in testimonies from Kierkegaard or Bonhoeffer or Chardin to the wistful ethicism of the "God-is-dead" adherents today. Even while rejoicing in the new detail and naturalness in which we now see Jesus of Nazareth, children and adults are well served with truth when they do find how to meditate in the limitless *wholeness* of the modern universe, finding God less manageable, less easily thinkable and describable than in previous generations of faith. As it is always a wondrous boon to the child to be confronted with the ocean — a mysterious, infinitely powerful and brooding force stretching to infinity, casting up a wondrous variety of living creatures and realized in a thousand sparkling or tempestuous moods — so in the modern, scientifically explorable universe, child and adult need more than ever to experience the limitless and aweful reality of God, in the cosmos as well as in Christ. The task of translation is a desperately difficult one.

A NEW INDIVIDUAL

Time-lag and imagination-lag in our cosmology is surely matched in our appraisal of contemporary man himself, as we seek renewal of devotion. The average educated citizen in our midst knows a good deal more about popular psychology than about theology, and spiritual *praxis* must come of age here too if faith is to be appropriated. What new discoveries about the person are relevant?

Some small part of our problem is an updating of terms about the individual and what goes on within him. Few will demand that we shall pray for our id or censor to keep checking our libido, or for deliverance from an Adlerian power-thrust or a Jungian drag of race memories! Yet the language of Christian devotion may well show that we are not simplistic in our analysis of man, and are aware of all the grim threats of Oedipus or Narcissus or De Sade or Masoch as we define our own approach to devotion. We must at the very least know the terms and claims.

Having this glossary is especially necessary as much psychological practice nowadays has outgrown the scorn or disbelief with which in past decades it once viewed theistic faith: a great many therapists now have a questioning acceptance of religion as an occasional ally or even a specific and essential resource. From the Christian side, of course, the "cure of souls" has readily adopted many of the terms and techniques of psychology and psychiatry. Yet, strangely, clergymen counselors most caught up in such therapeutic practice have often been those least likely to call upon the classic gifts of the mystical or devotional tradition: it seems a different world entirely from that of the clinic and the couch.

Yet some of the "givens" of contemporary psychology are richly useful in any approach to the life of devotion and worship. Look at several of these, very sketchily suggested.

Probably most determinatively of all, the *I-Thou* hypothesis of Martin Buber has found its way into both psychological and theological thinking. His pointing out that only person can "make present" or "affirm" person leads to his claim that such affirmation by Deity provides personhood among men. The specific qualities of the I-you relation, constantly in opposition or complement to the I-it, have become a part of the language of the time, and a useful category for considering prayer as well as inter-human exchange. Devotion has been lighted, even ever so slightly, by this fresh awareness of the unique account of person-to-person possibilities.

Similar has been the changing odyssey of the practice of "analysis" itself in recent decades, providing clues about the motive for prayer and the pitfalls of certain sorts of devotion and confession. Rollo May, a Manhattan analyst, published several years ago his account of the changing general assumptions of therapy at the depth level: in the first Freudian days the standard assumption was of course that *sex* is the chief human problem and motive; between the wars, this had shifted to the assumption that *hostility* is the key difficulty; now for twenty years, May suggests, analysts widely agree that *why to exist at all* (why seek meaning, why continue to bear life?) is the endemic question of the neurotic or hypochondriac or even the "normal" citizen. Thus it seems that "the new individual," at the very time when he seems to have conquered space and matter, is poignantly vulnerable at the very core of his self-realization. Accordingly, any devotional measures proposed for this generation must be significantly different from those helpful in the last century or even in the first half of our own. The startling new appraisal of man's state and stance shows that despair and meaninglessness — rather than, for instance, failure to fulfill a Victorian moral code or to like people around us — are the situation with which prayer must deal, if it is to be relevant to the condition of modern man.

At another point man's powers and equipment, explored with new inventiveness, affect his approach to devotion: the whole realm of communication *in intercession*. How, with twentieth-century hypotheses as to how the mind operates, do we provide even a clue about the transference of idea and intention between God and man? As our orisons go up that someone in a coma be healed, or an alcoholic restored, the modern mind demands some inkling as to what the process is, how the prayer is (as it were) "transmitted." A previous age, with more naive accounts of the God-man and man-man interrelation, could pray with little enlightenment in these areas. Many in our own time have actually redefined "intercession" as a process of our adjusting ourselves to what will take place anyhow — shrinking from the idea that we can wheedle the Deity into changing his will, by whatever means or whatever numbers of those praying. Thus we must have further research in the perplexing, tantalizing field of inter-personal conveyance of thought and concern, if for this psychologically oriented generation intercession is to be real and authentic. Professor J. B. Rhine and his Extra-Sensory Perception experiments at Duke University are "controversial" and his conclusions have not been widely accepted, but the phenomena with which he sought to deal are decidedly apposite in current questions about the life of intercessory prayer.

Probably the over-all consideration in most exploration of the "new individual" is what constitutes *personhood* in modern terms. Where philosophy and theology formerly were the only disciplines dealing with this question, the psychologist and social science experimenter, the anthropologist and the cybernetics expert, have tended to take over. But their data are largely the same old relentless dilemmas of man's destiny. David Reisman's familiar categories of tradition-directed, inner-directed, and other-directed man hark back ineluctably to questions about freewill and determinism. Erich Fromm in his researches points back to age-old options about who man is and whence comes his freedom to be or to love, even as he denies the necessity of any such transcendental dimension in human life. Paul Tournier's insight about the meaning of person and personage, in a frankly and creatively theistic setting, are eagerly grasped for by a host of modern readers who ponder the meaning of man. Fresh realizations as to what personhood means have prompted even reanalyses of the doctrine of the Trinity — another dimension in which devotion obviously has much at stake.

Somewhere between the *hubris* of Promethean man and the self-depreciation of the flagellant, the Christian role and image of responsible personhood becomes a proper basis for our dedication to our Maker, in Christ. Can I in devotion be liberated into the full stature of who I am, "casting aside every weight" and refusing to be "conformed to this world" as I present myself to him? We need as much informed self-analysis, or even professionally-contracted analysis, as possible, to search out the pitfalls, mixed motives, innate tendencies, and hallucinatory overtones which may beset our life of prayer. In the age of anxiety and interstellar exploration, it is imperative that we seek to know how free, how self-possessed, how eagerly childlike, and how come-of-age we can be in our confrontation by the Son of Man and the Lord of life.

A NEW EVANGEL

Certainly in all the Christian centuries, there has never been such a deep probing of our historical roots as our own generation has seen. We know more, and have technical tools to assay more accurately, than our ancestors. One result has been an almost radical revaluation of our own holy history as a movement.

To oversimplify, we might suggest that scholars today take us further and further to the left textually and historically — and at the same time further and further to the right in doctrine and liturgy. The very New Testament specialist who now knows that the accepted accounts of Jesus' life need serious revision is often the very man who is more and more deeply committed to incarnational dogma of a profound sort. Like a good many of us, he somehow emerges from the jungle of Heilsgeschichte and Interimsethik, Bultmann, Cullmann, Jeremias, Bornkamm, the Dead Sea Scrolls and Qumran, to join seriously with Karl Rahner or Karl Barth in new commitment to orthodoxy! The whole range of opportunity and difficulty related to the claims of *mythos* and symbolism in this process has much to do with our life of prayer. Barth once said that difference between Protestant and Catholic begins with the very first word of the Creed, *Credo* — difference having to do with acceptance over against creative assertion, assent rather than declaration, and so on. In the new day, he doubtless has revised this judgment: Christendom suddenly finds itself becoming *one* regarding authority and tradition and freedom of confession as it has not been for centuries, and the dialog is set in entirely new dimensions.

Not only the historicity, but the *availability* of God's life among men comes up for scrutiny in ways which are crucial for prayer. On the one hand there are wistful or relieved devotees of a sophisticated God-is-dead "theology," who take a leading part in the contemporary ritual of burying the teleological, cosmological, axiological approaches to the Deity — at the very hour when scientific progress constitutes an astonishing extension of these very arguments. Yet on the other hand a large modern tendency toward pan-entheism, "divine science," syncretistic amalgams of various religions, Zen, and ethical culture, all emphasize the claim that the Deity is more than ever present, more multiform, more Principle and less Person.

As has been mentioned, both these contrasting movements have their effect upon worship: Is God present with us? Is the incarnation an event in past history, unavailable in any real sense even through the ministry of the Holy Spirit today? On the one side we have the classic and uniquely Christian prayer, "Almighty God, who art ever more ready to hear than we are to pray . . ."; on the other are the Old Testament implorations that he "bow down and hear us," "vouchsafe his mercy," and harken to our repeated cry for lenience. In an epoch of aggiornamento in theology, such questions dealing with God's constant, unelicited presence and providence are of the essence in devotional life.

An area of "the new Evangel" in which Christians have more unanimously made up their mind, apparently, is our attitude to the "unsaved," the separated brothers, the others whose doctrine is unlike our own. "God loves the world, not the Church," is one of the insights Yves Congar and Hendrik Kraemer have lined out with new dynamism. Often the new tolerance goes hand in hand with claims that the atonement is revelation rather than transaction, that we know less about hell (in a modern preterition-by-preoccupation) than our forbears did. Karl Rahner, for example, seems to find a sort of atropying of the religious sense in our generation, while man is temporarily intoxicated by his wondrous achievements in science and invention; but he refuses to be judgmental, monitory, or minatory about this, choosing rather to wait for God to reach out to all his people. As we agree with him or disagree, the attitudes and even the wording of our prayer about the Church in the world are shaped by what we now believe.

Moves toward "contextual" or "situational" ethics are of course a part of the contemporary theological revaluation. Such doctrines as that of "the just war" have come in for serious reassessment among both Catholics and Protestants — partly because of pragmatic demonstrations of a non-violence which appears, at its best, to be uniquely that of the New Testament faith. Sex mores have shaped sex absolutes of an older day, family life has recast household roles in unaccustomed directions, the "affluent society" has necessitated restatement of asceticism, "anti-poverty" has challenged the ancient Christian assumption that we do have the poor always with us — and all these changes affect our worship and intercession.

Distinctly affirmative is the effect of the clearer, dynamic picture of our Lord which has come into focus in the past several decades: as modern man prays *en Xristo*, the demand and delight of obedience are sharper than ever. When the atonement is found to relate directly to the race struggle, or to labor relations or parent-child attitudes or rehabilitation of prisoners, the layman's practice of devotion does give promise of being quickened — if he prays at all as he gives himself to such concerns! It may be such existential, *ad hominem* understandings of the Gospel, replacing many a doctrinaire abstraction by dogmaticians, which can help millions of college-graduate seekers to discover fresh impulsions to piety.

A NEW CORPORATENESS

Through the ages of the Church, people have faithfully raised their prayers for "all sorts and conditions of men," with usually little actual idea of just how assorted and conditioned mankind could really be. Within our lifetime, we have been thrust into a new proximity and relatedness never known before.

We are closer by television to multitudes of people than most of our ancestors were to anyone outside their household. We travel and have friends abroad. Our churches have world connections which are constantly pictured and described for us. Our intercession for world leaders is informed by our seeing them within the hour on the screen. We experience nations and crowds, battles and cities and sunsets and interviews — admittedly, in one-way, non-participating communication — right in our living room at home. Whether we wish to pray for our neighbor or not, he is plainly right at hand.

Yet it is not mere spatial or pictorial closeness which characterizes our corporate identification with people everywhere. We have developed (especially in America, it seems) an unprecedented *xenophilia* and openness to new contacts, communicative, articulate, glad to relate, ready to identify easily with persons we meet. Business executives have had T-group training and "sensitivity training," in order to operate on group dynamics principles. Millions of middle-class people are "joiners," in community and nation. They have real identification with lodge, congregation, service club, fraternity or sorority, sports club, political grouping, P.T.A., credit union, labor organization, management enclave, or a hundred other sorts of membership. Most of all, probably, our nationalisms are really a religious affiliation for many modern citizens: "I am an American" Day or the pledge of allegiance to the flag represents a fealty often deeper than any they own for their theistic faith. Granted, that most of these human relationships, like that at work, are for the majority very shallow — even though they demand a lot of energy and do seem to be a defense against aloneness. But the variety and omnipresence of them is a contrast with former times when membership in the village or the family or the parish was the only acknowledged corporateness in most people's lives.

How do I pray, when in addition to television and supermarket and bowling, a constant succession of fellow-members, neighbors, and casual conversationalists go steadily trooping through my life? Sometimes, to be sure, their very proximity drives us to seek resources for them and for ourselves. Or on the contrary, we may neglect praying because nowadays we can talk out with others a problem which formerly we could take only to God. Our relentless fraternization does narrow down the amount of time and attention available for devotion. "The world is too much with us," we may well lament in such a sensate, gregarious time. The corporateness which modern man has enlarged beyond all past dreams of togetherness is a very large ecological environing fact for contemporary worship.

A NEW "LIBERTY"

Much of what has been said here might be summed up under the title, "the new freedom of man." From one standpoint, this strange, indentured liberty is a twentieth-century bondage to environment which should be written with quotation marks — "liberty" — in irony. In another perspective, it is wondrous freedom of an unprecedented kind.

For example, we are affluent, rich, in plenty. We produce a surplus of food and goods for everyone everywhere. We can buy and invent and compute and enlarge in fantastic ways, to enact The Great Society. We are — we think — out from under the rules of sex, with situational ethic or *Playboy*-type self-gratification as our writ of emancipation. We abound in art forms good and bad, phonograph records reproducing any noise ever made, high-rise buildings, sea-sleds and hydrofoils, global missiles, deployable armies of young men, fluoridation campaigns, lavish help for any human disaster. In the Church we are at liberty to put on jazz masses, or to speak with tongues at the university, proliferate coffee-houses, or claim that God is dead. A bishop is free to muse that three retreats a year might overbalance fifty-two isolated hours of worship for the faithful — or that the faith might be better served without an ordained clergy! Undeniably, this generation is abler to do or to change, better equipped for any plan, than human beings have ever dreamed we could be. Millions of us might almost join with Swinburne in his paean: "Glory to man in the highest, For man is the measure of things. . . ." Such is our "liberty."

If in the second half of the twentieth century we do indeed have a new universe, a new individual, a new Evangel, new corporateness, and this astonishing new freedom of opinion and action, each of these changes of terrain or of cultural climate is determinative of how we seek God and how he is known to us in Christ. No project of the scientist in matter, nor any adventure of the cosmonaut in outer space, is so imperative for the life of the race, nor so profoundly exhilarating for the seeker, as the discovery of these fresh channels of grace into the common life of the believer.

Problems and Perspectives: an Epilogue

Kilian McDonnell, O.S.B.

The purpose of this paper is not to summarize but to pose problems for future discussion. In order to indicate with clarity the nature of these problems no attempt has been made to blunt the offending point. On the contrary, the formulations have been given, perhaps, too fine a point.

The problem of prayer is, in both the Catholic and Protestant traditions, the problem of the Holy Spirit. "No one can say 'Jesus is Lord!' except under the influence of the Holy Spirit." Those who neglect the role of the Holy Spirit in the total economy will hardly be likely to concede that he has an important role in prayer. The perennial temptation is to speak of the importance of the Spirit and then to forget that he has any role. Origen expressed the firm conviction that the Holy Spirit is strictly a Christian concept, indeed the shibboleth of Christianity. Yet, as P. A. Florensky points out, the Holy Spirit is not an integral part of Origen's theological system. "It is, so to speak, a 'false window' for the sake of the symmetry of the structure, and nothing more."

If the Holy Spirit is a "living, real, personal kingdom . . . the kingdom of the Father and the unction of the Son," then his role in the economy of salvation and in prayer can be forgotten only at the cost of a radical distortion. Luther's theology, as shown by Regin Prenter, was completely dominated by the concept of the Holy Spirit. Werner Krusche has shown how the Holy Spirit was one of the normative centralities of Calvin's thought. Subsequent Protestantism has not always been true to the genius of the Reformation. One wonders whether the enlightenment and subsequent secular movements would have made the inroads they did if Protestantism had kept the Reformation pneumatology. The moralism, not to say Pelagianism, of much of later Protestantism was a sign that the Spirit had lost his kingdom. Whenever the Holy Spirit is neglected, moralism and Pelagianism is the lot of the Churches, Protestant or Catholic. Even the non-sacramental groups, such as the Quakers with their rich prayer tradition and their waiting for the Spirit, came to act as though self-reliance and individual responsibility were more to be trusted than a Spirit who moved with so little dispatch. The balance between the primacy of the Spirit and man's responsibility is precarious, and history is full of sad solutions which chose one of the poles of the paradox as a total dogmatic.

We may have reservations about the total dogmatic of the Pentecostal Churches and about their growing importance, but they did restore consciousness of the decisive place given in the New Testament to the experienced reality of the Holy Spirit. The Pentecostals take quite literally St. Paul's words "If anyone does not have the Spirit of Christ, he does not belong to Christ," and to this extent the Pentecostals are true witnesses to the spiritual climate of the apostolic Church.

Catholicism has its own sad history. On our library shelves one finds monographs in number on the Holy Spirit; one also finds oblique references to the Holy Spirit in our dogmatic tracts, but the Spirit does not permeate all our theological and devotional thinking as it did Luther's and Calvin's theology. One has only to think of that otherwise magnificent document, the Constitution on the Liturgy, to realize how deficient our pneumatology is. Here we have much to learn also from the Orthodox.

The noisy efficiency of much of Catholic devotional literature, the self-ennobling presuppositions to our piety betrays a veiled attempt at self-redemption. A few years ago I asked a class of 40 college juniors to write out a description in non-technical language of grace and of the relationship between grace and man's cooperation. What they gave expression to was an authentic semi-pelagianism. There were polite nods of recognition in the direction of grace (created) which was reduced to an object, something which helped and was in a real sense, to be sure, indispensable, but in the last analysis it was man who saved himself. There was no mention of uncreated grace, the Holy Spirit; indeed one had the impression that the students would have been highly surprised to hear that the Holy Spirit had anything to do with redemption, sanctification, or prayer.

This lack of appreciation for the role of the Holy Spirit surely accounts for the superficiality and, to say the nasty truth, the ritualism of much Catholic prayer. Catholic prayer and devotional life is often not characterized by a deep inwardness, that interiority which is not just psychological self-possession but a sensitivity in depth to the movement and touches of the Spirit. The Christian, Protestant or Catholic, who wishes to speak the name of Jesus and to declare his lordship must ask the Father to send the kingdom of the Spirit. The kingdom of the Spirit, according to Gregory of Nyssa, is the subject of an important variant of the Lord's prayer in St. Matthew 6:10 and St. Luke 11:12, which does not exist in the modern text. It reads both "Our Father . . . thy kingdom come" and "Our Father . . . thy Spirit come upon us and cleanse us." Only in the kingdom of the Spirit does the interior cleansing take place in us and in the Church which enables the Spirit to establish Christ as Lord. What is needed by Protestants and Catholics is not a theology of the spiritual life which is in effect an overblown pneumatology, but a truly trinitarian theology.

The concern for a greater interiority brings up the problem of the liturgy. Roman liturgical life has been held suspect by segments of Protestantism. The sacramental and liturgical life is sometimes seen, not without a measure of justification, as a kind of sanctuary busyness, a vastly elaborated sanctuary etiquette which confuses ritual movements with movements of the heart, a sort of prayer by proxy. The basic fear is that the liturgy is essentially ritual Pelagianism. Why all this parading around in lacey gowns, why all this bowing and incensing if Christ has redeemed us? Is this not a species of ceremonial self-redemption? More than that, the whole ritual-sacramental dimension is dominated by a sanctuary will-to-power, a sacramental imperialism, which attempts to make even greater and more exclusive claims on the spiritual life of the people. It is difficult for a man to meet his God and speak to him apart from the sanctuary externality of the official Church. Not only is there no salvation outside of the Church, but there is no salvation within the Church for those who withdraw from the organizational business of the sanctuary.

Cited is the Catholic tendency to think of the presence of Christ almost exclusively in sacramental terms. Little is heard in Catholicism of Christ's presence in the word, a concept which Karl Barth has brought to the fore. Does not Origen represent a true biblical tradition when he says, "One should not esteem the word of Christ less than the body of Christ." The very real presence of Christ through faith (and baptism), a presence which St. Paul expressed in a physical terminology to the embarrassment of a later theology, is slighted in favor of the real presence of Christ in the Eucharist. On the one hand, the real presence of Christ in the Eucharist is a substantial presence. On the other hand, the real presence of Christ in the believer by reason of faith is not substantial. This led theologians, enamoured of substance as the highest and most noble of the philosophical categories of being, to speak of the presence of Christ by reason of faith as presence improperly so called. Only the real presence in the Eucharist is presence properly so called. This, says the Protestant, with good reason, is unabashed sacramental imperialism. The accent in St. Paul is on what later theologians call a presence in the improper sense.

Beyond this is the tendency to make the presence of Christ in the Eucharist an ultimate end, instead of directing it to that continual presence of Christ in the believer. Certainly union with Christ is the purpose of the

Eucharist, a union which should hardly be limited to the sacramental moment. St. Thomas Aquinas has a highly elaborated sacramental and eucharistic doctrine, but he directs the Eucharist to union with Christ. This is in no way a devaluation of the Eucharist, or of the eucharistic presence.

The objections here are real. But they are objections to an abuse. We would hope that no Christian would reject free prayer, spiritual waiting, inward listening, simply because sometimes free prayer is pompous, and spiritual waiting is sometimes spiritual laziness, and quiet of the soul is sometimes the sleep of the body. Abuse does not invalidate the thing abused.

This brings us to another objection, not unrelated, which some Protestants raise against Catholic liturgical life. What they see as the unspoken presupposition is what they call raging objectivism. It is to the visible, the tangible, to objectivized reality, that incarnational Catholicism is drawn. The presence of Christ in the Eucharist is more highly esteemed than the presence of Christ in the believer because of the Eucharist's visible particularity. Shifting to the realm of vocal liturgical prayer, Protestants have pointed to the contemplative orders, especially of sisters, who have, for centuries, prayed the divine office in a language of which they understood scarcely a word. This is a scandal to the Protestants quite apart from the lesser problem experienced by those trained in Latin who pray in a tongue which is not their own. The theological basis for the practice of sisters saying their office in Latin was that this was the official language and the official prayer of the Roman Church. It was seemingly impossible to separate the official prayer from the official language. There was a hint of that peculiar and exasperating mentality which equates the Latin rite and the Latin language with the Catholic Church, as though the Orientals, deficient as they are in glories of Latin, were not also Catholics. The sisters prayed in the name of the Church, and therefore it was fitting that they pray in the official language of the Church, though they could understand almost nothing of what they said and sang. These Protestants would not deny that such contemplative groups have produced great sanctity. But they are appalled — the word is not too strong — at the lost opportunity for even greater sanctity. Had the contemplatives prayed as human beings are wont to pray, in their own language, or at least in a language which they understand, the convents and monasteries might have been even greater centers of spirituality.

Many Protestants are willing to admit some value of praying in the official language of the Church, but they are quite literally staggered at the price that is paid. To this end is sacrificed much — by no means all — of the essential personal qualities of prayer. That a whole life is devoted to prayer in a foreign language is not a wasted life, but it is certainly a wasted opportunity. This is the raging objectivism which Protestants note in Catholicism. The objective value of a rite which represents the Church's official prayer life, a rite to be gone through, is the end to which many human values and prayer values are sacrificed. Their objection is not to structured prayer, nor to liturgical prayer, but to a structured-liturgical prayer in a language one does not understand. They note that even after the Constitution on the Liturgy, this situation in contemplative monasteries remains largely unchanged; frequently the sisters are not free to make the changes they would want. The Constitution on the Liturgy places emphasis on understanding and moves away from exaggerated objectivism: signs and liturgical forms must be more than confected and performed; they should be understandable and understood. But contemplatives — indeed almost all who recite the office in choir — still chant the office in a foreign tongue, and this by those not granted the gift of interpretation.

What has been given here is but one example of an exaggerated objectivism. The Reformation polemic against the *ex opere operato* theology was a denial of an evangelical truth: that in every saving act the work of the sovereign Lord is decisive. However an objectivism which sacrifices human and personal values is hardly what the sovereign Lord demands. The Reformation distrust of and the contemporary unease with *ex opere operato* corresponds to a dislocation which is found at the heart of the Catholic ethos.

There is a profound dislocation of a sacramental nature found within Protestantism. In spite of the strong official declarations about the centrality of word and sacrament, when it comes to parochial practice the sacrament is far from central. Much progress has been made in this area, but even in those Churches where the liberal theology of the last century made little progress, one finds that high regard for the Eucharist is suspect. A Lutheran rector of a conservatively oriented seminary told one of his seminarians that as a Lutheran the Eucharist could never play an important role in his life. Luther himself would not have left such a statement unchallenged. And in the Churches of the Calvinist tradition, as in some Lutheran Churches, an undoubted Zwinglianism obtains — and Calvin was by no means a Zwinglian. The immediate effect of the Reformation was a more intensive eucharistic life within Protestantism. Calvin's parishioners complained that while they were under Rome they were bound to go to communion only once a year while Calvin demanded that they go four times a year. It was Calvin's personal conviction that the Lord's supper should be held weekly — he gradually reduced his demands under pressure from civil authorities.

There are large segments of Protestantism which have recovered much of their liturgical heritage; there are also some which never lost it. Yet there is in some Protestant Churches an insufficient appreciation of the nature of the liturgy, which is seen as a second-handed approach to God. This lack of understanding of the liturgy has led also to an impoverishment of private prayer. Protestantism has been reluctant to formalize private prayer by means of set forms. The pre-structuring of private prayer is often seen as a depersonalization and a mechanization of what is essentially a free movement of the heart. However, a Swiss Calvinist pastor told how he envied the Catholic devotional practice of the rosary. He had strong mariological objections to the rosary, and he saw the danger of repeating a formula, but he said that the parishioner not practiced in prayer frequently does not pray at all simply because he does not know how to begin. Set formulas are crutches but who of us is not a cripple?

On the other hand, the Catholic has much to learn from Protestant prayer forms. For centuries we dismissed the liturgical austerity and the intimate character of Protestant worship, especially in its more rigid Calvinist forms, as the rejection of all sacramental objectivity and therefore as ineffectual subjectivism. Some Protestant Churches do represent a ritual chastity which appears stark and antiseptic. But the Catholic who is able to have this Protestant experience of God will immediately recognize that what he had rejected as mere subjectivism is, in fact, deep personalism. And he may come to the end of his Protestant prayer experience with the discomfiting realization that he has never been so personally involved and so intimately committed in prayer as during his moments of prayer at a Protestant service.

The Catholic also has much to learn from the Protestant tradition of free prayer. The Catholic soul is slightly canonical in his approach to vocal prayer. What has not been approved by a competent authority he will not utter as prayer because the unguarded spontaneous spoken prayer might possibly contain doctrinal errors. When it comes to vocal prayer for even semi-public use the Catholic has an excessive fear of heresy. Public sermons need not be submitted for approval but even semi-public vocal prayer, he feels, must. This is not Church law; it is simply a Catholic complex.

But the problem is deeper than the fear of heresy. Quite frankly, free prayer embarrasses us. To expose the soul in public, even in a small gathering in a home, in so personal a manner makes us blush. It is not, we think, indecent, but almost. It is a form of improper exposure. This is an unfortunate commentary on the Catholic psychology of prayer and it gives some credence to the Protestant charge that our liturgical forms are really ritual exhibitionism, ritual Pelagianism, the mouthing of prayer without the heart's involvement. Is it not true that we want to pray without the prayer experience? Are we not truly embarrassed by religious experience and more specifically by a public religious experience, even though it be restrained and disciplined? This is not a problem peculiar to the Catholic; any knowledgeable Protestant will readily admit that it is a Protestant problem.

The practice of free prayer on the part of Catholics would seem to be a necessary supplement to their own structured liturgical prayer. The tradition of free prayer within the liturgy appeared very early, is indeed its earliest form. Hippolytus says of the prayers for ordination: "It is absolutely not necessary for the bishop to use the exact wording which we gave above, as if he were learning them by heart for his thanksgiving to God. Rather each one should pray according to his capability. If he is ready to pronounce a grand and solemn prayer, that is well; if on the contrary he should say a prayer according to a set form, no one may hinder him. But the prayer must be correct and orthodox." This is also true of the Mass text proposed by Hippolytus. There was at this time (the third century) no fixed formulary for the Mass liturgy, but only a fixed framework within which the celebrant formulated his own prayer. The collects were for a long time left to the celebrant to extemporize, as he did his admonitions to the people. He was also free to recite a text previously written down by himself or others. St. Augustine bears witness to both methods in his *De Catechizandis rudibus* (PL, XL:320). He also notes the pitfalls of free prayer and warns the well educated layman not to mock the ministers of the Church should they give utterance to a barbarism while extemporizing.

The third century is not the twentieth century, but we can recover a prayer form which belongs to so ancient a tradition without falling into liturgical resurrectionism. We need not set aside prayer forms which the Church has used for centuries. But within the context of the liturgy place should be found for extemporaneous prayer. Certainly free prayer could be used in the homes. Should it be surprising that Catholics also speak to their Father out loud?

Taking the norms of Hippolytus and Augustine, there should be both a framework and freedom. Without the framework the way is easily open to a prayer which is emotional, subjective, pompous; without freedom prayer becomes mechanistic, frigid, oblivious to the needs of the local Church. Freedom insures that the particular worshiping community has an avenue of expressing its character and needs; the Church is, after all, both local and universal. Catholics are afraid of this type of prayer freedom. They much prefer to have their vocal prayers carefully written down, codified, stamped and certified with a *nihil obstat* and an *imprimatur*, and, finally, promulgated.

There is also the problem of moments of silence within the liturgy. In Catholic liturgical history there is to be found a Gothic activism. We cannot endure just sitting, waiting, listening to God speak interiorly. Unless we are aggressively full of words we think that we are wasting our time. The pause between ritual actions we consider voids, and these we earnestly fill with liturgical chatter. If prayer, also public prayer, is a conversation with our Father, we might occasionally be silent so that our Father might speak his word to the interior ear.

This points up a deficiency in our theology of grace which is related to our prayer forms. Karl Rahner has called our attention to the Catholic formulation of the doctrine of grace as though it were a pure beyond-consciousness reality. It is a reality of which one knows something through the teaching of faith, but the reality itself is not accessible in such a manner that it can be noticeable in the conscious personal life of man. The "room" in which man himself is and experiences and lives, that which has to do with the data of his consciousness, is not filled with grace. This "room" we have identified with nature, that which we experience without the help of revelation. Grace is a certain externality to man's experience of life. It should not come as a matter of surprise when men have little interest in grace. Why should they show interest in something which is beyond consciousness, which is not to be found there where he lives and experiences? Contemporary man thinks existentially. He wants to experience the reality of grace in that room where he lives.

Also there is need to return to the pre-Tridentine tradition which gave greater attention to the Holy Spirit as uncreated grace. Because of polemic preoccupations the post-Tridentine theologians came to think of created grace (paradoxically, a construct of medieval theologians as a tool against Pelagian tendencies) as grace in the proper sense. A more experiential, personal approach to grace — such as found in Piet Fransen, among others — will make man's prayer life more related to the room in which he lives. He need not then strive to enter some beyond-consciousness realm when he prays. He can, rather, recapture that profound experience of grace and that immediate inspiration of the Holy Spirit as found in the apostolic Church. The presence of God in the depth of one's own existence can be a prayer experience and not simply a kind of objective state.

The Christian will sometimes feel the need for some kind of direction in this "secular" room in which he experiences God. Both Catholicism and Protestantism are faced with problems here. Classical Protestantism has never been able to work out a true Christian humanism, nor for that matter a viable theology of the body. What it does possess in these areas comes not from its own theological tradition, but are borrowings from the secular humanists. Catholicism, on the other hand, with its stronger sacramental tradition, feels very much at home, undoubtedly too much at home, with a Christian secularity. Yet the contemporary Protestant, paradoxically, has seen his vocation in the world more clearly than has the Catholic. The Catholic has come a long way from the monastic orientation of all devotional literature, but the Church is only now moving away from an ecclesiology dominated by monastic ideals: too much "come apart with me into a desert place" and too little "go preach the gospel to every creature."

The current attempt to break down the barriers between the secular and the sacred in which the sacred is extended to the secular in its totality amounts to a weakened immanentism. It is a type of pan-sacramentalism which ends up with everything a sacrament of the sacred. When the concept of *qadosh*, that which is set apart, is so weakened that it no longer has any special connotations, no reservation, no separation of function, then ultimately pan-sacramentalism ends up with nothing being a sacrament. Pan-sacramentalism lacks separateness, *qadosh*. It may be acceptable to the secular world but the Catholic cannot be at ease with it.

The Catholic, too, has a faulty solution. The medieval synthesis did break down the distinction between the sacred and the profane: the profane became absorbed in the sacred, lost its autonomy. Where the sacred dominates to the point that there are no valid secular or profane ends, the Catholic has been traditionally comfortable. However unfortunately, the identification of the sacred with the ecclesiastical finds a response in the Catholic soul. When, on the other hand, the secular and the profane — or perhaps, in more precise terms, the non-ecclesiastical — is the dominant reality, when the sacred is not made visible in forms specifically ecclesiastical, when the sacred speaks out with the voice of the secular world, then the Catholic says to himself "Soul, beware. This is secularism. Objective religious values are being denied. Where there is no sanctuary, no incense, no priest, there can ultimately be nothing sacred." The Catholic has his own peculiar vocabulary of the sacred, his own theological conceits. When this vocabulary and these conceits are rejected, the sacred is rejected. This is unfortunate but it is so.

The problem of the sacred and the profane complicates the task of giving spiritual direction. The Catholic director tends to place greater emphasis on ascetical discipline — the profane world which must be rejected — the Protestant director more on freedom. The Catholic director places more emphasis on structured life, and the Protestant more on the charismatic non-fixity. This is not to accuse the Protestants of depreciating discipline; it does define a religious posture. The Protestant director is less concerned with abstract principles and a formulated message, more concerned with persons and existential situations. The Protestant conception can lead to a spiritual perfection seen somewhat exclusively in terms of a fully developed personality, an authentic individual who might well be an integrated person but not yet a Christian. The distinction is dangerous but it has its validity. That the Protestant starts existentially and not from a religious principle does not mean that his procedure is any less religious, any less Christian. It does mean that he is open to the temptation of never proceeding beyond a humanism which is not specifically Christian. It is only a temptation, not a necessary fate. This procedure, however, does equip the Protestant to hear more readily God speaking with the voice of the secular world. He is less apt to identify the sacred with the ecclesiastical, and he is less inclined to dismiss the purely secular as without religious value because it is non-ecclesiastical. The Protestant is readier to meet and greet the Spirit where he moves and manifests himself, even in the secular world. The Catholic ties the Spirit to sacred places, sacred persons, and sacred actions. The Catholic is an ecclesiastic at heart, even when he is a layman.

Dr. Douglas V. Steere, the T. Wistar Brown Professor of Philosophy, Emeritus, at Haverford College, Haverford, Pa., is chairman of the Friends World Committee and of the board of Pendle Hill, the Quaker center at Wallingford, Pa., for religious and social studies. — *Rev. Barnabas M. Ahern, C.P.*, is a leading American Catholic scripture scholar. — *Rev. Jean Leclercq, O.S.B.*, a monk of Clervaux Abbey, Luxembourg, has specialized in the field of monastic spirituality. His essay was translated from the French by Sister Marianne Pomerleau, O.S.B., of the convent of St. Benedict, St. Joseph, Minn. — *Rev. Horton Davies*, a member of the Congregational Church, is the Henry W. Putnam Professor of the History of Christianity at Princeton University. — *Rev. John B. Coburn* is dean of the Episcopal Theological Seminary in Cambridge, Mass. — *Rev. Bernard Häring, C.SS.R.*, expert on moral theology, teaches at the Roman Redemptorist College and in this country. His paper was translated from the German by Rev. Warren Kulas, O.S.B., of St. John's Abbey. — *Dr. John Oliver Nelson*, a Presbyterian, is director of Kirkridge, an ecumenical retreat and study center at Bangor, Pa. — *Rev. Kilian McDonnell, O.S.B.*, teaches Protestant theology in the graduate school at St. John's Abbey. Princeton University Press will publish his book *John Calvin, The Church and the Eucharist*.